A Secret among the Blacks

A Secret among the Blacks

Slave Resistance before the Haitian Revolution

JOHN D. GARRIGUS

HARVARD UNIVERSITY PRESS
Cambridge, Massachusetts
London, England
2023

Copyright © 2023 by the President and Fellows of Harvard College
All rights reserved
Printed in the United States of America
First printing

Publication of this book has been supported through
the generous provisions of the Maurice and
Lula Bradley Smith Memorial Fund.

Library of Congress Cataloging-in-Publication Data

Names: Garrigus, John D., author.
Title: A secret among the blacks : slave resistance before the Haitian Revolution / John D. Garrigus.
Other titles: Slave resistance before the Haitian Revolution
Description: Cambridge, Massachusetts : Harvard University Press, 2023. | Includes bibliographical references and index.
Identifiers: LCCN 2022060237 | ISBN 9780674272828 (cloth)
Subjects: LCSH: Médor, –1757. | Macandal, François, –1758. | Traditional medicine—Political aspects—Haiti—History. | Antislavery movements—Haiti. | Slave insurrections—Haiti. | Haiti—History—Autonomy and independence movements. | Haiti—History—To 1791.
Classification: LCC F1923 .G26 2023 | DDC 972.94/03—dc23/eng/20230301
LC record available at https://lccn.loc.gov/2022060237

Contents

	Introduction	1
1	Médor's Town and Country Lives	13
2	Médor's Medicines	34
3	Poison and Panic	53
4	Makandal, Congo Diviner	75
5	An Epidemic of Their Own Making	97
6	Makandal's Ghost	121
7	The Haitian Revolution Begins	144
	Conclusion	171
	NOTES	181
	ACKNOWLEDGMENTS	223
	INDEX	227

Maps

MAP 1.1 Médor's Town and Country Lives

MAP 2.1 Events from Médor's Testimony

MAP 3.1 Poison Accusations after Médor's Death, 1757

MAP 3.2 Assam's Search for Medicine, 1757

MAP 4.1 Makandal's Life in Saint-Domingue, 1730s–1758

MAP 5.1 Doctors Diagnose Anthrax and Describe Its Spread, 1770s

MAP 6.1 Resisting Anthrax and Poison Accusations in the Coffee Zones, 1780s

MAP 7.1 Enslaved Labor Strikes on Sugar Estates, 1770s and 1780s

MAP 7.2 Prelude to Revolution

MAP 7.3 Early Days of the Revolution

A Secret among the Blacks

Introduction

This book tells the story of men and women who, alone and together, over thirty years, prepared the land they lived on for revolution. They toiled in fields and houses, tended cattle in remote mountains, stoked refinery fires that burned day and night, drove coaches on roads through the sugarcane fields, and kept vigil over the sick and injured, healing when they could. They were enslaved and freed Africans and their descendants who lived on the mountain slopes and in the coastal plains surrounding the French-controlled city of Cap Français—the commercial capital of a territory that would become the nation of Haiti. In a colony built on their submission, these people persisted and resisted in communities that were the seedbed for a revolution that would end slavery in the most profitable plantation economy in the Americas.

Introductions are in order because these few individuals, along with thousands of other enslaved people silenced by history, played a vital but misunderstood role in fighting against slavery. First comes Médor, an enslaved domestic servant who lived in the port city of Cap Français in the 1740s. When his enslaver moved the household to a mountainous coffee estate, he was forced to leave the friends who had helped him and others work toward freedom. The Seven Years' War erupted shortly thereafter, and a terrible drought struck the colony. During these years, a wave of unexplained deaths swept the region. Médor was accused of being a poisoner, and, after three days of interrogation, he confessed to secretly drugging his masters for freedom. He revealed that free Black people were using medicines to soften their enslavers and hasten their manumission. A growing community of freed people hoped to ultimately confront the colonists, he said. Médor's confession led to a spiraling investigation into poisoning that ensnared many free and enslaved Black people.

A plantation nurse named Assam was one of the next to be accused. Her enslaver had sent her away on foot in search of African-style medicines to cure other captives. After days of searching, she found and administered the medicines. When her patients died, she was tortured as a poisoner. Assam's confession pointed authorities toward an African man named Makandal, who had escaped slavery to live hidden in the mountains. Black men and women sought out Makandal to have him divine the future with the help of spirits. His rituals created the kinds of deep loyalties that could embolden a person to resist oppression. Makandal was arrested and unjustly convicted of running a network of poisoners who aimed to destroy the colony.

Makandal became known to history as a fearsome poisoner even though he denied it, and, within two decades of his execution, medical experts concluded that a newly diagnosed illness could have caused the unexplained deaths. As planters continued to accuse alleged poisoners, enslaved people across many communities found creative ways to resist. A free Black woman named Lizette went to court to save her freed adult son Kangal when his former enslaver levied a poisoning accusation calculated to return him to bondage. While fear and death navigated the colony, an enslaved woman named Kingué used African-inspired rituals to divine the identity of poisoners. An enslaved man named Nicolas undertook a dangerous journey with thirteen others from a coffee plantation to Cap Français and succeeded in filing a formal complaint of torture against their enslaver.

Resisting in obscurity on a sugar plantation that would become the cradle of the Haitian Revolution, enslaved foremen Jean-Jacques and Hippolyte led strikes among cane field and refinery workers that paralyzed the plantation. Nine years later, on the neighboring estate, a coachman named Boukman lit the first of the fires that within a month would burn thousands of acres of sugar to the ground. This was the August 22 revolt that ignited the Haitian Revolution. Historians have chronicled Boukman's fires but failed to illuminate the decades of resistance that preceded them.

Until thirty years ago, most historians of the only successful slave revolution in modern history maintained that it occurred in a colony with no tradition of organized resistance, for Saint-Domingue had no documented revolts between the 1720s and the revolution.[1] Even today, except for work focused on slave escapes, very little has been written about how enslaved men and women resisted captivity in Saint-Domingue. In some ways, this is not surprising; enslaved people are too often silenced in the sources that scholars rely on. Historian Tiya Miles calls this "the conundrum of the archive."[2] Thousands of documents record enslaved people's existence as economic assets, but almost none record their voices.

Historians have been able to reconstruct the resistance of colonized people elsewhere in the Caribbean and Latin America using records from religious trials. In Portuguese Brazil and Spanish America, Catholic missionaries worked to convert enslaved Africans. They punished those who refused to abandon their original beliefs. Documents from colonial-era religious trials have allowed historians to describe the lives of enslaved Africans in places like Brazil and modern-day Colombia.[3] Historians of French colonial Haiti, known as Saint-Domingue, have no such records because there was no Catholic Inquisition in France or any of its territories.

Records from criminal trials in Saint-Domingue might have provided a valuable window into slave resistance, but humidity, insects, carelessness, and violence destroyed thousands of documents. The Cap Français court was said to be especially disorganized, with no central archive. In 1734, a fire destroyed all criminal records in Cap. Many more documents disappeared in 1787 when the Cap Français and Port-au-Prince courts merged.[4] Fires set during the Haitian Revolution destroyed yet more papers. The legal sources that survived, for the most part, were those that colonists deemed important enough to send back to France.

Most significantly, courts in Saint-Domingue systematically destroyed the records of slave criminal trials. In 1717, the Superior Council of Léogane, the colony's oldest court, ordered employees to purge slave trial records up to 1715.[5] In 1724, the Cap Français Superior Council ordered the burning of "old criminal trials of blacks and other useless items." In 1744, the Léogane Council again ordered officials to pull all slave trials from their archives and burn them.[6]

Eliminating criminal trial records might have served the interests of colonial judges, who were nearly all planters. Evidence offered at trial could include descriptions of poor conditions on a plantation or abuses committed by enslavers. French slave laws directed courts to investigate masters who treated slaves "inhumanely and barbarically." This "Code Noir" instructed judges to prosecute colonists who tortured, mutilated, or murdered their captives. It also allowed enslaved people to complain to a judge about a master's cruelties, such as denying food to enslaved people or inflicting savage punishments.[7] In the roughly one hundred years of Saint-Domingue's history, only five prosecutions of an enslaver for cruelty can be documented.[8] Judges might have wanted to destroy documents that proved they had shown leniency to planters.

What we know of slave resistance throughout the Americas shows that some of slavery's most successful Black opponents were maroons, people who escaped plantations to set up communities in the wilderness. In Jamaica, maroon communities fought a war that forced the British colonial government to guarantee their liberty. However, their freedom did not mean an end to slavery. A condition of the agreement was that they would help maintain the colonial system of slavery. They were required to fight against slave rebellions and to capture escaped slaves.

In Saint-Domingue, there were undoubtedly thousands of captives who managed to escape bondage permanently. Maroon leaders such as Plymouth and Colas Jambes Coupées attacked plantations and killed French colonists. However, Saint-Domingue's maroons never united to wage a long and coordinated campaign. *Marronage* did deprive the plantation system of valuable labor. Enslavers published over ten thousand notices in Saint-Domingue's newspaper describing escapees and seeking their return. For fifty years, scholars have mined these notices to determine whether a rising tide of escaped captives might have caused the Haitian Revolution.

Most maroons in Saint-Domingue were newly arrived African men. Early scholars asserted that these men escaped because they had not adjusted to slavery. They also said that people who were *born* into slavery on the island only fled when there was a problem on their estate, most often a lack of food.[9] Later scholars strongly disagreed and cited the same notices to argue that Saint-Domingue's people never accepted slavery. All types of enslaved people, they showed, tried to escape bondage.[10] Some historians have concluded that maroons "may indeed have contributed to the basic groundwork and general form of the massive outbreak of 1791."[11] Others determined that "marronage was not, all things considered, a permanent threat against the established order."[12]

David Geggus calculates that "at any given moment less than one percent of Saint-Domingue's enslaved people had escaped and maybe one out of every 30 or 40 adults escaped in a given year." Most of these people, he estimates, were captured or returned on their own after absences ranging between several days and several months.[13] Crystal Eddins, in a sophisticated analysis of marronage notices, recognizes that "scholarly debate surrounding the role and relevancy, or lack thereof, of enslaved runaways before and during the Revolution seems to have reached a stalemate."[14] Eddins concludes, "The Haitian Revolution, although not wholly dictated by Africa-inspired rituals and marronnage, benefitted from maroon bands and ritual leaders at important moments of its unfolding."[15]

Until now, one man has epitomized prerevolutionary resistance in Saint-Domingue. Makandal is considered to be a poison conspirator who sought to drive white people from the island. Makandal is revered in Haiti and remembered as a rebel who resisted to his very end, leaping from his burning execution pyre to cries of "Makandal escapes!" The poison plot attributed to Makandal has been described as "the only hint of an organized attempt at revolt during the hundred years preceding the French Revolution."[16] Why and how Makandal fought oppression and inspired others to do the same is a complex question made more difficult to resolve by myths that have come to shroud his life and actions.

Over time, writers developed three different versions of the Makandal story, each reflecting and serving the political ideas of its era. The first myth was that Makandal was a colonist-killer. This idea emerged very quickly, appearing first in a pamphlet published in France in 1758, the year Makandal was executed. The pamphlet contained part of an anonymous letter claiming that "the slaves seek to make themselves masters of the country, by killing all the whites."[17] This became the central theme in colonists' descriptions of Makandal.

A second Makandal story appeared in France about thirty years later: Makandal was a madman. Makandal-the-madman appealed to Europeans and North Americans. This myth had a long life because proslavery writers in the 1800s used it to help explain the Haitian Revolution. The myth started in 1787 in Paris, when a writer known only as Larival published a work of fiction called "Makandal: True Story."[18] The story combines seemingly authentic details with obviously fictional elements. Larival combined the idea of a poisoning plot and exotic colonial words taken from a contemporary book with an unmistakably fictional plot: a doomed romance.[19] In the first paragraph, Larival wrote that Makandal was a "monster," and the story portrays him as a gifted healer who is driven mad by the cruelties of slavery. Madness is essential to Larival's story because Makandal is shown using poisons to kill and terrorize other enslaved people as well as colonists.

This story was quickly picked up by other journals and translated and published in Germany and Great Britain. A 1789 British version added sabotage and a race war to Larival's story, having Makandal's lieutenants confess that their leader planned to "destroy privately the greater part of the planters, or to ruin them, by poisoning all their slaves who appeared to be attached to them; and lastly to exterminate the whole race of white men by a general massacre which would render him the deliverer and sovereign of the whole island."[20] When Saint-Domingue's enslaved people launched their great uprising in 1791, the story found a second life in the United States, where readers were already consuming news that emphasized the horrors of the French and Haitian Revolutions.[21]

In the twentieth century, a third Makandal myth arose, as Caribbean writers of African descent began to portray him in mostly positive terms. One of the earliest was the Martinique-born abolitionist and free man of color Civique de Gastine. In his 1818 history of Haiti, Gastine argues that Makandal's "force of character and correctness of mind" showed that Black and white people are intellectually equal. For him, the lesson of Makandal's plans to purge Saint-Domingue of colonists is "Despots and tyrants, beware!"[22]

More than a century later, Trinidadian writer C. L. R. James wrote his highly influential *The Black Jacobins* (1938), which praised Makandal as the precursor of the Haitian Revolution. "An uninstructed mass, feeling its way to revolution, usually begins by terrorism, and Mackandal aimed at delivering his people by means of poison."[23] In *The Kingdom of This World*, a 1949 novel describing the Haitian Revolution, Cuban writer Alejo Carpentier created the most famous portrait of Makandal, one that symbolized the vitality of African and Afro-Caribbean cultures. Carpentier's description of Makandal's supernatural powers created the Latin American literary style of "magical realism." This Makandal was a man of great moral purpose who planned a massive slave uprising and taught an enslaved boy about the glories of African civilization.[24]

The myth of Makandal as a heroic revolutionary allowed other creators to imagine him on an even larger stage.[25] In 2012, multimedia company Ubisoft released "Liberation," the fourth installment of its popular video game *Assassin's Creed*. Set in Louisiana in the 1760s and 1770s, "Liberation" features enslaved and free characters of color, including two rival assassins who claim that Makandal taught them his lethal arts in Saint-Domingue.[26] As a rebel loosely aligned with Ubisoft's fictional Brotherhood of Assassins, Makandal is part of a secret centuries-long struggle against tyranny.

In the words of historian Annette Gordon-Reed, these Makandal depictions are "forms of fantasy written as fact." Gordon-Reed observes that "historians have a duty . . . to look beyond the presentations of people who deliberately forced obscurity upon others and portrayed the oppressed in a way that justified their rule over them. Privileging [enslavers'] documents has historians playing along with a rigged system, producing history that is indelibly marked by prejudice, a form of fantasy written in fact."[27]

Relying on carefully deconstructed archival sources, this book disputes that Makandal was a poisoner. He was a diviner in the

Congo tradition who formed spiritual communities for healing and self-defense. In doing so, he established one of the multiple cultures of resistance that emerged in the decades before the Haitian Revolution. Other enslaved people took vengeance against their enslavers or appealed to colonial courts to protect them from torture and abuse. Still others planned and participated in labor stoppages or strikes against plantation policies and leadership. Enslaved people were thinking strategically about their lives as they imagined and worked for a future in which French colonists would no longer dominate Saint-Domingue.

Ten maps reveal how resistance over a period of three decades was centered around mountainous foothills between sugar and coffee land. This terrain was overlaid by drought, epidemic illness, and poison interrogations. On the same ground, the revolution's first fires broke out on the night of August 22, 1791. This location was not accidental. Vincent Brown argues that rebel leaders in Jamaica were "keenly attuned to their spatial situation ... [and] worked to build alliances across mountains and across plantation lines."[28] They knew "who was on the estates ... who controlled particular regions." With this knowledge of the physical and political landscape, they could begin to persuade and pressure people to join the revolt, for this was not a "simple reaction to the fact of enslavement."[29] Social connections, shared ethnicities, membership in a local community, and loyalties to local leaders all combined to shape the coalition and determine the fate of the rebellion in Jamaica. The same processes occurred in Saint-Domingue before 1791. As Brown writes, "Paying careful attention to movements in space and over time offers a new perspective on the military maneuvers of the combatants."[30] The maps in this book offer that perspective.

This book is part of an ongoing scholarly debate about what constitutes resistance. After a wave of studies in the 1980s and 1990s that celebrated slave resistance, some historians have argued that the term has become too broadly applied, encompassing nearly all elements of enslaved people's lives.[31] French scholar Frédéric Régent champions a narrower definition of resistance, limiting its use to "any behavior by a slave that went against the economic system."[32] Régent considers slowing down plantation work, sabotaging equipment, injuring livestock, and escaping the estate as forms of resistance because these diminished production and profit. Participating in a dance ritual, tending a private garden, or growing vegetables to sell in a colonial market were not, in his view, cultural or economic resistance, because they helped enslaved people accept slavery. "Music, dance, and singing let the enslaved population unwind and diverted it from different forms of resistance."[33]

Historian Randy Browne studies enslaved people living under British colonial control in what is today Guyana. There, enslaved people were permitted to complain to a judge about abuses, and those records were preserved, culminating in "the single largest archive of first-person testimony from and about enslaved people in the Americas."[34] Browne found very few records of people fighting their enslavement. His evidence showed that people enslaved on Caribbean sugar estates had little excess energy to fight the plantation system. The best that most could manage was to survive the brutal work they were forced to do. Browne advocates for a narrow definition of resistance, while cautioning that "an exclusive emphasis on domination and resistance obscures the many other important relationships—and conflicts—that shaped enslaved people's lives."[35]

This book's position is that enslaved people's survival efforts can constitute resistance. In Saint-Domingue, resistance was a response to specific threats that were, depending on the case, personal, local, regional, and global. An offended plantation manager could imprison a free Black man on a pretext. Rivers dry from drought could spark a brutal production drive to recover lost refinery profits. Mysterious death could carry off enslaved neighbors living up and down a river valley. Deadly bacteria imported from foreign fields could infect an entire island's soil, livestock, and inhabitants.

Saint-Domingue's colonial plantation economy undeniably brought all these forces to bear against the enslaved. But the corps of enslaved resisters was not monolithic. They were from dozens of cultures in West or West Central Africa or had been born in the colony. They were men and women. Many were in positions of authority over other slaves: factory foremen, artisans, nurses, and household managers. They had a variety of political visions. As Brown and Browne recognize, people who resisted oppression did not necessarily seek to end slavery.[36] They were, however, looking to alleviate aspects of their suffering. Community was key to accomplishing this. A free Black woman together with her allies sued for her son's freedom in a campaign that ascended to the King's Council at Versailles. A crew of enslaved refinery workers walked into the foothills on a seven-day labor strike. An African diviner convened ritual communities across a chain of estates to stem a tide of illness.

These communities had years of practice resisting oppression, which made armed resistance possible. In the moment any coordinated rebellion begins, every man and woman must decide how they will engage. In his history of Tacky's Revolt, Vincent Brown describes how slaves present at the beginning of that rebellion were "compelled ... to make unbearable decisions about when to yield, how to protect themselves and others from harm, whom to align with, and when and how to fight back, if at all."[37] These decisions were not made alone. In the years preceding the Haitian Revolution, environmental pressures, epidemic illness, and poison accusations were a stress test for enslaved communities. Communities survived those tests if their members were connected by powerful bonds of loyalty and if they had determined their priorities and established their willingness to tolerate risks. Communities that survived were strengthened because their members had decided which risks they were willing to confront. In the poison zone, when the call came to join a revolt, many leaders and their communities were prepared to answer. On the night of August 22, 1791, thousands of enslaved men and women in Saint-Domingue made the "unbearable decision" to join Boukman's rebellion.

I

Médor's Town and Country Lives

MÉDOR TRAVELED against his will. War and capitalism wrested him from West Africa, forcing him across the Atlantic Ocean, past the reefs and shallows of the Cap Français harbor, over the sandy beach, and past the charred remains of the recently burned settlement, where other enslaved men worked to replace wooden houses with stone buildings. After living twenty years in the port town, Médor was forced into one last involuntary journey, rumbling on a wagon down thirty miles of road surrounded by cane fields, to later walk alongside laden mules up a river valley, deep into the mountains. For Médor, like hundreds of thousands of other enslaved people in Saint-Domingue, there was no retreat, so he endured these journeys, imagined how to improve his life, and worked to attain that change.

When Médor arrived in Saint-Domingue, probably in the early 1730s, French colonists made up about 9 percent of the population and held 89 percent of the colony's people in bondage.[1] The labor of those enslaved workers made the colony Europe's leading supplier of sugar and, eventually, coffee. Plantation labor in Saint-Domingue was so brutal that half of all Africans who arrived there died within eight years.[2] Planters replaced dead captives with new ones, paying slavers to unload thousands of shackled Africans in Saint-Domingue nearly every year. Médor wore those chains himself and then watched tens of thousands of people like him pass through Cap Français, the colony's leading port.

From 1700 to 1790, more enslaved Africans passed through Cap than any other single port in the Caribbean.[3] Most of those captives were on their way to the countryside, where they would face different kinds of living conditions depending on the type of plantation they worked on. A man enslaved on an estate that grew coffee or made indigo dye might live in the mountains with thirty to eighty other Africans and one or two colonists. On a sugar plantation, a captive might be one of three hundred enslaved workers on a coastal plain overseen by four or five white people.[4] On many plantations, enslaved people had little contact with colonists; they were watched, trained, and compelled to work by higher-ranking slaves called drivers.

By 1757, Médor had survived slavery for at least twenty years. He was still alive because for fifteen of those years, he was enslaved in a house in Cap Français rather than on a plantation. He and a handful of others were under the constant surveillance of their enslavers, the Delavaud family. He spoke French with the Delavauds, or Creole, an emerging language with African-inspired grammar and mostly French vocabulary. With other enslaved people, Médor spoke African languages, but not in front of the Delavauds. His African name is lost to history because the Delavauds imposed French names on all the enslaved household workers: Agnès, Élisabeth, Hippolyte, Adrien, Scipion, Venus, and Mercure.[5]

Médor worked as a valet or manservant to surgeon Philippe Delavaud. On Delavaud's order, Médor might have left the house alone to buy food at the market or the butcher stall, or he may have been sent to collect packages from merchants. He also would have carried messages from Delavaud to the surgeon's patients or other doctors. As the surgeon's personal servant, Médor likely experienced moments of autonomy and greater freedom of movement than other people enslaved by the family.

However, he and the others were all subordinate to Agnès, an enslaved woman who managed the household. For an enslaved person, occupying a position of trust or authority over others could be both advantageous and perilous. A personal servant could be the first accused of betrayal. A skilled driver leading a crew could be the first accused of conspiracy. Any woman under an enslaver's control could be used for sex.[6] This might have happened to Agnès.

Médor came from West Africa, perhaps modern-day Benin or Togo. We know this because his friend Venus said she heard him talking to a man named Gaou in "their language." The African name Gaou probably came from the Kingdom of Dahomey, in what is today Benin.[7] This suggests that Médor, Venus, and Gaou were probably swept into the Atlantic slave trade during Dahomey's military expansion, which flooded Saint-Domingue with captives in the 1720s and early 1730s.[8] In the first half of the eighteenth century, more than one-third of the Africans arriving in the colony came from this region, more than from any other part of Africa.[9] Médor, Gaou, and Venus probably spoke Fon, Ewe, or another of the Gbe languages of modern-day Togo or Benin.

Cap Français was Saint-Domingue's largest and most important settlement. When Médor lived there, it was more of a town than a city, with three to four thousand residents. If he had seen cities in Benin in the early 1700s, like Grand Ardra or Savi, with populations of up to thirty thousand, he would not have been impressed by the French settlement's size.[10] By the 1780s, long after Médor's death, Cap Français grew to fifteen thousand residents.[11]

In Médor's time, a great mass of humanity toiled beyond the city's gate. Forty thousand enslaved people lived in the surrounding parishes, and roughly 170,000 enslaved people populated the colony.[12] Cap was the main port for European cargoes and passengers. The city's booming economy was heavily dependent

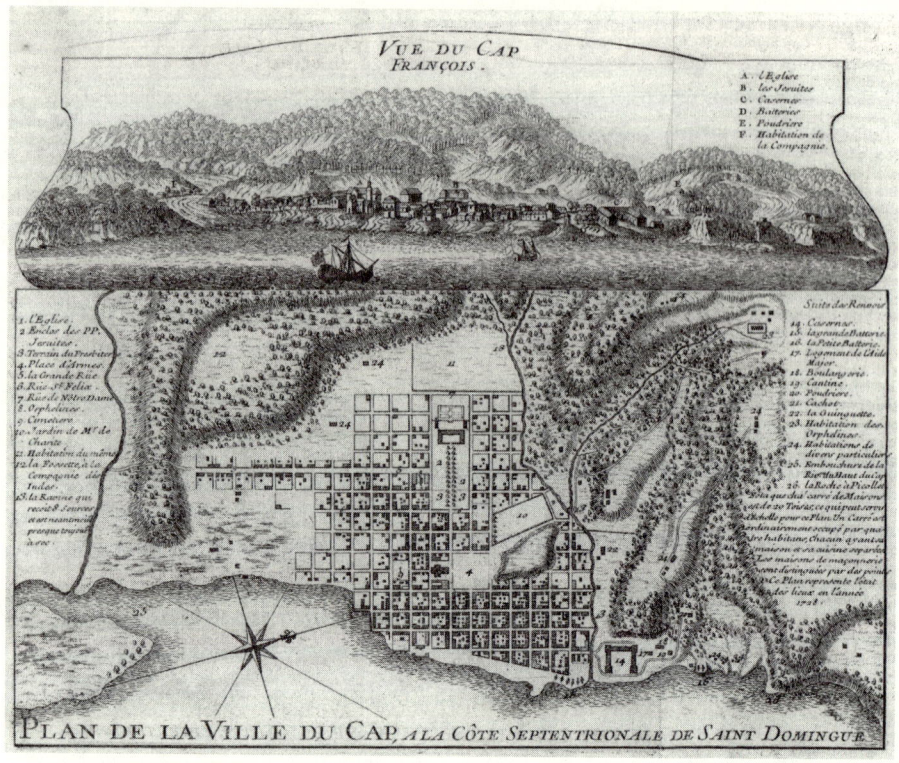

1.1 Cap Français in 1728. "Plan de la Ville du Cap, a la Côte Septentrional de Saint Domingue," from Pierre-François-Xavier de Charlevoix, *Histoire de l'Isle Espagnole ou de S. Domingue . . . Tome second*. Paris: Hippolyte-Louis Guerin, 1731. Reproduction courtesy of John Carter Brown Library.

on exporting plantation products and importing food, draft animals, enslaved Africans, and agricultural tools. Cap was also the center of the colony's provincial political and legal system, with courts that could condemn and execute free and enslaved people. But Cap was a space of relative freedom for freeborn biracial and Black people, and for ex-slaves, who were mostly African-born. They formed a free population of color and had identical legal rights to French colonists; in practice, however, their lives were heavily constrained by racism.[13]

Three-quarters of the people who lived in Cap Français were Black, and many of them, like Médor, had been born in Africa. As Médor walked past the harbor on any given day in the 1730s and 1740s, he would have seen dozens of ships at anchor. Half a dozen might have been slavers. The sight might have triggered memories of his own weeks of misery and terror in a slave ship's hold. He might have remembered being auctioned to a colonist, perhaps Philippe Delavaud, on the deck of that same vessel.[14] Years later, when Delavaud returned to the harbor to buy two dozen captives for his new coffee plantation, Médor would have served and accompanied him.

If time spent at the harbor made Médor reflect on the misery of the slave trade, it might have led Delavaud, a Paris-trained master surgeon, to think about disease. Ships from Europe, Africa, and other colonies carried diseases that spread through Cap Français and into the surrounding parishes. From the beginning of the 1700s, laws required that an official doctor inspect all incoming vessels, especially slave ships, for evidence of a shipboard epidemic. All ships arriving at Cap had to be cleaned and "perfumed," in the hope that this would disinfect them.[15]

Colonists particularly feared yellow fever, which could kill 40–50 percent of an unexposed population. If Médor had experienced a mild case as a child, he might have been immune to yellow fever, but he would have seen it cut down many of Cap's residents in the summer of 1733. The dreaded disease returned in 1735. Authorities canceled the "perfuming" requirement the following year, but yellow fever was back in 1742 and 1746.[16]

Smallpox was another scourge that arrived by sea. A physician in Cap Français noted in 1738 that many slave ships carried captives with the disease, which struck Saint-Domingue hard in 1741, killing many enslaved people. As smallpox epidemics became more regular, some colonists had doctors inoculate their slaves in 1745, although this was still a highly experimental practice.[17]

Of all the city's spaces, the Sunday-morning food market on the parade ground, called the Place d'Armes, held the greatest promise of community. On Sundays, enslaved workers streamed into town from surrounding parishes, doubling Cap's population for a few hours, to set up shop in front of the church. For many, Sunday was the only day they were allowed to leave the plantation.

Marketgoers started walking to town at dawn, carrying sacks of yams, squash, or cassavas; baskets of greens or beans; or fruits like guava, soursop, or pineapple. They had grown this food on small plots of land that planters considered worthless for sugar or indigo. Some brought eggs, live poultry, crabs, fish, or turtles. To sell in the market, vendors had to show constables a note from their enslaver. They spread their wares on the ground in the square and bartered with free and enslaved townspeople. In times of famine, enslaved people needed the coins they earned in the market to buy their own food.

The market also attracted free Black and white market gardeners and small farmers. They sold from wheeled carts or from tables mounted on sawhorses. There were peddlers too, including free Black people selling *tassau*, a jerky made of thin strips of sun-dried beef marinated in citrus juice to disguise its often-rancid taste. Tassau peddlers bought their meat from ranchers across the mountains in Spanish Santo Domingo. Constables who policed the market had orders to inspect the tassau for spoilage that could cause disease.[18]

Cap's cooks and housekeepers stocked their enslavers' kitchens at shops that sold staples from France, like olive oil and wine. They made daily trips to the bakeries that turned imported flour into loaves of bread, and to butcher stalls that sold beef, mutton, or pork. Every few years, the town auctioned off a single butcher's license, which gave its holder a monopoly on meat sales, while restricting the prices he could charge. Wholesale and retail merchants carried French imports: textiles; soap; medicine;

tools; kitchen items; tableware; writing supplies; and the occasional collection of books, musical instruments, or jewelry.

Sailors and newly arrived colonists brought trunks of goods to trade in Saint-Domingue, and Cap's administrators allowed them to sell their wares along a street near the port on Sundays. Colonists called this the Whites' Market, to distinguish its sellers and wares from the plantation slaves offering food a few blocks away. In Médor's time, the food vendors had expanded down a side street from the Place d'Armes, practically joining the two markets.[19]

For as long as Médor was enslaved in the port town, he was a part of its dynamic commercial economy. Philippe Delavaud gave him permission to buy and sell goods for his own profit, and he dealt in valuable bits of cloth. Médor said that Magdelaine, an enslaved woman, owed him 157 livres for Persian cloth and a cotton scarf; the free Black mason François Boucard owed Médor 247 livres for various goods. Many like Médor hoped to accumulate enough money to buy their freedom. The two debts Médor held would have amounted to roughly one-fourth of his freedom price if the surgeon allowed him to buy his freedom.[20] Delavaud never did.

Some enslaved people in the city were able to buy their freedom. Boucard, the mason, probably purchased his liberty by working and saving in this way. Officials complained that self-purchase arrangements encouraged enslaved people to steal from their masters. Other slaves, they claimed, "abandoned themselves to all kinds of [sexual] vices to collect the necessary sums, gathering and conducting their business in the houses of those who are already free, most of them working in taverns, even in the homes of whites who are low enough to receive them day and night, traffic with them and allow their infamous and shameless trade."[21]

Purchasing one's own freedom required cooperation from the enslaver, who could refuse the transaction or set an impossibly high price. If a manumission did proceed, the grantor or recipient would have to hire a notary to draft a legal deed, which the newly freed person could use to prove his or her liberty. The French Code Noir of 1685 allowed a master who was at least twenty years old to manumit a slave without official permission and gave "freed slaves the same rights, privileges and immunities that are enjoyed by freeborn persons."[22]

By the time Médor arrived in Saint-Domingue, however, authorities were beginning to regulate manumission and limit the rights of ex-slaves. In 1713 and 1736, the French Crown required masters to get the permission of Saint-Domingue's two top officials, the governor and the intendant, for any manumission. Six years later, the government sent seventeen people back into slavery after their master freed them without official permission.[23] The idea that ex-slaves would be equal to freeborn people was quickly dismantled by colonial prejudices. These were in plain view when, in 1724, officials created a free Black militia because white and biracial colonists refused to serve alongside Black men.[24]

Saint-Domingue tried to restrict free Black people, both by policing them and by making them into policemen. While Médor lived there, Cap Français reformed its police force to better control the free and enslaved Black people who made up three-quarters of its population. The town hired free Black constables to work under a white officer and allowed some enslaved men to earn their freedom by serving as policemen. Constables patrolled the streets at night, searching free Black or slave dwellings to look for stolen goods. They arrested enslaved people for gambling, carrying a weapon, or fighting. Constables were ordered to break up any gathering of four or more Black people and arrest them. When free women of color held private parties in their homes, if constables saw any dancing, the men who attended were arrested whether they were white or Black.[25]

Cap Français had a number of well-established free Black businessmen and women: fishers, masons, pastry chefs, wigmakers, and others. In the 1780s, free Black and biracial people owned 20 percent of the houses in the city, and more than fifty free Black residents of Cap bought or sold goods worth the purchase price of five to ten slaves.[26] Like others in the city, these people held slaves and profited from their labor; some adopted the common practice among French colonists of branding these people. Some free Black and biracial people bought relatives in slavery and sheltered them, while saving money for their freedom papers.[27]

Police raids occurred in Cap's free Black neighborhood, known as Petite Guinée (Little Africa), where affordable rents attracted white tenants as well. Médor said that one of his free Black acquaintances named Dainé lived "in the swamp"; this is undoubtedly a reference to Petite Guinée, which frequently flooded.[28] Médor admired the free Black people he knew in Cap, but he knew that colonists disapproved of them.[29] He said that he wanted to be free so he could "dress like them, by the bad business they conduct when they are free."[30] By "bad business," Médor likely meant the profitable trade in stolen goods received from slaves.

When constables arrested free Black or white people for a serious crime, the trial took place in Cap Français's local court, which had jurisdiction over the town and ten surrounding parishes. Local judges were legal professionals from France who came to the colony hoping to become rich planters. The provincial appeals court, known as the Superior Council, consisted of eighteen judges, many of whom were established planters. They heard appeals from the North Province, which was the wealthiest and most populous of the colony's three provinces. In Médor's time, the provincial governor, the governor-general, and the intendant also lived in Cap Français. This accumulation of high-ranking officials and judges meant that controversies in or around the town quickly attracted government attention at the highest levels.

The two largest buildings in Cap Français were the Jesuit compound and the church. Médor would have seen Jesuit priests walking the streets in their black robes, and he would have watched their order build its colonial headquarters, a two-story stone building roofed in slate. With its dormitories, offices, storerooms, and chapel, this structure, completed in 1748, was far more imposing than any government building. By way of contrast, at that time, the Superior Council heard appeals and debated laws in a royal warehouse at the edge of town.[31]

Although the Jesuit headquarters showed the order's considerable wealth, the church on the Place d'Armes was tottering when Médor lived in Cap. Religion was a low priority for most colonists, and the physical condition of the Cap Français church symbolized this. Under the Jesuits, Black men and women gathered privately in the church. At night, a worship leader usually "taught or preached to the others; the same slaves frequently went into the surrounding area, to teach religion to slaves in houses and plantations."[32] They also created a formal organization, "rais[ing] up some of their number as lead singers, ushers, and sextons." When their community attracted official attention, they were locked out of the church at night. They continued to meet there, coming at noon and at other times when colonists were absent.

In 1761, the council forbade slaves from gathering in churches when colonists were not present. It also prohibited free or enslaved people of color from instructing people about Christianity. The prosecutor for the Superior Council reported that this community was gathering "without permission" and "pretending to operate like a parish council."[33] With no evidence of actual harm, the prosecutor's rationale was that gatherings like these "inevitably damage good order and public safety."[34] This was two years before the Superior Council expelled the Jesuits from the colony for being too sympathetic to enslaved resisters.

Under 1700s French law, all religions except Catholicism were illegal. The state required its Protestant and Jewish subjects to convert before letting them come to Saint-Domingue. Some of these converts attended Catholic services but secretly practiced their own faith. Africans who wanted to follow Islamic teachings or traditional African religions had to hide their practice as well. However, the prosecutor's report about the Black worshippers in Cap's church describes them practicing Catholicism, which suggests that the lockout was not aimed at religious control but was an effort to prevent enslaved people from forming a community.

Jesuit priest Father Boutin taught Christian doctrine in Creole on the steps of Cap's church every Sunday evening. He was responsible for ministering to the tens of thousands of people enslaved in the North Province. He baptized hundreds of slaves every year, heard thousands of enslaved Christians confess their sins, and learned several African languages so he could give last rites to slave trade captives who died right after arriving in the colony. During the yellow fever epidemics of the 1730s, Boutin convinced the town to create a new cemetery so he could bury poor people and slaves on hallowed ground.[35] Médor was living in Cap Français in 1737 when the Jesuits dared to refuse a Christian burial to a profane white merchant named Jérôme Olivier. The decision enraged colonists because Father Boutin had recently performed a full burial service for an elderly enslaved woman who had been publicly executed.[36] Even if they appeared to advocate for slaves, the Jesuits were not against slavery.[37]

Colonists accused Jesuits of illegally emancipating some enslaved babies by describing them as free in the baptismal register, which served as an official record of their status.[38] They claimed that the missionaries wanted to control Saint-Domingue's Black majority. According to one traveler, "Eager to establish their domination, [the Jesuits] worked to gain slaves' confidence by instructing them very specifically about religion and telling them about their sublime being, man's majesty, and his hopes for the future."[39] After Father Boutin died, his successor, Father Duquesnoy, counseled an enslaved woman accused of poisoning to resist her interrogators. This attracted so much controversy that Saint-Domingue evicted the Jesuit order.

Away from the Place d'Armes, some forms of association among slaves were tolerated in practice if not in law. Officials outlawed the slave dance known as the calenda in 1704, but planters in the countryside tolerated it, seeing it as merely a form of entertainment. In the Congo, a *calundu* or *kilundu* was a ritual to summon the spirits. In Angola, the word *quilundo* means "any ancestral spirit that possesses the living."[40] Colonial writer Moreau de Saint-Méry described the calenda as Saint-Domingue's most popular slave dance, noting the participants' extraordinary eye movements, which suggested they were experiencing spirit possession.[41] In 1757, seeking mercy under interrogation about slave resistance, Médor told colonists that they should not let slaves leave their plantations at night to attend calendas.[42]

The town of Cap Français and the surrounding countryside differed in many important ways, but they were not remote from each other. From the market square out through the city gate, sugar fields were just a half hour walk away. Enslaved coachmen, domestic servants, market gardeners, and peddlers regularly traveled between the port town and surrounding plantations. The nine parishes surrounding Cap had 712 plantations in 1739. Over 150 of them were sugar plantations, clustered in the largely deforested coastal plain. People leaving Cap Français could traverse thirty miles of sugar fields with canes standing six feet tall at harvest. These sugar estates were Saint-Domingue's largest, most profitable, and most complex agricultural operations. Plantations in Saint-Domingue's other two provinces, the West and the South, were far less developed, in part because these regions were farther from Atlantic shipping lanes than Cap Français.[43]

Colonists came to Saint-Domingue to extract wealth from its land and return as quickly as possible to France. They wielded their professions and privilege; acquired land through marriage, purchase, or government grants; and leveraged any foothold

MÉDOR'S TOWN AND COUNTRY LIVES

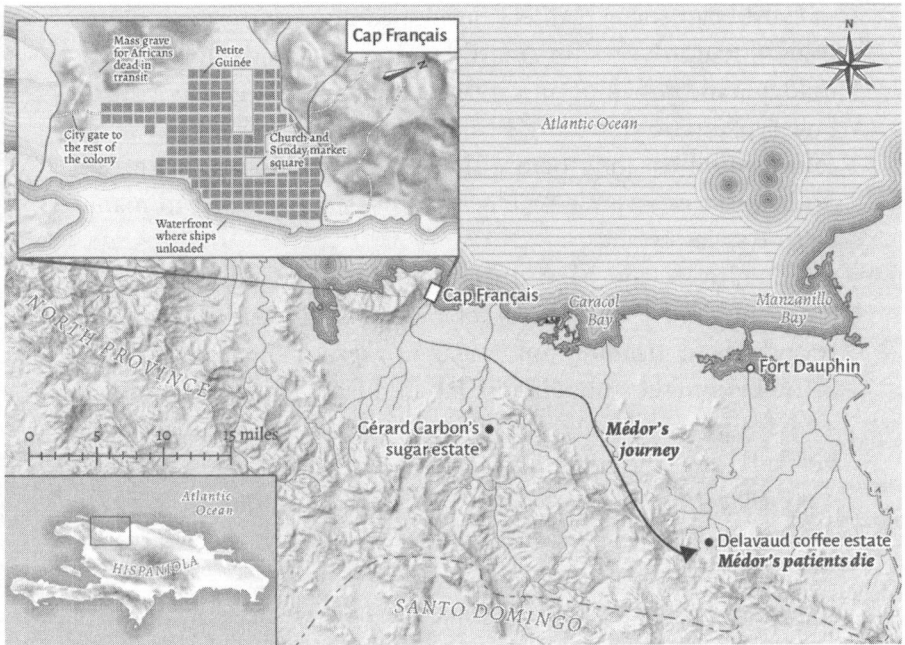

MAP 1.1 Médor's Town and Country Lives

they had in officialdom to their personal advantage. Those who defeated their neighbors in the competition for good land and scarce resources might return to France with vast riches. Those who failed could struggle with unproductive land, drought, and disease and die in Saint-Domingue. Gérard Carbon, one of the most powerful planters of Médor's time, followed the first path. Médor's enslaver, Philippe Delavaud, took the second.

Thirty-two-year-old Gérard Carbon arrived in Cap Français in 1719, when Saint-Domingue's plantation economy was beginning its first phase of rapid growth. He worked as a lawyer in the town's admiralty court and acquired by marriage some of the most fertile lands in Saint-Domingue, about twelve miles from Cap. He became an influential figure in the colonial legal world while he built a sugar estate.[44]

Caribbean sugar planters developed an early form of industrial agriculture, maximizing their profits by investing in technology and trafficking in captives to create a large labor force. Sugar plantations were farms that grew sugarcane, but those canes would rot long before they could be shipped to Europe. To have an exportable product, sugar estates needed to manufacture sugar crystals.

To cultivate and harvest the cane, Gérard Carbon exploited three hundred enslaved workers. They endured lives of poverty and heavy, grinding toil. Sugar workers, about 40 percent of Saint-Domingue's population, labored from sunup to sundown, six days per week, digging holes, planting cane, and weeding fields. During the sugar harvest, when time was critical to profits, enslavers forced them to work eighteen-hour days, seven days a week.[45] This killed dozens of workers on estates of this size every year.[46]

For an aggressive capitalist like Carbon, ensuring a supply of enslaved Africans to work the land was a major priority. In 1740, he bought stakes in three slave ships sailing from France to West Africa. Two of them, *L'Américaine* and the *Patriarche*, unloaded around five hundred captives in Cap Français in 1741.[47] As an investor, Carbon (or his agents) likely would have been accorded first choice of the journey's survivors.

In addition to hundreds of enslaved workers, Carbon needed a sturdy mill to crush the syrup out of thousands of canes, a machine that could turn day and night for weeks. He constructed an expensive waterwheel to power his mill and had his slaves dig canals to supply it with water. He also expanded the property with a royal land grant.[48] Carbon contentiously defended his estate's water supply. He sued seventeen neighboring planters who built an irrigation system that drew from the same river, claiming they had not left enough water to turn his mill. He sent his slaves out at night to damage their irrigation canals. A judge ruled that Carbon could limit his neighbors' water use, but he had to compensate them for the damages to their canals.[49]

Carbon also needed a boiling house where multiple fires could thicken the watery cane juice in big copper vats. Workers would pour the concentrated syrup into hundreds of clay pots with holes at the bottom. When the remaining liquid drained through the holes, it left behind sugar crystals that could be shipped to Europe.

In the early 1750s, Carbon returned to France a very wealthy man. He sold his plantation and used some of the profits to obtain noble status, buying the office of counselor-secretary to King Louis XV. He died in Paris in 1762. His daughter married into a noble family that had just purchased a newly built palace in Paris, which later became one of the world's most famous luxury hotels, the Hôtel Crillon.[50] Through Carbon's descendants, the misery of colonial slavery underwrote the glamour of cosmopolitan Paris.

By the time of Carbon's death, the land he had left in Saint-Domingue was seeded for the kinds of resistance that would eventually overtake the plantation system. A plantation like Carbon's, with three hundred enslaved workers, might have employed five or six white people as bookkeepers, sugar refiners, or managers, but the estate's productivity depended on the leadership of a small cadre of enslaved Black people to control and motivate other enslaved workers. In the fields and in the refinery, these men were called drivers, and each one directed a crew of up to thirty other enslaved workers. Drivers carried a whip and a rod and used them to make other slaves work harder. Forcing a crew to dig more holes or cut more cane could mean the difference between a profitable and unprofitable plantation. In the plantation house, an enslaved woman known as a *ménagère* (housekeeper) was much like a driver because she was responsible for directing a team of perhaps twenty others.

Planters rewarded drivers and housekeepers by giving them better housing, clothing, and food than other slaves. In a position of relative privilege, these workers might live to age sixty, while field-workers, for example, died closer to age forty.[51] Plantation owners or, if they were absent, estate managers chose leaders from the enslaved population after searching for people who could create a community and exercise authority over it. These same men and women could lead fellow workers against their oppressors.[52]

Within the plantation system, some enslaved people, by virtue of their work, experienced greater autonomy or freedom of movement. A coachman ferrying passengers could have regular contact and form relationships with city dwellers and with workers on distant estates. Skilled artisans like blacksmiths, sugar boilers, barrel makers, carpenters, and brick masons could form ties with others while working away. If allowed to take side jobs and earn for their own account, they might be able to save money toward their freedom.

Far away from the plantation, livestock guardians were practically unsupervised. They might be older or disabled workers who could no longer meet the demands of field or factory work. Watching livestock that was pastured on a separate piece of property, perhaps a day's walk away from the plantation, these workers could use the natural elements that surrounded them to make medicines as well as drums and other instruments used in African-style rituals.

Still farther from the plantations, maroons, or people who had escaped from slavery, took refuge in unsettled mountains, and some created hidden villages where they could live in relative freedom. One such man was known as Colas Jambes Coupées (Colas Cut Legs), probably because an enslaver cut his hamstrings to stop him from escaping. He became a focus of planters' fears in the 1720s as he conspired with other maroon leaders, led attacks on travelers and estates, and practiced

African-style rituals. He was captured and sentenced to death for "having secret plans to abolish the colonies . . . [and for using] spells and magic [and] for having repeatedly escaped from irons and prisons and for having poisoned several blacks." In his case and others, using spells and potions gave rise to an accusation of "poisoning." A few years after Colas was executed, another maroon leader named Polydor led similar attacks.[53]

It was not into this wilderness but *beyond* it that Médor was forced to move when his enslaver, Philippe Delavaud, abandoned his medical practice in Cap Français. Delavaud had married into ownership of some mountainous property forty miles from Cap; it was terrain too rugged for a sugar plantation, but the surgeon believed he could grow coffee there. Unlike sugarcane, coffee bushes did not need flat land and they thrived in cool temperatures. This crop did not require industrial machinery or a massive workforce, and coffee beans did not rot quickly like sugarcane. A small slave crew could harvest the crop, crush the ripe coffee berries to extract beans, and wash away their pulpy fruit. No heavy rollers were required, and the coffee beans, once extracted, did not need to be boiled or roasted. They dried in the sun and were ready for export.

Colonists established the island's first coffee plantations in a hilly district south of Cap Français, and soon after enslaved people were forced to cultivate coffee in almost any location where sugar would not grow. Coffee planters made a fortune in the 1740s, and in the 1750s, many colonists rushed to imitate them.[54] Delavaud was one of them.

After twenty years in a bustling port, Médor was removed to a district called Les Perches around 1751.[55] At that time, and some thirty years later, it was so remote and rugged that the French military had not completely mapped it. Les Perches was so unpopulated that maroon groups used it as a refuge up to the 1780s.[56] For Médor, the rest of the household, and the twenty-four additional people Delavaud enslaved for this

1.2 Sorting coffee on a mountain plantation. J. J. Patu de Rosemont (1767–1818). La culture du café à l'île de Bourbon, aquarelle, début du XIXe siècle, ancien Musée National des Arts Africains et Océaniens, devenu Musée national de l'histoire de l'immigration. Cité nationale de l'histoire de l'Immigration[1], Palais de la Porte Dorée, Paris. Reproduction © RMN-Grand Palais / Art Resource, NY.

venture, it was an arduous journey. They walked for miles alongside laden mules into the mountains, toward unsettled lands where they would struggle greatly to survive.[57]

When Médor had been in Les Perches for five years, the Seven Years' War broke out, magnifying the stresses and deprivations that all enslaved people in Saint-Domingue faced. The British mounted the tightest blockade they had ever imposed on French shipping. British cruisers captured French merchants who dared to sail from Bordeaux or Nantes to the Antilles. In 1756 and 1757, British colonial administrators instituted new antismuggling policies, fining American captains heavily for feeding France's plantation colonies.[58] In March 1758, one colonist wrote, "We have never seen the colony in such misery. . . . There are more than 50 English privateers [sailing our coast] and we see them every day. They take everything that is coming in or out [of Cap Français] and neutral captains cannot help us; they capture the Dutch and Spanish [ships] as if they were French."[59]

The blockade meant that planters could not afford favored food products such as wheat flour and red wine for themselves. A barrel of imported flour sold for more than five times its normal price,[60] which was particularly out of reach for planters who were now unable to export their crops. The blockade also meant they could not buy low-quality imported salted beef and fish to feed their slaves. Colonists were reduced to eating slave fare: boiled root crops and bread made from cassava flour. Enslaved people drew nearer to starvation than ever before.[61]

Around this time, the Delavauds probably began to realize that Les Perches was not a good place to grow coffee. A manuscript map from 1760 shows almost no coffee plantations there, suggesting that other colonists had decided the challenges were too great.[62] Water was a major problem, for Saint-Domingue's annual rainy season often bypassed the district. The climate of the North Province was drying in the mid-1700s, which would have made water even scarcer in Les Perches. In 1756, annual rains failed throughout the North, and drought continued into 1757.[63] Slaves' gardens shriveled up. Some root crops like cassava or yams might have survived, but there was less of the millet and plantains that some plantations grew for slave provisions. The drought hurt livestock too. Grazing animals tore at the ground, nibbling on roots below the soil line. They grew thin and prone to disease.

Les Perches and other mountainous border regions were way stations in a critical livestock trade. All of Saint-Domingue ate beef raised in Spanish Santo Domingo, and sugar planters brought thousands of cattle from across the border every year to pull heavy carts and turn sugar mills. The North Province was particularly dependent on the cattle trade. Colonists in Les Perches and other border regions bought cattle from Santo Domingo, fattening them in the mountains before selling them to sugar planters in the plains. When Médor was living in Les Perches in 1750, livestock disease struck both sides of the border.⁶⁴

Médor had already been exposed to the deadly sweep of livestock epidemics during his city life. In 1739, a physician named Jean-Baptiste Pouppé-Desportes reported that diseases had killed many enslaved people and livestock around Cap Français during an extreme drought. Two years later, a massive livestock die-off nearly closed the city's butcher stalls. Then, in 1743, an unusually high number of animals and slaves died during another drought. Another epidemic struck in 1745.⁶⁵ Over a few months in 1751, two thousand horses died in the Cul-de-Sac plain, north of Port-au-Prince. Doctors concluded that this was "an anthrax [outbreak] caused by drought, stagnant water, and bad grazing conditions."⁶⁶

Livestock diseases that worked their way into Saint-Domingue's human food supply proved deadly. In a 1756 petition, eighty-six Cap residents declared that in 1750 or 1751, the quality of beef sold in the city market declined noticeably. In 1755, under a new city butcher, the meat got even worse. Cap residents accused him of slaughtering any ox that could drag itself to the abattoir, no matter how sick. The butcher even sold meat from carcasses found along the roadside. They believed the meat carried a mysterious illness that was killing "a very large number of residents of every age." The meat, they claimed, was "carrion . . . only fit to give to the dogs." As if to verify this, the city's dogs died in great numbers in January or February 1756. So many dog carcasses floated in the harbor that the governor outlawed the sale of fish.⁶⁷

Even in normal times, disease, overwork, and malnutrition made the Caribbean deadly for newly arrived Africans. On the Delavaud estate in the 1750s, the surgeon was driving his slaves to transform one hundred acres of mountainous forest into a plantation.[68] For the first two years, they cut down trees and burned stumps. Delavaud would have supplied them meager rations to save on hauling food through the mountains where there were few roads. After planting gardens, they might have expected to eat better, but the drought drastically reduced their homegrown produce.[69]

Médor tried to help Delavaud's newly purchased coffee slaves survive the strain of heavy labor under conditions of near starvation. We don't know what illness struck them, but Médor administered African-style medicines to people, livestock, and even poultry. There were many healing traditions in the colony that African people practiced, though they were controversial among white people. Colonial physician Raymond Delaborde noted skeptically, "I have often seen their drugs . . . that they call *piails;* it is a pile of 20 or 30 different drugs closed in a box or little sac; each has its different properties . . . this piece of wood will make any girl fall in love with the man who wears it; this piece of earth will infallibly cure that disease."[70] Another physician, Nicolas Bourgeois, praised the skill of Saint-Domingue's enslaved healers: "Our colony has an infinity of black men and even women who practice medicine," practitioners "more ingenious than we in the art of procuring health through simple and natural cures."[71]

Médor's efforts were less skilled than that, or he faced an insurmountable set of circumstances, for his patients died within days of consuming his medicines. He felt remorseful and angry at the people who had given him the cures. Under interrogation for two days, Médor told his enslaver that bad medicine—he said "poison"—had killed them. With those words, the Makandal affair began.

2

Médor's Medicines

MÉDOR'S ATTEMPT TO DOCTOR other enslaved people on the coffee plantation during the famine was a disaster for him and, eventually, for enslaved people throughout the North Province. In May 1757, as people and animals began to die suddenly on the Delavaud estate, the surgeon and his wife, Augustine, confronted Médor about the mysterious deaths.[1] He told them that he had given "poisons" to many of the people and animals who died. Alarmed, they locked him in a room and shackled him to a bed. Saint-Domingue's top civilian administrator, the intendant, explained seven months later, "This *nègre* no sooner found himself in chains than he made a confession that threw the entire district into a state of terror."[2]

Médor's interrogators caused that terror by using the French word poison to describe his African-style medicines. In West Africa, where Médor was from, words that might be translated as poison referred to objects that affected living bodies, either positively or negatively. Like people in many eighteenth-century cultures, he believed that substances had both physical and spiritual properties and that ingesting them could produce negative as well as positive results. Médor got many of his medicines from an enslaved West African man named Gaou, who worked on a ranch in Les Perches. The two men spoke the same language, but that language is unknown. If Médor and Gaou spoke the Fon language, they might have called Gaou's preparations *atin* or *atinken*, words that can be translated into English as powder but also as medicine or poison.[3] If they were Ibo or Ibibio people from southern Nigeria, they might have used the words *nshi* and *nysha*, which are often taken to mean both poison and medicine.[4] Médor was speaking French or Creole to interrogators, but he was likely thinking in the concepts of his native language. While his language history does not rule out a harmful intent, neither does his use of the word poison rule it in. A man of Médor's background could have used the word poison to describe the herbs or powders he gave his neighbors to cure them.

In Médor's time, French legal definitions of poison reflected changing ideas about physical and spiritual harm. In France, poison had long been identified with magic. In 1682, Louis XIV announced a new law that separated the crimes of poisoning and witchcraft. By Médor's time, royal courts considered witchcraft a serious crime only if spells involved blasphemy or potions hurt someone. After redefining poisons as substances that were physically but not spiritually dangerous, the 1682 law established new requirements for storing or selling chemical toxins like arsenic, which was widely used to kill rats, or mercuric chloride, which doctors used to burn off skin ulcers.[5]

As a master surgeon, Philippe Delavaud had internalized the emerging chemical definition of poison. He earned his professional credential by passing a series of rigorous exams in France after working for several years as a medical apprentice.[6] His training included work with drugs, and his wife, Augustine, was a master surgeon's daughter, so she was probably also familiar with the new definition of poison. In Saint-Domingue, master surgeons sold medicines as part of their practice.[7] When the couple lived in Cap Français, they had a cabinet where they stored medicines and, presumably, poisons like arsenic. Delavaud was certain that Médor had confessed to premeditated murder.

Delavaud summoned six of his neighbors to his coffee plantation and asked them to write down Médor's testimony. The

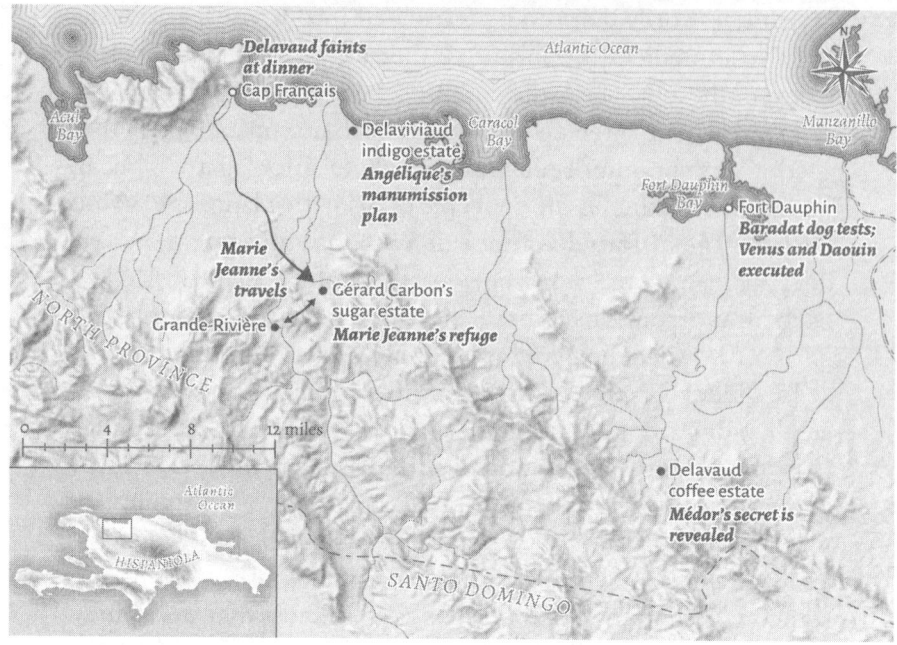

MAP 2.1   Events from Médor's Testimony

nearest court was located in Fort Dauphin, a rugged mountainous journey from Les Perches. The neighbors interrogated Médor in Delavaud's house, shackled, while his fellow house slaves presumably worked nearby.

Delavaud's neighbors questioned Médor in different groups over two days. They were not court officials; they were amateurs creating a document they hoped the court could use for its investigation. All of them apparently lived nearby, since they were able to arrive at the home one day after being asked. Four men heard Médor's account on Thursday, May 25, 1757. One of them, Augustin Richer, was likely Augustine Delavaud's half brother.[8] There are no records describing the three others, Francois Borel de Neuilly, Louis August Aymar, and Jacques Hamelin. Two different men came the following day, Friday,

May 26, to join Philippe Delavaud. One of them, named Balamien, left no documentary trace. The other, Bonnement, was a planter who enslaved Médor's countryman and accused coconspirator Gaou.[9]

The document that Delavaud and his six neighbors created from Médor's words requires considerable interpretation.[10] It is unknown whether Médor spoke to them in French or Creole, the colony's lingua franca. The colonists did not transcribe his words but summarized his stories and revelations in French, referring to him in the third person. They wrote from their own frame of reference, never questioning, for example, what Médor meant by poison. Nor did they transcribe their questions, which must have shown Médor what they wanted to hear. They were not interested in how or why Black people and livestock had perished. They only wanted to know about poisoned masters and the slaves who killed them. They did not ask Médor to describe the substances he administered; they only wanted to know who made them. Médor's interrogators recorded that he got "powders" from a free Black man and that he knew of an enslaved woman who gave her master "herbs" as well as "powders." But the record mostly discussed "poison."

As an enslaved person accused of conspiracy, Médor knew he was negotiating for his life.[11] So the whites would see him as an ally, he named sixteen people who he claimed made or used poison. As he tried to win the colonists' trust, he improvised, at times revealing information that was against his interests. As he searched for stories to illustrate his good faith or his regret about past actions, he exposed secrets that the household staff had concealed from their enslavers for years. His urgency and his need to sway his captors were obvious when, on both days, he called interrogators back from lunch early to give them new information.[12]

Médor began his first day of testimony by expressing his motivation for confessing. He was trying, he said, "to repair the wrongs he had committed against his master and several neighboring planters." In practical terms, however, he needed to convince Delavaud that other people, including the medicine makers, were the real criminals, so he could avoid being sent to the court at Fort Dauphin. For twenty years, Médor and other enslaved people had learned that influencing and even misleading Delavaud was crucial to avoiding punishments. Médor hoped and had reason to expect that he could persuade his master to protect him from the colonial courts.[13] A judge would give him no chance to present his version of events, except under hostile questioning. He knew that court officials would probably torture him, as French law permitted.[14] Persuading Delavaud and the neighboring planters was his last chance; from Fort Dauphin, there would be no return.

Influencing a powerful person, Médor would reveal, was the goal of most of the poisonings he knew about. These occurred, he told his interrogators, because enslaved people wanted to get freedom "sooner." For most enslaved people, freedom was absolutely out of reach, but nearly all enslaved people knew of local free Black people who had been manumitted by their enslavers. They might be women who bore their enslaver's child or people who performed extraordinary acts of loyalty or bravery to help their enslaver. They might be workers who were permitted to earn and keep their money, which they paid to their enslaver for freedom. For Médor and others who worked closely with an enslaver, influencing him toward manumission was a tantalizing possibility. An outright promise of manumission could become an enslaved person's North Star. Writing about an enslaved African man in eighteenth-century Brazil, James Sweet described promises of manumission as "a tool used by masters to exact a steep financial, human, and psychic toll on their slaves, especially Africans."[15]

Promises of freedom, once uttered, were difficult to enforce without a willing enslaver. In 1785, an unnamed woman in Cap

Français persuaded a lawyer to sue her master, Arnaud. Arnaud had promised the woman that he would free her, and he had drafted a power of attorney to that effect. The woman's lawyer argued that when Arnaud wrote this document, he made a legally binding promise to her. The court rejected this interpretation, ruling that the woman was still Arnaud's property because he had never dated the papers and had explicitly revoked them eighteen months later.[16]

Manumission required considerable paperwork that only an enslaver or his legal representative could complete. An enslaver had to write the governor for official permission to free a slave and give reasons for wanting to do so.[17] The Naval Ministry disapproved of self-purchases, so masters' petitions usually claimed that the manumission was a reward for faithful service, never mentioning any financial transaction. To complete the manumission process, a master or his representative would have to announce the ex-slave's freedom after mass at the local church for three consecutive Sundays and have the priest document these declarations in writing.[18] Sometime around 1760, the colony started charging enslavers a freedom tax for each manumission.[19] Each step had to be completed correctly, or the freedom papers would be invalid.

An enslaver might provide for manumission in his or her will. But when that master died, an estate executor could ignore the will's manumission instructions, and an enslaved person could not challenge that. In the late 1730s, a colonist who had promised to free an enslaved woman named Marie-Catherine traveled to France and died there. His executors in the colony refused to free Marie-Catherine, pointing out that the deceased had not applied for the necessary government permission. She was only freed when the colonist's brother in Paris ordered her manumission in writing and asked royal authorities to help.[20] In 1742, the colonial government canceled sixteen testamentary manumissions granted by a colonist who died without applying for official permission. His widow sued to overturn the provisions so she wouldn't lose control of her human property. The court ruled in her favor.[21] A slave's surest route to legal manumission was to have the favor of a healthy and enthusiastic master, not to have a dead one. To attain freedom, an enslaved person needed to boost motivation and change minds among the living.

This was true for three enslaved women who, Médor testified, had dosed their enslaver in Cap Français. Médor said, "Dame Larue was poisoned by her domestics Magdeleine, Margot, and Angelique, who today belong to Sieur Latapy."[22] His information came to him thirdhand from a friend who had heard it from Thereze, an enslaved woman who now belonged to the Larue heirs. Médor did not say that the three women wanted to kill Dame Larue, only that they had poisoned her and that she died. If Magdelaine, Margot, and Angélique were seeking manumission, they may have been secretly giving Dame Larue African-style medicines. If manumission had been their goal, her death would have put a foreseeable end to their influence over her. Although we don't know what killed Dame Larue, Médor said that Magdelaine, Margot, and Angélique remained enslaved.

After reporting Médor's allegations against the three women, the interrogators wrote that "he knows only one way to stop the course of these poisons and malefices which is [to address] what led him to do what he did, which is to not promise liberty to nègres, négresses, or mulattos; and that it was only in order to get it earlier that they poisoned several whites." In light of what Médor and other enslaved people understood about how to obtain freedom, this supports the conclusion that the three women secretly administered African-style medicines to increase Dame LaRue's motivation to launch the manumission process.

Colonists were accustomed to the idea that people used deadly poisons to get what they wanted. Hundreds of eighteenth-century French publications retold the story of Marquise de Brinvilliers, a noblewoman executed in 1676 for poisoning her wealthy father and two brothers.[23] In a grim joke based on her crime, the French press nicknamed arsenic the "inheritance powder."[24] Hers was a fearsome example of a person excluded from legal standing administering a deadly dose to gain power.

Inexplicable, sudden death also prompted suspicions of poisoning in French popular culture, especially when the deceased was a powerful person. Rumors of courtiers poisoning each other at the court of Versailles reached a peak in the early 1700s when Louis XIV's son and grandson both died within a few years of each other. It was widely rumored that the king's nephew, the Duc d'Orléans, had poisoned them to leap ahead in succession and claim the crown for himself. In fact, they died from smallpox and scarlet fever.[25]

Over the course of his interrogation, Médor admitted that he had been giving medicines—"poisons"—to the Delavauds for many years. He obtained them from one community when he lived in Cap Français and from another community after he moved to Les Perches. In Cap Français, he obtained "powders" from Dainé, a free Black man who lived in the city's Petite Guinée neighborhood. It was probably there, among ex-slaves, that Médor learned of the secret that he confessed to interrogators: "a secret that can only bring about the end of the colony, of which the whites know nothing." Free Blacks were the driving force behind this conspiracy, he said, "using all these means to increase their numbers, in order to be able to confront the whites if necessary."[26]

In other words, Médor and a free Black community in Cap sought to shift the balance of power in Saint-Domingue, using medicines that would make masters more willing to keep their manumission promises. They aimed to increase the free Black population over time, so that, eventually, ex-slaves and their freeborn descendants would be strong enough to force colonists to negotiate with them. Médor and other Africans were imagining a political process led by free Blacks, backed by the implicit power of a massive enslaved population.

When the Delavauds moved Médor to Les Perches, he lost his Cap Français network of friends like Dainé. Looking for new medicine makers, he met three men enslaved on nearby ranches: Gaou, Daouin, and Ferou. Like many other people trying to re-create African healing arts in the New World, they were keen observers of local plants and animals.[27] They supplied Médor with the powders he confessed to giving "his master, his mistress, his [master's] children," and "20 slaves some of whom are dead, as well as animals and poultry, some of which died."[28] Importantly, the lives lost on the Delavaud estate by poison or bad medicine were those of enslaved people, animals, and poultry, but not Philippe, Augustine, or their children. If Médor was trying to kill his enslavers, he was a very poor poisoner. Philippe died in 1763, and Augustine in 1788.[29] Médor's testimony suggests that when the medicines Gaou, Daouin, and Ferou gave him turned out to be deadly to Delavaud's enslaved coffee workers, he regretted the suffering he had inadvertently caused. He wanted authorities to arrest the three men for giving him bad medicines.

Leading up to midday at his first interrogation session, Médor explained how enslaved people in the countryside were able to build relationships and rapidly share information during nighttime visits with friends and neighbors at other plantations. Suitors and their intendeds visited between plantations, and enslaved people from different estates gathered at calendas. Médor's interrogators wrote, "As soon as a new black understands French, he is told that everything the whites do or say is known within two hours [by Blacks living] in a ten-league circle." Médor advised colonists to curtail this by forcing Black men and women to stay at home and to forbid them from having outside visitors. In the moments before his interrogators left to eat their noon meal, Médor was pressed to name poison makers, and he implicated men who lived on three different estates: Jean Yoquo, Adrien, and Christophe, who Médor said worked with two other enslaved people making substances that were too expensive for Médor to buy.

Before long, Médor sent someone to ask the interrogators to come back. He may have still hoped that showing his remorse and providing more information could bring him leniency. Over the next day and a half he described how an enslaved mother sought freedom for herself and her family, how Delavaud's household workers escaped blame after he fainted one night, and how Médor and a larger community of enslaved people rescued a child from bondage.

Médor described an enslaved woman named Angélique, her son François, and her daughter Catin, captives on the estate of François Delaviviaud, an indigo planter.[30] Angélique had gained her enslaver's favor, probably working as a domestic servant. He allowed her to sell goods on her own account in exchange for a monthly sum. Even if the arrangement served to enrich her enslaver, the net proceeds were crucial to an enslaved person saving for her freedom. Angélique also wanted to see her daughter Catin become Delaviviaud's concubine. A woman in a sexual relationship with an enslaver might be able to influence him to free her family. To that end, Angélique secretly gave powders to her enslaver. Médor testified that he encountered François on the road during an errand, reminded him of the "secret among the blacks," and asked where his mother got her "herbs and magic powders." François said that every Saturday evening, she sent him to the Fournier plantation to buy preparations from a man enslaved there.

When Delaviviaud died after a long wasting illness, Angélique's manumission plans were likely destroyed. It is unknown whether she was ultimately able to entice him toward Catin. During his illness, she may have even worked to heal her enslaver, but when he died, her leverage ended, and her family was reduced to being an asset on the estate's balance sheet. Angélique had already endured dislocation after the death of her previous enslaver, which culminated in her family's sale to Delaviviaud.³¹ On his death, Angélique, Catin, and François faced being sold and separated, or worse. The worst happened when Médor's interrogation made her into a "poisoner." The colonial court likely burned her at the stake.³²

Agnès, the head housekeeper enslaved by Delavaud, had also worked toward freedom. Twenty years before Médor's interrogation, she ran the household and directed its staff, and she was possibly in a sexual relationship with Philippe Delavaud. Médor said that, when they lived in the port city, Agnès was dosing Delavaud with powders "to procure liberty for herself sooner." She did not prepare her own powders; she bought them after they had passed through many hands. Often, the makers lived in the countryside, where they could harvest needed materials unobserved and prepare them in privacy.³³

Médor told his interrogators what he knew about Agnès's supply chain. Jean Yoquo, an enslaved barrel maker who lived and worked in the hilly woods near the Carbon plantation, made powders. He might have given them to André Carbon, who was the biracial son of the prosperous sugar planter Gérard Carbon. André was born in Saint-Domingue to an enslaved mother; he had close and enduring ties to the enslaved community, and he also had some wealth and the ability to move freely in the countryside and the city. Médor claimed that André Carbon gave Agnès powders. Médor also knew that a man named Jupiter living on the De la Selle plantation made powders. De la Selle's male servant was Quessy, who traveled from the plantation to the city. According to Médor, Quessy was Agnès's lover, and he gave her powders. In exchange, Médor said, Agnès gave Quessy five of Delavaud's shirts.

One night in 1737, when De la Selle was staying in the Cap Français house, Delavaud fell ill at the evening table. He drank from a bottle of wine and suddenly collapsed, unconscious. When he regained his senses, he gasped that his throat and chest were burning and called for oil, which he swallowed in great gulps. He recovered and assembled the enslaved household workers: Médor, Agnès, Scipion, Hippolyte, Adrien, and Élisabeth, who was called Zabeth. He demanded to know what they had given him to drink. Agnès, Médor, and the others told Delavaud that they had seen his wife, Augustine, pour his wine after taking something from the apothecary cabinet. Delavaud believed them and punished his wife by sending her away from her birthplace, Saint-Domingue, to live in France. She remained there for years.

Médor was convinced that Delavaud had been poisoned, although the surgeon might have suffered an actual medical crisis. Médor confessed regret for Augustine's banishment, twenty years before. Likely addressing Augustine's brother, who was one of his interrogators, Médor begged forgiveness for having blamed her. In a surprising reversal, Médor said that the lady was innocent. It was Agnès who had prepared the wine, he said. Médor reported that Agnès, deceased by the time of the interrogation, had poured powder into Delavaud's wine bottle right before he drank. It was poison, Médor claimed, that she received from André Carbon.

Médor's coerced confession describes several enslaved people in positions of relative privilege, who had money, special freedoms of movement, and personal access to their enslavers. Agnès, like Angélique, wanted to use African-style medicines to speed her manumission, and enslaved Africans in other colonies used substances in this same way. In the Swedish Caribbean colony of Saint-Barthélemy in 1811, one woman paid another large sums for love potions to mix in her enslaver's food, so he would free her. In Brazil, enslaved people bought substances from African-inspired healers who told them the medicine would "tame" their masters; the plant *petiveria alliacea* or guinea weed was one of several species that enslaved Brazilians called *amansa-senhor* or master-tamer.[34]

Agnès relied on intermediaries and ultimately on distant and unknown makers to obtain the substances she needed. Loyalty and commerce held her network together until Delavaud's poison investigation forced Médor to negotiate for his life. Agnès and Médor had little motive to kill the enslavers they were dosing for manumission. They also may have lacked knowledge of the substances they were administering. Agnès knew and trusted André Carbon and Quessy, but they were intermediaries; they didn't make her powders. The same applied to Médor, who was forced to rely on Gaou, Daouin, and Ferou, men he didn't know well, when he arrived at the unsettled territory of Les Perches.

If Médor's account is to be believed, a yearslong household conspiracy protected Agnès by blaming Augustine Delavaud for her husband's collapse that night. The bonds of loyalty and secrecy within that household community withstood all the usual tensions that arise among family members, neighbors, and workers with differing needs and viewpoints—until the full scrutiny and power of his enslavers overwhelmed Médor. One explanation for why the twenty-year-old incident of Delavaud's blackout became a focus of interrogation might be that, when enslaved people and animals started dying on his estate, the surgeon began to doubt the colonial adage that enslavers could never be harmed by enslaved people's African-style magic.[35]

As Médor grew increasingly desperate to gain leniency from his interrogators, he also revealed the hidden work of a community that had rescued an enslaved child from Augustine Delavaud's abuse. In 1750, Augustine had returned from her expulsion to France and was again living in Cap Français in her husband's household. Every night before Augustine went to bed, she ordered an enslaved girl named Marie Jeanne to be chained to the bedpost. This child was André Carbon's daughter, born of a Delavaud domestic slave who had died some years earlier. In his testimony, Médor did not name the mother, but it was probably Agnès.³⁶ Marie Jeanne had tried once to escape, and André had repeatedly tried to buy the child, but the Delavauds refused to sell her.

Frustrated by the Delavauds' refusal, André Carbon convinced Médor and Venus, another enslaved Delavaud servant, to arrange Marie Jeanne's escape. During the night of June 26, 1750, Médor testified, they removed the girl's chains, led her out of the house, and took her to stay with Gene (Jeanne) Baudin, a free Black woman in Cap Français. After three days, they escorted her to the Larue house, where Venus knew several enslaved women, including the three who dosed Dame Larue. A day or two later, they smuggled Marie Jeanne out of town to the Bauval plantation, where she had been captured in her previous escape attempt. Médor testified that she stayed in the hut of an enslaved man named Bouquement.

Marie Jeanne finally reached Gérard Carbon's sugar plantation, roughly twelve miles from the city, and lived there in hiding with André. Five enslaved women in four households knew she was there, and Médor named them all: Monsieur Dufoucher's Madeleine, Monsieur Carbon's Babeth and Angélique, the Larue heirs' Jeannot, and Sieur Latapy's Magdelaine.

At the time Médor was testifying, some seven years after the rescue, Marie Jeanne was still in hiding. André Carbon's offer of payment to the Delavauds was still outstanding, and, unless they agreed to accept it, Marie Jeanne would remain a fugitive. Médor testified that André Carbon occasionally took his daughter on short excursions to visit Bouquement's hut and to the free Black town of Grande-Rivière. Until Médor's interrogation, André Carbon had relied successfully on at least twelve people to keep the secret of his daughter's escape.

Médor said that Carbon paid him and Venus for the rescue, giving them money gradually. He did not name the amount, but he did say that Marianne Poissy, a free Black woman in Cap Français, was holding twelve hundred livres for Venus. This would have been enough for Venus to buy her freedom, but in May 1757, she was still enslaved to the Delavauds. It seems likely that Augustine Delavaud suspected but could not prove that Venus had helped rescue Marie Jeanne and so refused her self-purchase, just as she had refused Carbon's money for Marie Jeanne.

On Friday, the second day of interrogation, Médor lost confidence that he could save himself. It was the first day that his master, Philippe Delavaud, joined the interrogation. That meant Médor could appeal directly to him and scrutinize Delavaud's face and bearing to measure his chances for success. Following French legal custom, Médor was also forced to confront some of the people he had incriminated the previous day, to see if he would change his testimony. Médor's words early in the interrogation suggest that Gaou was present to confront him. Médor recanted when asked about his claim that Gaou supplied him with poisons. No, he said, Gaou had not given him anything that could have harmed his master, mistress, or their children. Gaou only supplied a potion for Venus: a scrub for her face and hands that would make Augustine Delavaud like her.

Venus was also brought into the room. The interrogation text suggests she had been interviewed the previous day. A note appears to confirm that three enslaved women had poisoned their mistress. Another note indicates Venus denied that a free Black woman was holding twelve hundred livres for her. Venus immediately contradicted Médor on the question of poisons. Gaou had produced two potions, not one, she said. Gaou gave her a bottle that would make her mistress like her better and gave Médor a bottle, telling him "in their language" that it would "finish off" Madame Delavaud. Venus said Médor pressed that bottle into her hands and urged her to kill her mistress, but she emptied its contents into the dirt behind her hut because her conscience pricked her.

At noon, Delavaud and the other interrogators went to another room to eat. As Médor waited, he lost hope. Delavaud's presence as an interrogator or Venus's testimony may have convinced him that his enslaver would not protect him. He had implicated himself in multiple acts of resistance, and the iron cuffs around his ankles surely felt firmer than the bonds of influence he had cultivated over many years with Delavaud. At two o'clock, Médor sent Catin, an enslaved woman, to tell Delavaud "that he did not know his fate . . . for the crimes he caused and for which he had declared his guilt, and he understood that his master had condemned him to be sent to the judge at Fort Dauphin for . . . his trial."

When Delavaud left the interrogation room, he did not return. Bonnemain, one of Gaou's enslavers, took his place. Interrogators brought Venus back into the room and sat her face-to-face again with Médor, urging them to reconcile their conflicting stories. The interrogation document suggests that, at this moment, he and Venus agreed to a text drawn up by the interrogators. In part, it said, "In revenge for some punishments received from their master and mistress, they used several slave poisoners in Trou parish, Cap Français, and in Les Perches to acquire herbs and magic powders that they used in all types of drinks, broths, stews and others by intervals and at different times and even in the poultices that their masters needed."

The interrogators' influence becomes more obvious as the statement proceeds. Médor and Venus admitted that they "caused their masters several serious illnesses and forced them to stay in bed and in their rooms, unable to do anything for two, four, and six months at a time, and that the illness of Dame Delavaud, who has been languishing and moribund for several years, notably for close to five years with suffering and pain in all her internal parts, has been caused only by the magic powders which they say they have served daily to her, as well as to her husband, their children, and to nearly all their slaves."

Médor's and Venus's final statement included three confessions that neither had made previously: they wanted revenge against the Delavauds for punishing them; they poisoned various foods and medicines; and they deliberately sought to kill their masters, other enslaved people, and livestock. These contradicted Médor's earlier testimony and the logic of his situation. The final statement likely bore no trace of Médor's or Venus's voice; it was a perfect chorus of the fears of enslavers all over Saint-Domingue.

On the next day, Saturday, Médor did not testify but asked to make another statement about Venus. Delavaud contacted the first four interrogators, asking them to return to his plantation. When they arrived at about nine o'clock Sunday morning, they went to the room where Médor was imprisoned. Médor lay dead on a pallet, a knife in his ribs and a chain around his neck, an iron *barre* still cuffed to his feet. Besides the protruding knife handle, the chain, and the barre, the interrogators claimed that there was only one sign of violence on his body: white scars on his buttocks, healed over from a whipping weeks or months earlier. They concluded that there was no evidence that Médor had been recently tortured.

Delavaud's explanation was that Médor had confessed to "put his conscience at rest and to save innocent lives." He killed himself, stealing a knife from one of his guards and plunging it into his right side up to the hilt. Delavaud's explanation is just one possibility. Other people had a strong motive to keep Médor from testifying before the court. His revelations had already ruined the lives of dozens of people, including Venus, Gaou, and Daouin, yet after his confession, he had asked to say more.

Soon after Médor's death, court officials began to round up the people he had named. Colonists' alarm about Médor's "secret" grew when authorities found evidence that two of Médor's suppliers did possess fast-acting toxins. When constables went to the Juchereau ranch where Gaou was enslaved, they found that he had died just before they arrived. They concluded that he had taken one of his own poisons to avoid arrest.[37] They arrested Daouin and collected gourds and bottles from his hut. The royal judge in Fort Dauphin ordered a local physician, Antoine Baradat, to test these objects for poisons, accompanied by a local surgeon, Etienne Lhér, and Jean Cruon, commander of the Fort Dauphin garrison.[38]

Baradat's team found that most of Daouin's gourds contained traditional remedies. They identified African pepper, licorice seed, brown sugar, powdered charcoal, rock alum, and Gaillac bark, which French doctors used to treat sore joints. They focused their poison tests on two mysterious items: a packet of dried leaves that they could not identify and a square flask containing leaves soaking in rum. Based on the odor of this mixture, they suspected that Daouin's flask contained leaves from *absinthe bâtarde*, a plant that closely resembled the European absinthe plant. Colonial doctors used these leaves in poultices for joint pain and administered them orally to fight worms or fevers.[39]

Baradat ground the unidentified dry leaves into a powder and mixed them with the contents of the flask. The experimenters fed the mixture to four dogs, in progressively more dilute concentrations. The dog that received the strongest dose "fell down dead."[40] When Baradat opened its body, blood in two ventricles of its heart appeared to be coagulated. The dog that took a weaker dose vomited, convulsed, drooled for six hours, and then recovered. Dogs that took the weakest doses suffered no effects.

However, when Baradat collected his own absinthe bâtarde leaves, he could not replicate these results. Although Baradat concluded otherwise, his results suggest that the dogs were afflicted by a powerful toxin that was not inherent to the plant but may have been deposited on it. Years later, Baradat found similar symptoms—thick black blood—in the hearts of cattle who died rapidly in a livestock epidemic. In some of the cattle, he said, the blood was so thick that it would not come out of their veins when doctors tried to bleed them.[41] If naturally occurring toxins were deposited on Daouin's leaves, it is noteworthy that he was enslaved on a farm next to a large communal pasture and that Gaou was a caretaker on a ranch.[42]

Médor's confession set colonists searching for Black poisoners. Médor's secret, they believed, was a plot to kill all the whites. In a surge of poisoning investigations that unfolded over eighteen months, Saint-Domingue's doctors never again found anything like Daouin's leaves. For another twenty years, Saint-Domingue's physicians and botanizing colonists tried and failed to find a local poison that would have an immediate deadly effect without any distinctive taste.[43]

It would take decades before colonial doctors could explain the mysterious deaths that prompted Médor's confession. Colonists never did understand the values underpinning Médor's "secret that reigns among the blacks." They did not see that he described a plan that would change the balance of power in the colony one person at a time, using manumission to slowly and nonviolently increase the free Black population. A larger vision drove them, he explained: the eventuality of free Blacks "confronting the whites if necessary." Médor's words suggest that some free Black and enslaved people saw individual manumission as a form of collective resistance; one person's liberty could move all free Blacks closer to the goal of challenging white control.

3

Poison and Panic

IN THE WEEKS AFTER MÉDOR'S DEATH, the royal prosecutor of Fort Dauphin made ample use of the interrogation document penned by Philippe Delavaud and his neighbors. He arrested many of the people Médor named and used Médor's testimony to convict Venus and Daouin of poisoning.[1] A royal official visiting from Cap Français attended their trial in August and noted that "the main culprits have said nothing." Venus and Daouin resisted, refusing to succumb to torture and implicate others. On the strength of Médor's confession, they were sentenced to die, and less than four months after his death, they were burned at the stake.[2]

André Carbon escaped death, and his daughter Marie Jeanne eluded capture, but Fort Dauphin authorities arrested André and Jean Yoquo, the enslaved barrel maker. A visitor writing to André's white father in France, said, "They are both accused of poison. I do not know how they will get out of it, they could be burned like so many others who are in the same situation, it is a great scourge in the island."[3] Six months later, the Fort Dauphin court dropped the poisoning charge against André and transferred him to Cap Français on the charge of stealing a slave—his daughter Marie Jeanne. Except for Médor, no one in the community who had aided in Marie Jeanne's rescue betrayed her. After keeping André Carbon in prison for almost a year, the authorities could not prove the kidnapping and were forced to release him.⁴ Marie Jeanne, who would have been in her early twenties, had vanished.

André Carbon's community held a calenda on Sunday, July 23, 1758; the date suggests that it coincided with his release. There would have been drumming, singing, and dancing. Ritual leaders would have offered food and drinks to the spirits and redistributed these offerings to attendees. Field-workers, plantation artisans, and domestic workers from all the neighboring estates would have attended. If the women and men who had helped Marie Jeanne escape were still alive and free, they might have dared to come. The calenda was so loud that Charles Fournier de la Chapelle, the Cap Français prosecutor who had pursued André, fined Gérard Carbon's plantation agent three hundred livres for permitting it. The agent complained to Gérard Carbon that Fournier levied the fine "even though he allows calendas everywhere on his property."⁵ It is unknown whether Fournier was angry about the noise and disruption or the fact that André Carbon had triumphed over Fournier's attempts to convict him of poisoning and kidnapping.

The 1758 calenda would have been a welcome release for the people enslaved by Gérard Carbon. They had survived two years of ongoing famine, unexplained deaths, and poison trials. Every enslaved or free Black person in the region around Cap Français and Fort Dauphin had experienced deep hunger due to a terrible drought and their enslavers' war with Britain. The drought had likely destroyed many slaves' gardens, and the British blockade made local food much more expensive. Colonists had started to eat slaves' food, such as plantains and manioc. Without food imports, enslavers also stopped providing salted fish and beef to workers. Some enslaved people might have eaten their own poultry, pigs, or other small livestock. Others could have bought meat discarded from the slaughter yard that colonists wouldn't eat. Or they might have chewed on *tassau*, the sun-dried jerky from Santo Domingo sold by Black peddlers who walked from plantation to plantation.

Even if enslaved people were able to feed themselves in conditions of near famine, they saw strong, healthy neighbors dying suddenly and mysteriously. Gérard Carbon's plantation agent described these swift and unexpected deaths in October 1757: "A number of planters have been ruined by losing most of their slaves in this manner; the poison has reached several whites who have died of it."[6] Regardless of the danger white people thought *they* were in, Black people were dying in far greater numbers as death swept through plantations. Some planters had fifty or sixty slaves working on their estates. In less than two weeks, only four or five remained, and sometimes not a single one.[7] In June 1758, Saint-Domingue's governor-general, by then convinced of the cause behind so many deaths, reported, "For the last two to three years, the use of [poison] has become so common in the northern part of the island that besides a very large number of white persons who have died from poison . . . we count at least *six to seven thousand* slaves who have been destroyed by this wretched practice."[8]

At a time when food scarcity, disease, and plantation conditions were life-threatening, enslaved people found themselves shackled, tortured, interrogated, accused of poisoning, and burned to death in a spiraling investigation fueled by colonists' fear. Saint-Domingue's planters had an established culture of torture, despite the Code Noir's prohibition. For at least fifty years, French royal officials knew that colonists tortured their slaves.[9] In 1727, for example, the royal minister in charge of the French colonies noted "that there are colonists who, on the suspicion that they have slaves who are sorcerers, give themselves permission to kill them under their own private authority, some by fire, and others by breaking their bones with sticks or hammers."[10]

Slaves accused of poisoning were subjected to extrajudicial torture before any legal process began. They were locked away in plantation outbuildings and abused during interrogations by their masters and others. Raymond Delaborde, a physician who worked in Saint Domingue in the 1760s, described how slaves accused of poisoning were made to confess: "The plantation master has no trouble finding the causes [of unexplained deaths]; poison is all he knows; suspicion falls first on the most intelligent slaves, it fixes on the one the master trusts the most; he is put into irons and all kinds of tortures are used to make him admit the crime; they will definitely manage to make him say what they want."[11]

It is not surprising that desperate prisoners implicated many more people in an attempt to save themselves. Torture was a hallmark of poison investigations, not just on estates but also under the auspices of high colonial courts. Under French law, torture was legal when conducted by the courts. In conspiracy cases, torture was provided for under the law even after a person was convicted and sentenced to death. Prisoners were subjected to one last round to elicit the names of alleged coconspirators. Under this regime, an ever-expanding roster of suspected poisoners proliferated, and colonists grew convinced that poisoning threatened every master.

In December 1757, Saint-Domingue's intendant explained to the naval minister that "last May we suddenly discovered in the region of Cap and Fort Dauphin a nearly universal practice of poisoning carried out by slaves against their masters as well as on slaves and livestock."[12] Some colonists interpreted Médor's revelation of a "secret . . . that must surely result in the end of the colony" as a declaration of war.[13] The district attorney whose prosecutions launched the poison scare described that time: "The situation in Saint-Domingue's North Province in the years 1755, 1756 and 1757 was so dire . . . in the middle of an unfortunate war with the English, who devastated the coasts of this island, colonists were fighting an internal slave war that was all the more dangerous because it was often waged with unknown poisons."[14]

The threat of a British invasion meant that white plantation employees had to leave work for weeks to mount watch along the coast and practice military readiness. If, before the war, seven white men dominated two hundred enslaved people on a sugar plantation, under the burden of militia service, there might be only four white people left to keep control. Just weeks before Médor was accused of poisoning, one of Gérard Carbon's correspondents wrote him that "things are so bad here [in the North Province] that no one leaves home except to mount watch [with the militia] . . . it has been 18 months since I have been to Cap Français."[15]

Perceiving themselves as embattled from abroad and within, enslavers feared a murderous backlash against their brutally oppressive regime. A colonial critic in 1776 explained that "most whites live in fear [of poison]; nearly all feel that their slaves are right to hate them and to take justice into their own hands."[16] One colonist wrote in 1757, "We are frightened to see that almost all the guilty [slaves] are those who work in the big house, those we trust the most, the coachman, the cook and other domestic servants."[17]

All these factors—mysterious deaths, white fears, and tortured confessions—produced a fruitless, spiraling investigation that blinded authorities to causes other than poison for an epidemic of death that enveloped the countryside. When colonists heard Médor describe a future where free Black people would be numerous enough to confront colonists and "end the colony," it was proof that enslaved people were plotting to kill them or drive them off the island. They would or could not imagine that Médor was describing a negotiation process that might "end the colony" by transforming it, and they were deafened to slaves' testimony that African "poisons" were medicinal or magic powders not intended to kill.

For over two years, judges in the North Province interrogated hundreds of suspects and burned more than two dozen people at the stake.[18] Forty years later, a planter recalled that time as "a veritable slaughterhouse. They executed [convicted poisoners]

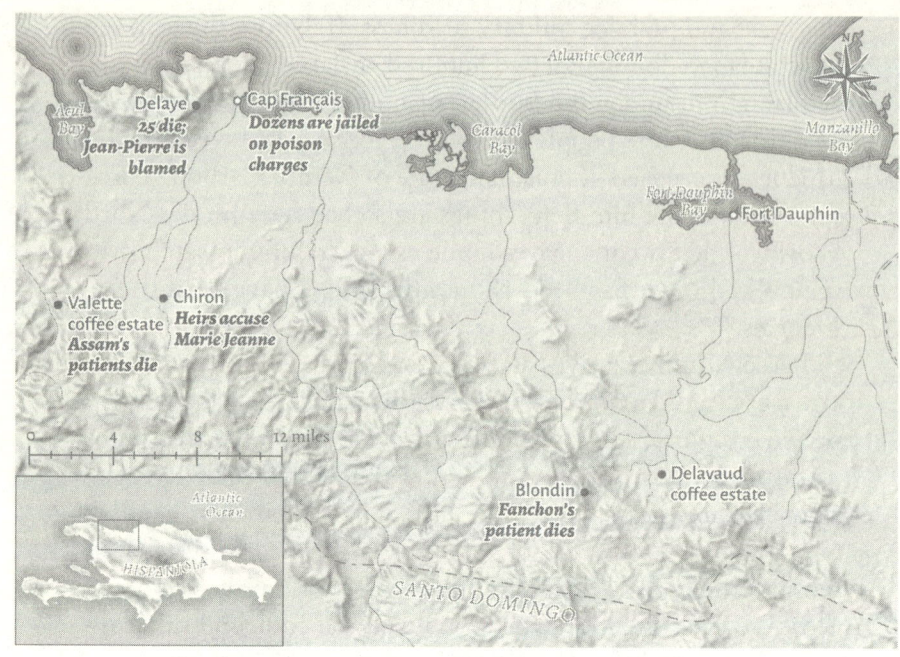

MAP 3.1 Poison Accusations after Médor's Death, 1757

from morning to evening."[19] These proceedings would have generated many documents, including slave testimony, but judges deliberately purged slave criminal trials from court archives. There are records of only six poisoning investigations out of the dozens conducted in the weeks and months after Médor's death. Those six cases survived because Saint-Domingue's intendant copied court documents, bundled them together with Médor's testimony, and, on December 12, 1757, shipped them to the French Naval Ministry to illustrate the poison crisis.[20]

The testimony of the accused people in those cases echoes Médor's confession in several ways. Like him, most of the accused were West Africans, as opposed to Congo-born or island-born people; most were enslaved for domestic work rather than fieldwork. They were often *ménagères*, who directed a household staff, or *hospitalières*, who nursed sick slaves. All were interrogated on the estates where they were enslaved, usually by their enslaver or neighboring colonists. They spoke about dosing slaves or masters with substances that might have been medicines to heal slaves or to tame an enslaver's mind. Some of the accused admitted giving toxins that killed. Nearly all got their doses from Africans who worked away from the enslaver's house, tending animals, cutting sugarcane, or making barrels.

In an example of how quickly the poison scare spread, only ten days after Médor's death, an enslaved man named Jean-Pierre was arrested near Cap Français. Jean-Pierre's enslaver was a farmer and a lawyer who practiced in town,[21] so he would have heard about the Médor case. Jean-Pierre was a "Congo," or person who had been enslaved at a port in West Central Africa, and he was one of several dozen people enslaved by Pierre-Alexandre Delaye. Most others on the farm were likely West African. Delaye's land was in Morne Rouge, in the hills that formed Cap Français's western border.[22] The farm had a large greenhouse for seedlings, irrigation channels controlled by iron gates, and 260 irrigated garden plats covered by barrels. Even during the drought of 1757, a spring flowed on the estate, and Jean-Pierre with other workers grew vegetables that were sold for Delaye's profit in Cap Français. Whereas drought and war meant commercial downturns for coffee and sugar planters, demand for Delaye's lettuce, eggplants, watercress, and other produce was higher than ever.

Over time, twenty-five of Jean-Pierre's coworkers died mysteriously—traumatic losses for Jean-Pierre and the others. Not only did they lose friends and family; everyone wondered who would die next. Delaye seems to have accepted such high mortality among slaves as part of colonial life. But the lawyer's perspective changed dramatically one afternoon when a healthy woman named Pelagie, who may have run the household, died suddenly.

Delaye concluded that someone on his estate had poisoned Pelagie and her twenty-five coworkers. Within a day of Pelagie's death, Delaye hired two surgeons to open her body, and he filed an autopsy report with the royal prosecutor. An interrogation surely took place on the plantation, but no record of it survived. Delaye blamed the deaths on Jean-Pierre, who might have been suspected or even named by other enslaved people. As a West Central African, Jean-Pierre was culturally different from the West Africans who likely made up the rest of the enslaved crew. "Congos" like him represented only 38 percent of the enslaved people trafficked to Saint-Domingue from 1713 to 1756. There is no testimony from Jean-Pierre, but the Cap Français court convicted him of poisoning twenty-six enslaved people and burned him at the stake.[23]

By September, a colonist named Sebastian Courtin was pursuing multiple poisoning investigations. He was a lawyer in Cap Français, temporarily appointed to be the local judge. In the French system of the day, he interrogated suspects to build cases and also decided their guilt or innocence. Death penalty judgments rendered by Courtin were reviewed by the Superior Council. On September 10, the Superior Council upheld a death sentence Courtin had rendered against an unnamed man and woman, both found guilty of poisoning. The council confirmed another poisoning conviction on September 21. A royal official describing these two cases in a letter said that poison cases were becoming more common every day. The trials, he said, revealed that slaves became poisoners because masters were granting too many manumissions.[24]

Fanchon, the enslaved hospitalière on Philibert LeBlondain's sugar estate in a parish close to Les Perches, was also ensnared early in the poison scare.[25] Fanchon kept remedies in her hut that she needed to heal other enslaved people. She may have used French medicines provided by her enslaver or African-style medicines to help her patients. For a slave to make or distribute any remedy or to try to cure any illness, except for snakebites, was illegal under French law.[26] But colonists often made healers like Fanchon responsible for the well-being of other slaves, either providing medicines or looking the other way while demanding results. African cures often worked as well or better than French remedies and cost less. Fanchon got powders and herbs from Thomas, an enslaved man who made sugar barrels for LeBlondain. Thomas's wife, Marguerite, also gave Fanchon remedies to use, as did Suzanne, who worked in the sugar fields.

In September, one of Fanchon's patients died unexpectedly. This was not unusual in Saint-Domingue, especially on a sugar plantation when food was scarce. But LeBlondain was on alert because Médor had testified that he got some of his powders from a man named Christophe living on LeBlondain's estate.[27] When Fanchon's patient died, LeBlondain blamed her. He hired a local plantation surgeon to autopsy the body and then searched Fanchon's room and Thomas's hut. He found "various herbs and drugs that he did not recognize" and gave them as evidence of poisoning to the court at Fort Dauphin. Physician Antoine Baradat had evaluated poisons for that court before, so he likely tested Thomas's herbs. Although Fanchon was not exonerated, the court held that LeBlondain's statement of facts did not furnish sufficient proof and a more thorough investigation was ordered.[28] This delay in convicting Fanchon probably meant that Thomas's herbs were innocuous.

Although the use of African-style medicines was widely known and important to both enslaved people and enslavers, the fate of an enslaved person dosing their enslaver to gain influence depended on the world beyond his or her control. Healing slaves was one matter; working to obtain freedom by dosing a master was another. The work of gaining favor took time; if an enslaver died of any cause, that was wasted work. Even if an enslaver granted manumission, after he died, terrible trouble might ensue. Suspicious or greedy heirs could attack a free person's liberty.

Two enslaved women, Nanon and Marie Jeanne, experienced this on the Chiron estate in Petite Anse parish, twelve miles south of Cap Français. Monsieur Chiron was said to have sternly declared that he would never manumit any slave, but his wife had shown favor to Marie Jeanne. Nanon worked as a maid, and Marie Jeanne was a poultry keeper. Marie Jeanne's brother Mathieu, who knew how to make powders, was also enslaved on the plantation. After a time, Chiron sold Mathieu to a planter in Mississippi, an extremely rare course of action that suggests Chiron felt threatened by Mathieu.[29]

Powders and other preparations circulated on the Chiron estate and the nearby Galliffet and Delacoursière estates. René, a Foeda man from West Africa enslaved on the Galliffet plantation, made medicines, and some newly arrived Yoruban men on a nearby plantation also traded and sold drugs. On the Delacoursière estate, when the master died—inconspicuously it would seem—without any accusation of poison, the household accepted and understood his death.[30]

His death did not endanger Hauron, a Yoruba (Nago) man who lived on the estate and made powders. Hauron was one of many other makers and sellers, including three Yoruban men who practiced as he did. He also knew a free Black man named Gambois, who stole powders from Hauron's hut. There was Vincent, of the Arada people, and several others who distributed the same medicines as Vincent. After Delacoursière died, his valet St. Jacq, who still needed "some drugs that would bring his freedom," turned to Hauron. If the powders worked, St. Jacq promised to pay Hauron either a horse or the equivalent sum of two hundred livres.[31]

Hauron gave powders to Marie Jeanne on the Chiron estate in exchange for a coin worth eight livres. Marie Jeanne and Nanon, the maid, had a contentious relationship. Nanon said that Marie Jeanne had used poison on Nanon's father to force Nanon into an unwanted marriage. The attempt failed, but when Nanon's father died, she blamed Marie Jeanne. The two women also disagreed about giving powders to Chiron. Marie Jeanne had mixed powders into Chiron's food, and, at least twice, Marie Jeanne had obtained medicines for Chiron that Nanon refused to give him.[32]

Chiron died unexpectedly on the first Saturday of Lent in 1756. Chiron's widow and heirs did not raise any claims of poison. Marie Jeanne was, as she had hoped, manumitted by Chiron's widow, and she lived for months as a free woman. She might have been admired by enslaved people for whatever role she had in securing her freedom. Whether she had improved her condition using medicines or through virtue, loyalty, or special service, Chiron's widow had let her go. By the time Médor's case gained notoriety among colonists, Chiron was more than a year in the grave, and Marie Jeanne was living free. But when Médor's testimony became public knowledge, Chiron's adult children suspected foul play in their father's death. They confronted Nanon, who was still enslaved, and they took Marie Jeanne captive. Before four neighbors who recorded testimony, Nanon and Marie Jeanne were accused of killing Chiron.[33]

Three confessions emerged from the interrogation. Nanon quickly confessed to poisoning Chiron by carrying him poisoned coffee on the first Friday of Lent in 1756. Marie Jeanne had supplied a gray powder, she said. She did not know what it was and did not want to kill her employer. She gave Chiron the doctored coffee because she feared Marie Jeanne.[34]

Marie Jeanne confessed to giving Nanon powders that killed Chiron. She liked her master, she said, but she poisoned him because "after his death, I was sure to obtain freedom from his wife." Her interrogators wrote that Marie Jeanne had "heard him say he would never give freedom to any slave." No one promised her freedom, she said, she just knew that her mistress had a soft spot for her. The powders came from Hauron.[35]

Hauron testified that he didn't know why Marie Jeanne wanted the powders.[36] He gave a long list of names, allegedly all poison makers and wrongdoers, though none had been involved in the Chiron affair. He implicated them in theft, in poisoning, and in the offense most prized among interrogators: master-killing. Hauron said that Barbe, Françoise, and Pierre, three freed Black people formerly enslaved on the Gallois plantation, had killed several slaves and were complicit in their master's death. Within two weeks, Nanon, Marie Jeanne, and Hauron were in the prison in Cap Français, sharing a cell with other poisoners condemned to burn at the stake.[37]

To Chiron's heirs, Marie Jeanne was the living embodiment of a slave who killed her master to gain her freedom. But hers is the only documented conviction with that outcome. Moreover, Nanon's testimony suggests that Marie Jeanne's powders may have been medicine or witchcraft, not toxins. Marie Jeanne had been asking Nanon to give Chiron powders for some time, becoming increasingly insistent. Marie Jeanne had twice given Nanon medicines for Chiron that she had not used; two other times, Marie Jeanne had mixed powders into Chiron's food. Perhaps Marie Jeanne, like Médor, thought she was giving him medicine and then changed suppliers. Her brother Mathieu had given her some medicines before Chiron sold him to an enslaver in Mississippi. Another man named René, on the Galliffet estate, provided her with some. She may have finally sought out a toxin after her earlier powders did not soften Chiron's attitude about manumission.

Enslaved people's testimonies suggest that many of them were confused and panicked by the deaths that surrounded them. Médor and others must have speculated about the different people who supplied them with medicines, wondering what or who was killing the other slaves. Even so, when pressured to unveil a conspiracy, they could only reveal a diffuse chain of individual or small-group contacts, not an agreement to kill.

Roughly five miles west of the Chiron sugar plantation, one healer living on a struggling coffee estate was forced to rely on an

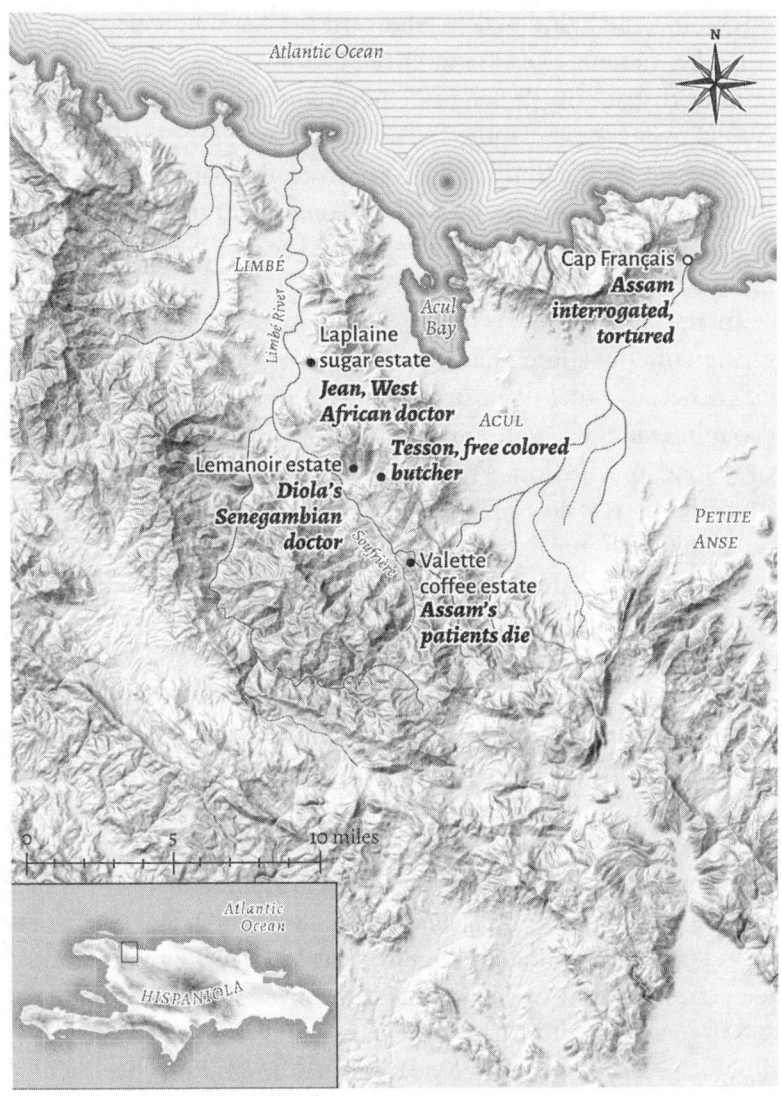

MAP 3.2 Assam's Search for Medicine, 1757

unfamiliar medicine maker. She suffered terrible consequences when her patients died. Assam lived in Soufrière canton, a mountainous district on the edge of Acul, a sugar-producing parish. About twenty-seven miles away from Cap Français, Soufrière was named for the Soufrière River, which flows north-northwest through the mountains, away from Acul and into the neighboring parish of Limbé. Assam lived in slavery on Jean Valette's estate, overlooking the river valley.[38]

In the 1750s, undeveloped mountain districts attracted aspiring coffee planters, but many coffee plantations in Soufrière failed because of soil unsuited to that crop. In some districts, drought came often and unpredictably, which could fatally disrupt food production. Where Assam lived, however, the Soufrière River was so reliable that planters could grow food and sell it in Cap Français, even during drought.[39] Assam did visit the port town of Cap Français on errands.[40] The trip to town would have taken over nine hours of walking.

Before Assam lived in Soufrière, sugar planters established grazing pastures there for draft animals. Livestock also habitually occupied fields in nearby Petite Anse to the east, the parish where the Chiron sugar estate was located. Cattle merchants transporting animals over the mountains from Santo Domingo to sell in Cap Français brought them to corrals in Petite Anse. The animals in these holding pens were notoriously unhealthy, so diseased that the enslaved cattle workers frequently died from contact with them. When the cattle died, dogs and hungry people scavenged their corpses for meat.[41]

Fifteen years after Assam told her story, doctors noticed that illness spread from estates near the cattle-holding pens when planters transferred animals, workers, or even harnesses between properties.[42] In 1772, a deadly livestock disease struck the line of sugar plantations that backed up to the Limbé foothills and the edge of the Soufrière Mountains. (See Map 5.1.) There, the Dupaty sugar plantation lost eighty mules and an unknown number of horses and oxen over three months. Doctors concluded that Dupaty's manager or his horse brought the disease into Acul parish from a second estate, miles to the east, in Petite Anse. Once established on the Dupaty property, the contagion spread to neighboring plantations, from the Noé estate in the south to the Bréda Haut-de-Cap estate in the north.[43]

Assam worked as an enslaved *hospitalière* on the coffee plantation. Like Fanchon, she cared for workers in the estate's hospital, which was essentially a room where sick and injured slaves were locked away until they were strong enough to work. Assam brought them basic meals and reported their condition to Valette, so he could summon a so-called plantation surgeon to perform bleedings, amputations, and other basic European medical procedures. A diplomaed physician from the city would be much more expensive and take days to arrive. For most of the enslaved patients, Assam was their only contact. She combined these duties with errands to buy food for the household, helping with the coffee harvest, and breastfeeding Valette's three children.

In 1757, the Valette coffee plantation was nearly destroyed by an inexplicable illness at the same time Médor was giving powders to animals and workers in Les Perches. It was a mysterious swelling that Assam said killed "all [the] slaves."[44] In the 1770s, physician Raymond Delaborde described such a disease: "[Slaves] are especially subject to a particular sort [of sickness] that is ridiculously called stomachache. It is a lymphedema [*leukophlegmacia*] or general swelling . . . more than half of slaves die of this cruel disease. I have seen it depopulate entire plantations in less than a year; it is caused by excessive work, bad food, and especially sorrow. . . . I have seen a great number of planters lose every slave this way, down to the last one."[45] He and Assam used the same word to describe its chief symptom: *bouffissure*, or swelling.

In March 1757, the swelling disease subsided on Valette's plantation, then returned in July, afflicting an enslaved man and child,

François and Victoire.⁴⁶ Valette was "in despair," Assam said; curing François and Victoire would fall to her. Valette gave her a one-day pass and ordered her "to look for and find some remedies to relieve and cure the sick slaves." She likely didn't know where to look but was advised to find the Black doctor known only to a man named Diola, who lived about three or four miles from Valette's property. Assam would have hoped that Diola's doctor, who was enslaved on the Lemanoir (or Lamanoye) plantation, could tell Valette where the illness was coming from.⁴⁷

Assam did not know Diola, but she remembered his visit to the Valette plantation. He was a free Black man who owned land nearby and seems to have been well known locally because a mapmaker in the 1760s listed his name on a map. His name, Diola, was a French transliteration of Jola, the name of an ethnic group from the Senegambian coast in Africa. Assam was from a neighboring area—"of the Poulard nation," as she described it, from the middle valley of the Senegal River. Diola's visit may have been especially memorable for Assam because there were so few Jola or Poulard people in Saint-Domingue compared to other ethnicities.⁴⁸

When Assam left to find help, she was met at the gate of the Valette plantation by a man she knew named Pompee. He was a free Black man, a former slave who leased nearby farmland. Pompee told Assam that Diola's doctor was dead. He recommended a West African healer, an enslaved man named Jean. To make sure she found Jean, Pompee walked with Assam north and west through the Soufrière hills into the Limbé valley. Once they could see the Laplaine plantation where Jean lived, Pompee gave Assam directions to Jean's cabin, then left.⁴⁹ Jean, the healer, spoke in the Fon language, meaning he was from West Africa. Assam, from Senegambia, might have had trouble understanding him, and his remedies might have been unfamiliar.

Jean told Assam that he could help her cure the Valette slaves if she would wait four days in his hut, where three enslaved women were already waiting for their medicines. At least two of them were West Africans: Marie Jeanne, a Tiamba, and Madeleine, a Yoruba.[50] Assam did not hear the third woman's name. All were enslaved by merchants in Cap Français, and Assam had seen them selling cloth and salted meat in the market there. Jean was sometimes joined by a big man with bad feet who walked with a stick and guarded the estate's cattle.

On Sunday, the day of rest for field-workers, Jean found the roots and herbs he needed to make Assam's medicine. She described how he combined the leaves of *losange* and blue vervain with the peeled root of *pois puant*. He added egg yolk and pot black, then rolled the mixture into a ball half the size of her fist.[51] He told her to break off a piece when she got home, mix it with warm water, and add more vervain and pois puant. After adding these ingredients to his mixture, she should give the preparation to her patients as a drink or an enema. To help her find the herbs, Jean also gave Assam a packet five inches long, tied with a string. If she held the string, he said, the packet would tell her which herbs were good. He also gave her a small packet the size of an almond to help with the same task. As she was leaving his cabin, Jean scratched her on the shoulder with a piece of sharp glass and rubbed a coarse powder over her cut. With his knife, he scraped up the blood-powder mixture and dropped it into a piece of ram's horn that he stopped up. He told her that this was for her good fortune.

When Assam finally returned to Valette's estate, she told him she had been delayed by sickness. She administered Jean's medicine to her patients, François and Victoire, as an enema. Both got worse. Jean had instructed her to keep his medicine secret, so she said nothing to Valette about these treatments. Two days later, when the planter sent her to buy meat from the free mulatto butcher Tesson, she ran into Pompee. He asked her how her patients were doing, and she said they were worse. Pompee urged her to give them a second dose of Jean's medicine, which she did when she returned to the estate. François and Victoire died soon afterward.

As hospitalière, Assam was forced by her enslaver to take responsibility for an enslaved population undergoing epidemic illness, but she did not have the tools to heal them. Médor faced a similar dilemma in Les Perches. Médor knew some sources of medicine in Les Perches, but Assam was even less connected in Soufrière. Although Valette had witnessed dozens of enslaved people die on this plantation from the swelling disease, when François and Victoire also perished, Valette accused Assam of poisoning. This was four months after Médor's confession.

Assam said nothing about Jean's drug to Valette and threw away the bag containing his medicine. Valette had his workers retrieve it. He arrested Assam and brought in two neighbors to help him question her.[52] The record of her local interrogation was five pages long, beginning not with an explanation of how her patients died but with a story about the free Black man Pompee urging Assam to poison her master. After propositioning her, Assam said, and being rejected, Pompee insulted her, calling her a fool. He said that all the local slaves were fools, especially house slaves like her.

They could all be free, Pompee said. Soufrière's masters were wretches (*coquins*) who treated their slaves unfairly and lived far too long. Some people understood this, he said, and they used poison to shorten their masters' lives. When the masters were on the brink of death, they manumitted these trusted slaves. According to Assam, Pompee claimed this was how he and other local free Black people had gotten their freedom. Pompee offered to help her poison Valette, saying he would surely free Assam on his deathbed, for she had given her own breast milk to nurse three of Valette's children.

Assam told the interrogators that she rejected Pompee's suggestion, claiming she had good relations with her master and didn't want to be free. In her testimony, she characterized Pompee as a manipulator and the driving force in her choice of a doctor. He was also responsible for the final dose she administered to her dying patients. For all the talk of manumission and poisoning of white people, Assam's case didn't involve either of these issues. The dead on the Valette estate were enslaved people, and there was no allegation that Assam had sought to poison her enslaver.

Pompee's speech to Assam about Black doctors and manumission may have been evidence of Médor's secret. Certainly, a servant who sickened an enslaver could earn favor and possibly manumission by nursing them back to health. A promise of manumission on an enslaver's literal deathbed, however, would be difficult to enforce. Alternatively, Pompee's speech may have been Assam's attempt to shift her interrogators' attention away from her. She was likely aware that Médor had implicated free Black people as conspirators and that colonists might respond with leniency if she provided proof of it.

Within two weeks of Assam's interrogation, Valette sent her to Cap Français, where she was imprisoned with dozens of other accused poisoners and interrogated by Sebastian Courtin, the Cap Français investigating judge. Courtin's priority was to root out the identities of poison makers and their clients on his way to finding the ringleader. Assam's urgent need in providing testimony was to influence her judge toward leniency. One day of interrogation by Courtin yielded twenty-five manuscript pages of testimony. His questions, transcribed, were penetrating and specific.

Courtin had total control over the interrogation. What help Assam could give was unclear, though she insisted that she had never given drugs to her master or to other slaves. She also noted that many slaves had perished before François and Victoire, and she wasn't sure if those people had been poisoned. She, like Médor, may have been baffled by the rapid, inexplicable deaths of so many slaves. Courtin asked if she had killed Valette's slaves to force her master to abandon his coffee plantation and therefore to sell her. No, she said.

Pompee emerged again as an exemplar of free Black people who corrupt slaves and give them bad ideas about white people. Assam said that Pompee insisted that "all the whites of Soufrière... inflicted cruelties on their slaves without judicial authority when they suspected that they poisoned their [other] slaves and that one day her master would do this to her and that she would need to find justice." She replied that she "did not know justice."

Assam told Courtin that Pompee described slave doctors who would give her drugs to stun or daze Valette (étourdir l'esprit) so that he would free her. This was what all free Black men and women had done, Pompee claimed. She said she refused him, that she was not interested in those drugs. When Courtin confronted her with her earlier testimony, Assam admitted that Pompee had also talked about killing masters who lived too long and how they would only free their slaves when they were about to die.

When the interrogation ended, Judge Courtin had obtained the evidence he sought, and Assam failed to find mercy. Courtin convicted Assam of poisoning and sentenced her to burn at the stake. She spent three months in prison before the Superior Council reviewed her death sentence in December 1757. An anonymous letter written six months later and published in a pamphlet describes how, after her death sentence was confirmed and while she awaited execution, authorities decided to exercise their right under the law to torture Assam.[53] Because she had been convicted of a conspiracy, Assam would face a further round of interrogation to reveal her coconspirators.[54] According to the pamphlet, before her torture began, Assam offered a new confession. Courtin and Fournier de la Chapelle questioned her for two days and two nights.

According to the pamphlet, Assam confessed to crimes that her earlier testimony barely mentioned, saying that "since the whites have never done anything bad to her, she would like to contribute to their security." For the first time, she confessed to killing a number of Valette's slaves and to poisoning the three Valette children, whom she had nursed. She was suddenly able to identify fifty poisoners for Courtin to question, though when she left Valette's plantation for help, she needed Pompee's help to find a single Black doctor.

The Cap Council suspended her execution. Six months later, Assam was "still in prison, her feet in chains but despite her crimes she shows such sincerity, gives such good information, that we owe the colony's safety to her." That she was alive six months after conviction suggests that she earned the lenience she had bargained for. The anonymous letter writer in 1758 predicted that the council would commute her sentence to life imprisonment.[55]

Last-minute revelations may have saved Assam's life, but her coerced confession was clearly a product of her desperate desire to avoid torture. Having provided as much information as she could in the two earlier rounds of interrogation, her only source of valuable new information would have been fellow inmates in the Cap Français jail. At the time, the jail held eighty prisoners, including twenty other accused poisoners. In the overcrowded jail, Assam shared a makeshift cell with Marie Jeanne and Nanon from the Chiron case and two other women accused of poisoning.[56] Other prisoners likely gave her the names of the dozens of people she denounced.

Assam's December testimony set off deep reverberations in the North Province's religious establishment and toppled the Jesuit missionary order in Saint-Domingue. She revealed that Jesuit slave priest Father Duquesnoy had visited her in prison and advised her, for the sake of her soul, to suffer all the torments the judges inflicted without revealing the names of others.

Duquesnoy's deep engagement with enslaved people in the North Province may explain his intervention in Asssam's case. The Jesuits knew more about enslaved people's lives than most colonists did. One missionary explained that he might hear one hundred slave confessions in a morning, including "a thousand irrelevant things in minute detail." Many slaves talked about their poverty in the confessional or asked the priest to intervene in their disputes.[57] With this kind of insight into slaves' lives, missionaries likely realized that many accused poisoners were healers, not killers. Father Duquesnoy may have counseled Assam to be silent, to spare the lives of innocent people.[58]

Cap Français's Superior Council eventually accused the Jesuit order of supporting the poison conspiracy. It evicted them from Saint-Domingue in 1763, citing "the report of the royal attorney general on the Jesuit doctrines and moral teachings to the slaves, which observes that these doctrines and teachings were the principal cause of enormous crimes, notably the desecrations and poisonings committed by the slaves."[59]

As Assam's denunciations brought in even more poison suspects, Saint-Domingue's intendant wrote that "the courtrooms of the Northern province echo with these charges and I cannot adequately depict for you the horror of this situation."[60] Assam's coerced testimony fueled colonists' fears about the enslaved people who surrounded and greatly outnumbered them. An investigation that began with the deaths of enslaved people on Valette's estate was transformed by Courtin into the search for a network of colonist-killers. But the judge's evidence showed only tenuous connections between the individuals drawn into his wide-ranging investigation. Courtin needed to find a ringleader for the conspiracy, and this was shortly delivered in the arrest of an African man known as Makandal. It only remained for him to argue that an African spiritual leader with a deeply loyal following posed an existential threat to the colony.

4

Makandal, Congo Diviner

THE ENSLAVED HOSPITALIÈRE ASSAM FACED many challenges in trying to save her patients. She was ordered to find an African doctor, but she didn't seem to know any. She had heard of Diola's doctor, then, after learning he was dead, she let a free Black farmer lead her to another healer, Jean, enslaved on the Laplaine estate. Despite ethnic differences and the danger of poison charges, Jean agreed to help Assam, working with her to divine the source of the problem. He had to rely on her descriptions of the sickness, her patients, their circumstances in life and work, and the community surrounding them. For Jean and other enslaved African doctors, healing was an act of discernment that required an understanding of all the forces working on his patients. Saint-Domingue's healers, African and European alike, would not succeed without training, practice, and an informed view of the problem.

Although Assam did not know it, a Congo-inspired community in Soufrière had been developing for at least a decade to help and protect its members. The people that colonists called "Congos" came from different homelands than many other enslaved people in Saint-Domingue. Whereas in the first half of the eighteenth century, West African ports like Ouidah in modern-day Benin supplied many of the colony's captives, by Assam's time, French slavers were sailing south to ports near the mouth of the Congo River. Enslaved people from Congo ports began arriving in Cap Français regularly and in small numbers in 1737.[1] After 1748, French slavers began buying a majority of their captives at Congo ports like Malemba and Cabinda.[2] This shift eventually changed the balance of ethnicities in Soufrière, giving rise to communities whose practices were inspired by elements of West Central African culture.[3]

In Soufrière, a man known as Makandal was creating spiritually powerful objects—bundles of natural and man-made materials—that his followers called *makandals*, and teaching those followers how to work with them. His kind of healing inherently challenged the colonial system, for in African societies, "rituals of healing are political because illness is considered a product of social relations gone awry."[4] In other words, he was making objects that could heal the new land he lived in.

Makandal created a deeply bonded community in Soufrière based on Congo ritual practice. He served newly arrived Central Africans from many different ethnic groups as well as island-born people. Many of his followers lived on the growing number of coffee plantations in the region, but others came from farther away: Cap Français or Port Margot and Le Borgne parishes to the west.[5]

Nearly all Black people in Saint-Domingue carried charms, packets that took different forms and were sometimes called *gry*.[6] But Congo-inspired makandals were not charms; they were considered to be alive. Makandal's community believed the bundles moved, spoke, revealed the future, and worked on behalf of those who fed and praised them. Most of them were two to four inches wide; French colonists said they were shaped like a short, fat sausage. People often carried makandals inside a ball of wool cloth with a small crucifix on the outside, a description that sounds strikingly like the bundles that modern Haitians call *pakets congos*.[7]

To make his packets, Makandal collected bone fragments from a cemetery, preferably from a baptized child. Other ingredients included the grated roots of the plantain and *figuier maudit* trees, black scrapings from a cooking pot, and objects used in colonial church services: consecrated candles, incense, Communion bread, and holy water. Some makandal packets contained crucifixes made of lead, which were distributed by Jesuit priests as part of their mission. For one follower named Geneviève, Makandal broke the crucifix off the end of a rosary and assured her that it would be a powerful protector.[8]

Makandal wrapped these ingredients in a cloth, tied the bundle with carefully knotted twine, and smeared it with dirt and holy water. He then chanted over the object, inviting a spirit to take residence there. Then he gave it a name, and the person who received the bundle was known by that name among the community members. From then on, that person was prohibited from eating beans and fresh meat, except for poultry, and from drinking wine. If someone drank wine, his makandal would lose its power, but he could restore it by rubbing his hands with basil and washing the makandal with holy water from the church.[9]

Those who possessed a makandal had to care for it. Makandal showed people how to mix eggs and broken eggshells with holy water, incense, and the dark scrapings from a cooking pot. After soaking the makandal in holy water, they rubbed it with animal fat and daubed it with the egg mixture. Colonists said it was easy to tell a makandal from other charms because of the bits of eggshell embedded in a dark, greasy coating.[10]

Makandal instructed his followers on how to make their bundles work for them. Before asking the makandal for help, a follower tied the bundle tightly. Makandal spoke to the bundles using West Central African words, "instructing them to spread out, hunt down, and strike abusers and soothe" the men and women who carried them, who, in daily life, were "insulted, yelled at, hated, and considered to be stupid brutes."[11] Then he ordered the makandal to make its carriers strong in combat, to help them win at gambling, and to save them from punishment for leaving the plantation or other infractions. Members of the group believed their makandals could "make [the master's] heart as soft as water."[12] That kind of power could ease the burdens of an enslaved person and their family, or it might enhance the possibility of manumission.

To bring misfortune to an enemy, people tied the makandal to their thighs, then insulted it and described all the bad things they wanted to happen. After this, putting the makandal under a heavy stone guaranteed that the chosen victim would be hated or whipped or would suffer other setbacks. Makandal and his followers insisted that their bundles could not cause serious illness or death. Brigitte, described as Makandal's wife and a ritual leader in her own right, claimed that a makandal bundle "consulted by its servant" could reveal the location of "an escaped slave, who had stolen something that was missing, the poisoner, and other [things]."[13]

Makandal regularly assembled his followers for a ritual feeding of their talismans. In one kind of gathering, they met in a hut where they would not be disturbed. After speeches and singing, they put their makandals into a special bowl. They covered the bowl with a white cloth and set it in a corner next to another bowl filled with the best food: boiled chicken, rice, salt cod, and rum. After some time had passed, the attendees feasted on these ceremonial offerings. Another type of meeting involved speeches and dancing. It began with a female priest cursing white and uninitiated Black people, which served to define the boundaries of the group. After dancing and "many speeches," each participant performed feats of skill and Makandal spoke or performed for the group.[14]

Another ritual was called *faire diable* or play the devil, perhaps from a French expression meaning to cause disorder or make a lot of noise.[15] Holy water, a crucifix, a cloth, and some cords were placed on a table. A member of the group tied up the makandals and recited prayers. Then the group wrapped all the bundles in the cloth and put it into a hat, dousing it with holy water. As the group sang Creole songs, each attendee held the hat on his or her head for a while, and the makandals danced inside the hat. After this, they drank rum and "made a lot of noise," which may have been a description of spirit possession.[16]

One ritual was celebrated in the morning. Makandal's followers knelt around the largest makandal, the size of a man's forearm. They called this bundle Charlot, a French folk name for Satan.[17] The group prayed to Charlot "and kissed the ground as in the [Christian] adoration of the cross." After rising from their knees, the group collectively proclaimed that there was nothing in the world greater than God in heaven and Charlot, and that after them was François Makandal. They called small makandal packets "God's children."[18]

Makandal's community-building probably began with people enslaved on Soufrière's coffee estates at the upper reaches of the Limbé River valley. By 1757, it extended to Cap Français in the east and Port Margot and Le Borgne in the west. A woman named Marianne may have been the leader of the Cap Français branch of the community. Enslaved by a wigmaker, Marianne performed rituals in the wigmaker's kitchen with two enslaved men named Michel and Jolicoeur. Jolicoeur could read and write French. Brigitte carried packets to Marianne in Cap Français once a week. A follower named Leveillé was enslaved to a rug maker and then a saddlemaker, which suggests he also lived in Cap Français. Jean à Tessereau, another close associate, eventually broke with Makandal and took his family into the hills behind Cap. This suggests that he was enslaved near the city. Far to the west of Cap Français, a follower named Geneviève was enslaved in Port Margot.[19]

Makandal's life in Africa and later in Saint-Domingue left a faint but legible archival trail that has never been traced. Makandal was probably sold into slavery at Loango, but we don't know where in Central or West Central Africa he originally came from. Historian Kathryn de Luna argues that because

Makandal's name is missing a final vowel, he may have been from the Central African interior rather than a western coastal region, as other scholars have surmised. She believes Makandal was captured and enslaved in a period of attacks by Ruund-speaking people against territory controlled by Yaka-speaking people. Makandal was probably enslaved in this region adjacent to the Malebo Pool and sold to the French sometime after 1730.[20]

De Luna's analysis of the name *Makandal* suggests he was involved with resistance and, perhaps, spirituality. For people who spoke one of the more than fifty languages in the Kikongo family, his name suggested he could make the spirits "press out . . . strike . . . or punish from afar." De Luna "hear[s] in Makandal's name a set of arguments about the mechanisms by which the world is made right."[21] Makandal would have found much to make right in Saint-Domingue's North Province.

Makandal was first enslaved on an indigo plantation near the mouth of the Limbé River, fourteen miles west of Cap Français. The Limbé River originates in the Soufrière Mountains to the south and descends to the sea, carrying fertile soil to a valley eight miles long and one and a half miles wide at its broadest. A ridge of hills separated the Limbé River valley from Cap Français and its surrounding parishes.

Indigo dye was quite valuable, and Makandal's first enslaver, named LeTellier, was already wealthy a decade before he purchased Makandal from slavers in Saint-Domingue.[22] Growing and manufacturing dark-blue indigo dye on LeTellier's land, Makandal likely had his first experiences of plantation labor. He may have been instructed how to harvest leaves from indigo bushes and soak them in a series of large watertight masonry vats. As the leaves rotted in the water, they gave off a blue silt that settled on the floor of the vats. Enslaved workers like Makandal would have scooped out the powder, let it dry in cone-shaped sacks, and packed it for shipment.

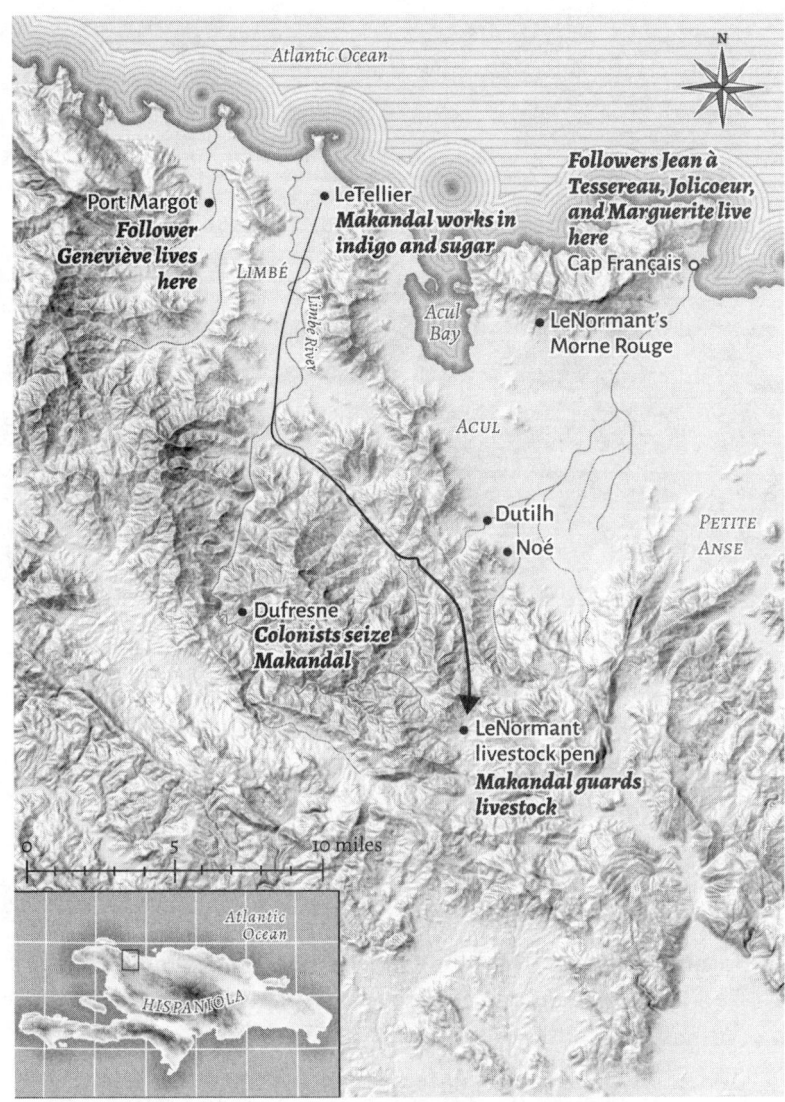

MAP 4.1 Makandal's Life in Saint-Domingue, 1730s–1758

4.1 Indigo Refining in the French Antilles. M. Chambon, *Commerce de l'Amérique par Marseille . . . Tome premier.* Avignon, 1764. Courtesy of John Carter Brown Library.

In the late 1730s, when Makandal likely arrived, his enslaver was converting his indigo estate into a sugar plantation. Under the new regime, workers planted sugar by digging hundreds of six- to nine-inch holes, placing a small piece of sugarcane into each one, and covering it with soil. They worked in unison; each person moved thousands of pounds of dirt per day. At harvest, crews bent low again and again to cut ripe sugarcanes six inches from the soil. Then they trimmed the leaves from each six-foot-long cane. Speed was crucial at harvest because ripe canes rotted quickly, so drivers pushed the workers to cut and trim faster and faster. The slower that canes moved from harvest to crushing, the less syrup they yielded. Sugar workers cut and hauled cane for twelve to fourteen hours at a time and then worked at night in the sugar mill. Some fed harvested canes into the rollers of

4.2 Sugar mill in the 1720s. Jean Baptiste Labat, *Nouveau Voyage aux Isles de l'Amerique* (Paris, 1722), vol. 3, between 222 and 223. Reproduction courtesy of John Carter Brown Library.

a crushing mill turned by teams of oxen or mules, while others stirred massive cauldrons of boiling syrup.[23] It was dangerous, exhausting work, and one writer claimed that Makandal's hand was caught in a sugar mill and cut off.[24] It is not clear if Makandal really did lose a hand, since no eyewitness description survives; the story of his accident was published thirty years after he died.

Manufacturing sugar required many more oxen and mules than LeTellier owned, and those animals needed land for grazing. In 1742, he purchased property in the mountains about ten miles up the Limbé River valley. LeTellier died shortly after, and his widow, Elisabeth Lescoffier, expanded the grazing pastures, buying a nearby corral from a free Black man and using two government land grants to connect all her hillside acreage.[25]

Perhaps because he was disabled by injury, around 1744, Makandal was sent to guard livestock in the Soufrière Mountains, miles from the coastal plantation. Colonists closely supervised the Limbé sugar works, but in Soufrière, Makandal lived alone or shared a hut with one other man. Plantation employees might occasionally show up to deliver new livestock or remove the strongest animals to work on the sugar estate, but from day to day, a livestock guardian was unsupervised. Living on land so thickly wooded and so cut through with ravines that some neighbors described it as "uninhabitable," Makandal's job was to keep people from stealing cattle while they grazed on rugged, uncleared slopes.[26]

In the mid-1740s, there were few enslaved people in Soufrière. Some tended livestock, like Makandal, and there were a few small indigo operations holding around twenty slaves each, but coffee planters had not yet moved in. Landowners of color did settle there, perhaps because there were no large slaveholding enterprises nearby. These included free Black people named Cadiz and La Rouderie, and Philippe Baudin, a biracial man who lived near the corral.[27] The relative autonomy that Makandal experienced in this setting increased when his enslaver, Elisabeth Lescoffier, married an ambitious naval administrator named Le Normant de Mézy. The couple moved from Limbé to Cap Français and later acquired a second sugar plantation in Morne Rouge, closer to Cap Français than the Limbé estate.[28] Makandal's autonomy, privacy, and mobility grew between 1744 and 1748 when his enslavers' newly acquired ventures and distant professional obligations drew their attention away from his orbit. Before they knew it, he was gone.

Makandal walked away from the corral and is said to have lived in *marronage* from around 1748.[29] He escaped but stayed nearby for ten years, living and working among dispersed communities of enslaved people who joined him in rituals. Around this time, colonists who arrived from France too late or too poor to buy a stake in the sugar industry began to buy land in the Soufrière Mountains to grow coffee. Assam's enslaver Jean Valette was one of them. To work these operations, colonists bought people trafficked from Congo ports who could be enslaved at a lower price than West African captives.[30] As the mountains grew more settled, rows of cultivated coffee bushes replaced tangled trees and vines, and Makandal, who had lived in a sparsely populated district, now had hundreds of enslaved Congo people as neighbors.

From the high hills he inhabited, Makandal could follow a northeasterly route to descend into the fertile sugar plain south of Cap Français. There were the plantations that would later be called Noé, Dutilh, Laplaigne, and Dupaty, which consumed whole populations of enslaved people who died from abuse, crushing industrial work, hunger, and illness. Theirs was a world in great need of healing. Pressing on, Makandal could penetrate the bustling port of Cap Français. There, he may have looked like a free Black man while he moved around town to meet with people enslaved in the households of merchants and artisans.

To the northwest, Makandal could have traced the Soufrière River to its junction with the Limbé River and entered a valley filled with well-established sugar and indigo estates as well as coffee plantations newly emerging in the hills. A veteran of the colony, he would have been received there by newly arrived Africans from the Congo River region. Although their ethnicities and languages were not all the same, Makandal's name contained meanings they might have discerned and felt confidence in.[31]

Pushing even farther west, Makandal would find Port Margot and Le Borgne, where enslaved people lived on the poorest, smallest, and most isolated estates, much like Médor did in Les Perches.[32] Whereas Médor was forced to abandon his alliances in town and was not able to re-create them in Les Perches, Makandal succeeded in building a community. Makandal's decision to walk away from slavery but remain in the Soufrière district was a critical act of personal resistance that allowed him to work over many years building associations to which the fathers of the Haitian Revolution would be indebted.

The end of Makandal's life as a diviner came when he gathered with followers on Julien Dufresne's coffee plantation in Soufrière. In attendance were enslaved adults and children who had arrived at the estate in 1756 or 1757. Their enslaver lived in Cap Français, where he was the business manager for a series of absentee-owned sugar plantations on which 360 people were enslaved.[33] Dufresne's older brother had been a slave ship captain since 1748.[34] In June 1755, he sailed his ship *Le Cerf* from the family's home city of Saint-Malo, France, to the Central African port of Malemba. It was his fourth slaving voyage to this region. He boarded hundreds of captives and crossed the Atlantic Ocean. On June 28, 1756, *Le Cerf* docked in Cap Français with 181 men, 33 women, and 334 children onboard.[35]

The ship anchored there for eleven months. The British blockade may have caused a delay, but it is also likely that the slaver could not sell all his captives.[36] Saint-Domingue's prosperous sugar planters didn't want to buy African children; they were too weak for sugar work. Coffee and indigo planters were Saint-Domingue's biggest purchasers of African children.[37] Julien Dufresne may have bought at least some of the children for his coffee estate in Soufrière. After a long voyage and months of captivity in Cap Français, the children would have arrived in Soufrière with no way to cope with the troubles that awaited them.

In the coffee region, imported food had grown scarce. Many enslaved people had died, and the mysterious swelling disease was killing Assam's patients only two or three miles from Dufresne's land. Illness was not the only threat to enslaved people; for over six months, colonial constables had been scouring the region for poisoners. After Assam made her third and final confession in November 1757, arrests accelerated. In December, the colony's top legal official explained, "The culprits have multiplied and there is almost no session of the Superior Council [at Cap] that does not furnish examples [of poisoners]."[38] The Congo children in their new community were living through a perfect storm of threats.

In December 1757, the Dufresne workers organized a calenda.[39] It was traditional that, at the end of the year, masters briefly suspended plantation work and distributed extra food, rum, or cloth among enslaved workers. Because of the war, there would be no cloth, salt fish, or other imported foods to distribute. Many people attending the gathering would have wanted to know what was causing these frightening levels of hunger, illness, and death. Enslaved people may have suspected that a witch or sorcerer was at work, harming their community.[40]

Makandal came to the calenda that night. By this time, he had been living free, in hiding, for roughly nine years. He had built a community that revered him for his ability to communicate with the invisible world of the dead, invoke their protection, and divine their secrets. In a time of inexplicable sudden death, this skill was priceless. The Dufresne workforce likely invited Makandal to their December calenda to learn who or what was the mysterious killer.

The night of the calenda, Julian Dufresne's father-in-law, Louis-François Trévan, was managing the estate.[41] A surveyor named Duplessis was also there. As the enslaved workers drummed, danced, and sang, a boy approached the two Frenchmen and told them that a poisoner was at the calenda. Trévan and Duplessis distributed more casks of cane liquor for the dancers, which, for a while, might have intensified the music. When Makandal eventually went to rest in a slave hut, the two colonists captured him. Unable to find shackles, they clamped his feet into a horse hobble and tied him to a fifty-pound weight behind his back.[42] They dragged him to a room in the main house where they planned to take turns watching him until daylight, along with two house slaves. One of the white men drafted a letter to Cap Français reporting that they had captured a poisoner.

As the hours passed, all four guards fell asleep. Makandal freed himself from the weight and doused the candle. A pair of loaded pistols lay on a nearby table, but he left them untouched. He pulled himself out of a window and dropped to the ground, still hobbled. When the night breeze rattled the window hook, the colonists awoke. It took them minutes to rekindle the light and discover that their prisoner had escaped. They searched outside the house, then called in dogs. When they found Makandal, he was still scrambling through the coffee fields.[43]

Makandal was held in the Cap Français jail for weeks awaiting interrogation. He was prosecuted in a judicial investigation that started on Tuesday, January 17, and lasted just four days. It was not a trial; there was no defending attorney. Judge Courtin—who had convicted Assam, together with prosecutor Fournier de la Chapelle, who had pursued André Carbon—interrogated Makandal, at times using torture. Makandal never admitted to making or using poisons.[44] He did name some of his followers, though, and the court sent constables to arrest them. Makandal, Brigitte, Leveillé, Mercure, Jolicoeur, and Geneviève were arrested and interrogated.[45]

Nearly all judicial records of this process have disappeared.[46] However, Courtin and Fournier each wrote a legal memorandum about the investigation. Courtin's memorandum aimed to convey the grave danger of poisoning faced by the colony at the hands of a powerful ringleader. If Courtin could bring Makandal's "conspiracy" to an end, he might be rewarded by the Naval Ministry in France.[47] The memorandum shows that Courtin possessed no evidence to support his death sentence against Makandal for "making and selling poisons of all sorts." Makandal also was convicted of seducing and corrupting slaves and of impiety and desecration.[48] The Superior Council reviewed

Courtin's judgment on Friday, January 20, 1758, and, before the day ended, Makandal was at the stake, flames rising.

In a moment that would become a stirring metaphor of resistance and the unexpected power of the enslaved, Makandal nearly escaped execution. The earliest printed account says that he pulled his shackles out of the post as he was burning, and slaves in the square began to shout that Makandal was a sorcerer who could not be burned.[49] "Makandal sauvé" they cried: Makandal is escaping! Another said that Makandal broke the post.[50] But his freedom was short-lived. Soldiers quickly recaptured him, restrained him, and heaved him back onto the burning pyre.

In the months that followed, many of Makandal's followers were executed as poisoners. Jean à Tessereau was arrested and interrogated two months after Makandal's execution.[51]

While presenting little evidence of poison, Courtin's memorandum decried spiritual practices that were understandable to people from West Central Africa but that Courtin invoked to shock and disgust high officials in France. The properties of Makandal's charms suggest that they were *minkisi*, objects that have been a part of West Central African cultures from modern Gabon to Angola, with significant local variations, for perhaps a thousand years.[52]

A *nkisi* or single object was not an idol, charm, or fetish. As Wyatt MacGaffey explains, "In Kongo thought a nkisi is a personalized force from the invisible land of the dead; this force has chosen, or been induced, to submit itself to some degree of human control effected through ritual performances."[53] The nkisi spirit inhabited a bundle, also called a nkisi, made for it by a ritual specialist. Because the nkisi spirit inhabited the world of the dead, it could heal, fight witches, and tell the future "but only at the command of the priest or *nganga* who operated on behalf of individual clients."[54]

Minkisi collected by European ethnographers in the late nineteenth century and early twentieth century all had distinctive names, each "represent[ing] a personality in the land of the dead."⁵⁵ In the late nineteenth-century and early twentieth-century Congo River Basin, local people described how the power of a nkisi "depended on the rules of alimentary and sexual avoidance that it imposed on its owner."⁵⁶ African minkisi required periodic feeding as well.⁵⁷ Priests in Africa spurred their minkisi into action by shaking, striking, and insulting them. In the nineteenth century, they hammered nails into some larger minkisi for the same effect.⁵⁸ These were elements common to Makandal's practice.

Ritual specialists made minkisi in many sizes and shapes, but the most typical nkisi was "composed in a basket, a bag, a ceramic pot, a calabash, a case or a bottle."⁵⁹ Missionaries reported that most people in the western regions of Central Africa wore a nkisi, perhaps several, for personal protection. They used larger ones to unite people into communities with important functions like healing, community justice, and economic affairs. The oldest-known nkisi, for example, was housed in a communal shrine and used in rituals against epidemics described in 1697.⁶⁰

People in West Central Africa gathered in associations around minkisi to achieve material as well as spiritual goals. This might have been the case among Makandal and his followers in Soufrière. One well-known society on the north bank of the Congo River served economic and legal functions. It grew around a nkisi known as Lemba, which emerged in the seventeenth century as a spirit of healing. Lemba priests performed ritual marriages that connected members of merchant and judicial families from different regions. The resulting Lemba network performed many of the functions of government in the lower Congo River basin, as traditional monarchical states weakened. As some families prospered and others suffered from the growth of the Atlantic trade in slaves and copper, Lemba officials established market rules, served as a court of appeal for trade disputes, and redistributed money collected from newly rich traders.⁶¹ If Makandal and his followers were working to create their own method of governance, it would have been a powerful form of resistance to their subjugation.

The centrality of Christian symbols in Makandal's practice allowed Courtin to charge Makandal with sacrilege, a crime punishable by burning at the stake. The judge's memorandum focused on Makandal's use of bound crucifixes and the rituals surrounding the large bundle named Charlot. The so-called faire diable ceremony was conducted in a slave cabin his followers called the "*caze à diable*" or devil's hut. Courtin charged that this was "not a consequence of their way of speaking but a true impiety which verged on sacrilege."[62]

Makandal and people in the Congo River basin incorporated Christian symbols into their minkisi practices in similar ways. By Makandal's time, there was a history of 250 years of Catholic missionary activity in the Kingdom of Kongo and the surrounding regions. In the seventeenth and eighteenth centuries, Kongolese ritual specialists used the crucifixes distributed by missionaries to strengthen the power of the minkisi they made.[63] Kings erected large crosses in public spaces, and Central African metal workers created bronze crucifixes in their own distinctive styles. Hundreds of these objects survive today, some of them as small as the ones Makandal wrapped with cloth and twine, others a few feet high.[64] Tying knots and wrapping cord around spiritual bundles was a way that African priests controlled a nkisi spirit, but they also used this bondage to increase its power. Some Kongolese crucifixes include the image of a cord that encircles the Christ figure.[65]

Congo people enslaved in nineteenth-century Cuba also developed distinctive minkisi and communities that served them. Scholar Todd Ochoa explains that these spirit objects, called *prendas*, are at the heart of Cuba's Palo religion. Cuban Palo is close to its Congo roots, so it may illuminate what Makandal was trying to create with his community. Both communities combined materials such as bones, wood, and holy water in spiritual entities with distinctive names that were fed and ritually insulted by their priests.[66]

Like Makandal, practitioners of Cuban Palo recruited elements of Christian religious practice to their own spiritual ends. In nineteenth-century Cuba, Paleros embraced symbols that the Church taught were evil. According to Ochoa, Congo people enslaved in Cuba understood that "the monstrous beings that unsettled Catholics and drove them to despair . . . were the devil, the witch, and, concretely for the Spanish Catholic Church in the nineteenth century, the Jew."[67] Palo practitioners studied these archetypes to learn the "secrets to their power" and developed a minkisi known as a *prenda judía* or Jewish prenda to access that power. For Ochoa, these were "a cultivated form of defiance" against Spanish masters and a way for Congo people enslaved in Cuba to "appropriate the Catholic nightmare."[68]

Makandal's follower Mercure claimed that he served Charlot, an entity that Courtin took to be the devil. It seems that venerating Charlot was a way Mercure, Brigitte, and probably Makandal himself appropriated French stories of the devil and claimed this power as their own. Ochoa's portrayal of Congo religion in Cuba may reflect what Makandal was trying to create: "Community, friendship, trust, song, dance, drums, knowledge, and, most of all, confidence in the realm of the dead."[69]

Enslaved people likely joined ritual communities seeking help to survive food shortages, brutal work regimes, epidemics, and poisoning investigations. Communities could supply strategies for finding food, practices to avoid or cure disease, hope for the future, mentors or allies in the skills of avoiding enslavers' anger, and a sense of spiritual and social belonging. Ritual communities that arose after Makandal's death won people's loyalty for many reasons, one of them being protection from terrible enemies, seen and unseen. For decades after the Makandal affair, enslaved people in Saint-Domingue's North Province suffered the double scourge of mysterious deaths and colonists' ferocious search for poisoners. The conditions that helped give rise to Makandal's community would remain in place over the next thirty-five years.

Throughout Courtin's judgeship, waves of mysterious death unfolded across the North Province of Saint-Domingue. Courtin claimed that "slow poisons are the cause of nearly all the languishing illnesses that attack the whites and blacks." If he were to vindicate this claim, convicting one man or even a chain of acquaintances would not suffice. The judge needed to portray community bonds as suspicious and make the qualities of leadership, loyalty, self-defense, and ritual devotion into threats against the colonial order.

As evidence against Makandal, Courtin depicted him as a "captain in his country," describing him as a man whose "gaze was alert, confident, and terrifying for the slaves, his movements quick, decisive and imperious, unlike a slave."[70] In dozens of poisoning interrogations, they had never faced a prisoner who was so self-possessed. According to Courtin, "He had such a hold over the slaves that they did not believe he could be taken.... And when they were brought before him, they were already condemned to the fire and were only awaiting the moment of their execution. They should have been to some degree preoccupied by the horror of their situation, but when they were brought before him, their surprise, their laughter, and what they said, especially Leveillé who knew him the best, made a singular impression."[71]

Colonists' fear of a community rising against them was sparked by Médor's confession about the "secret of which the whites know nothing," and Courtin's memorandum only inflamed those fears. Courtin retold a story about Makandal performing a trick using a cloth that changed from olive to white to black. According to Courtin, Makandal said that each color represented the masters of the island over time. Olive represented indigenous people, white represented the French colonists, and black meant that, in the future, Black people would rule the island. Courtin included the story in his memorandum, although he admitted it was "not well verified in the investigation." The origins of the story are not known, but, in foreseeing social change that could overturn the colonial order, it was Courtin's only evidence to link Makandal to the kind of race war that supporters and opponents of slavery for two hundred years would associate with his name.

Within two months of Makandal's death, the acting judge of Port-de-Paix, west of Cap Français, wrote the naval minister asking to be rewarded for his work investigating the poisoning conspiracy.

> Milord is undoubtedly informed that this colony swarms with slave poisoners, so-called diviners, and sorcerers, who have long planned to gradually kill all the whites, that these slaves belong to a cult or religion newly formed by two leaders, longtime maroons named Makendal [sic], and Tassereau; fortunately these two fanatics have been captured, one has already been convicted and burned alive, with thirty others, and the other is about to undergo the same punishment; unfortunately they have a considerable number of followers and disciples; there are currently more than 200 in the Cap Français prisons: in Port-de-Paix we have thirteen of them in prison two weeks into our [poison] investigation and 22 suspects [to round up].[72]

Courtin's own memorandum closed with a similar tribute to the many ongoing trials his investigation had produced. He designated seven enslaved poisoners, including Makandal's followers Jolicoeur and Leveillé, and seven unnamed slaves or groups of slaves who were also accused of poisoning. Nineteen white people were named as poisoning victims, some of whom survived. There was, Courtin wrote, "a great number of slaves charged with having made and distributed poison and of having killed their comrades and livestock. Some have been condemned."[73] In the wake of Makandal's death, poison investigations would spiral across the North Province, drawing in more and more suspects.

Reports show that the center of colonists' fears was shifting. Colonists long believed that Black people inflicted poison on each other, but they had always told themselves that these malefices—a word that included spells and poison—would not work against white people.[74] Under torture, in the glare of poison scrutiny, enslaved people gave planters and judges a glimpse of their political visions and their communities of resistance, like Médor's "secret of which the whites know nothing" and Makandal's loyal following. The poison scare both arose from white fear and deepened it.

Colonists who had propelled a tide of humanity taken from African ports expected that tide to turn against them. An anonymous letter writer in 1758 perfectly expressed colonists' fears of an enveloping race war. He announced that eight slaves had tried to poison the water supply for the soldiers' barracks at Cap Français. "Their plan was to put poison in the canal that carries water to the fountain, and in that way, cause the deaths of the soldiers who are the only thing holding them back and prevent them from killing all the whites."[75] Although the plan would have been a startling threat to the security in Cap Français, none of the colony's officials reported any such incident to the Naval Ministry. Significantly, though, the story warned all readers that poisoners were not aiming to kill one white or some whites but all white people.

Capturing and executing Makandal assigned blame for an outbreak of mysterious deaths, but it did not end those deaths. They continued for decades, as did the search for poisoners. The power of the Makandal-as-poisoner myth seemed to grow. Decades after his death, colonial lawyer Moreau de Saint-Méry would claim that Makandal's agents reached throughout Saint-Domingue.[76] When, in 1773, a new wave of livestock deaths prompted intense anxiety among enslaved and free people in the North Province, a respected physician offered a medical explanation. Despite the consistency and explanatory power of his diagnosis, colonists and the people they enslaved continued to search for the next Makandal.

5

An Epidemic of Their Own Making

THE TWELVE YEARS FOLLOWING Makandal's death were a period of relative plantation prosperity in the North Province. Mass death subsided when two years of wartime food shortages ended in 1759 after smugglers found ways to evade the British blockade and supply Saint-Domingue. The British naval commander at Jamaica estimated that in a single year, two hundred smugglers had traded with the French at the Spanish town of Monte Cristo, just down the coast from Fort Dauphin and Cap Français.[1] A South Carolinian merchant wrote, "We are well informed that the French, who were during the late embargo almost starving throughout Hispaniola, are now plentifully supplied."[2] Although the war had not ended, this revival of imported food meant that there was an ample supply of wheat flour and, presumably, protein like salt fish for enslaved people. At the same time, administrators' correspondence stopped mentioning the drought; as the normal rains returned, slaves' gardens could grow and livestock could graze widely.

At the highest levels of colonial government, the idea of a conspiracy to kill all the white people was losing ground. On Christmas Day, 1759, Saint-Domingue's governor wrote that the poisoning trials had ended roughly six months earlier. The investigations had stopped because there was a "lack of sufficient proof against the slaves who were still in prison, who have been released and sent back to their masters. Since then, Milord, everything appears calm in the Cap region and there is no talk of any criminal activity by the blacks."[3] The governor's correspondence shows that by this time, accusations of poison had left the public sphere of law and administration.

Although prosecutions abated, poison fears had crystallized in planters' minds, and they took measures into their own hands. Physician Raymond Delaborde arrived in 1760 and found that every sick colonist he treated claimed to have been poisoned by a slave. As a result, "no one trusted any slave; those who had provided the best service were those who were most mistrusted. There were pyres on every plantation. The planters immediately burned their allegedly guilty [slaves] at the stake; to intimidate the other slaves even more, they forced each one to carry a packet of wood for the pyre and all of them to witness the execution."[4]

Planters did not target only individuals for abuse in poison inquisitions. Some planters terrorized whole communities with acts of brutality for disobedience or suspected poison. In the North Province, some communities mobilized to resist in an astonishing way: they mounted legal challenges against their enslavers. They were aware of French law and correctly identified a judge who might enforce it in their favor. Article 26 of the Code Noir, enacted in 1685, forbade masters to torture or mutilate slaves. In the early 1770s, enslaved people on at least three occasions approached Cap's local judge Jean-Baptiste Estève, asking him to enforce that statute.

To seek protection from a judge, enslaved people first had to break the law by leaving the plantation. A man named Pantin, who walked away from a plantation on which eight to ten other slaves had been brutally burned, expressed this dilemma when he arrived at Judge Estève's residence and said he was "placing himself in the hands of justice so that he could be punished if he was guilty and protected if he was innocent."[5]

On a plantation owned by a colonist named Cassarouy, enslaved people were overworked and starved. When a group of them escaped, constables who were free men of color caught them and handed them over to their enslaver. Cassarouy took custody of them in the city of Cap Français for just two hours before delivering them to prison, and, in that time, he burned five or six of them with molten wax on their hands, arms, and backs. The constables told Judge Estève that the group left their custody healthy but had entered prison "subdued and covered with round spots and burns."[6] From jail, those people were returned to the plantation, but two people escaped again and sought protection from the royal prosecutor in Estève's court.

Their improbable strategy produced results. After an investigation, Cassarouy was charged with mutilating enslaved people. The court sent bailiffs out to the plantation, where they found clear evidence of torture—on their arrival, a woman was being hung by her arms. Cassarouy fought the charges, and Estève's decision went up for review. On October 2, 1770, in a holding that legitimized Cassarouy's abuse, the Superior Council nullified all the legal complaints and ordered the escaped people sent back to the plantation. They had succeeded in recruiting French law to their own purpose *and* in finding a judge willing to prosecute an enslaver for his illegality, but the Superior Council was made up of planters who treated abuse as an enslaver's prerogative. Estève noted that the council had been convinced to give masters a free hand because that approach seemed to have produced a declining number of slave poisonings in recent years.[7]

On May 28, 1771, ten more enslaved people appeared at Estève's residence and reported that their enslaver, Dessources, was conducting a brutal poison inquisition. He had tortured an enslaved man with fire and made him confess. Using that confession as evidence, Dessources claimed that all of the enslaved people on his estate were "*macandals*." He burned a driver named Jauncton, and he tortured enslaved people named Cézar,

Fanchette, and Jaunette by burning their feet and legs and burying them alive. An unnamed pregnant woman also died in a dungeon, where she had been imprisoned with burned legs and feet.[8]

The ten people who left to seek protection lived as fugitives at Estève's residence for a month while he arrived at a decision. Citing the Superior Council's decision in Cassarouy's case, he determined that it forbade local courts from getting involved in questions of punishment of slaves by masters. Estève held that his hands were tied, and he returned the petitioners to their enslaver but cautioned that Dessources would be held accountable if any of them died or were sold.[9]

Although the Superior Council gave planters wide latitude to manage sickness, death, and punishment on their estates, an epidemic of animal disease that began in 1772 drew French attention to the problem of plantation conditions. In late 1771, cattle being pastured at the southern edge of the plain in Petite Anse were struck by disease. They belonged to the Cap Français butcher, and when they all died, he was forced to give up his business.

In 1772, on the Carré sugar plantation only three miles away, sixty mules died within two days.[10] French physician Jean Louis Polony autopsied several of the animals and told a waiting crowd of planters that the mules had been killed by a highly contagious disease that would strike their animals too unless they took precautions. Polony had arrived in the colony in 1766, well after the end of the poisoning trials, but he understood the dangers of the poison mindset. Planters, he said, "preferred to ... blame the disease on the wickedness of the slaves; the disease spread far and wreaked terrible havoc, [however] most planters for a long time saw the slaves as the authors of this public scourge. The madness of some went so far that they did everything possible to mislead the governor and intendant."[11] Polony was a believer in new medical approaches to epidemic disease. He was well known in Cap Français for inoculating his entire family against smallpox in 1771.[12]

Physician Jean-Marie Regnaudot described the sixty dead mules on the Carré estate as the beginning of a livestock epidemic, but planters suspected poisoning because the mysterious sickness infected one estate and then jumped to another seven miles away. Regnaudot described how the epidemic moved across the sugar plain south of Cap Français, killing healthy animals with startling rapidity.

> In these different districts it showed the same irregular progress, the same virulence and constancy in its principles; in several places it made rapid, deadly, uninterrupted progress; in other places it moved more slowly, and it left fairly long intervals between its different attacks. There was quite a bit of drought when the disease invaded; the grass in the pastures was burned, the ponds were fetid; but the different seasons did not seem to bring much change in its character. Nothing kills more rapidly than this disease; it does not seem to have any early signs: many animals that had been pronounced in the best health were found dead several hours later; often the illness appeared [only] at the moment of death.[13]

Contrary to planters' beliefs, the epidemic's first mysterious leap was not due to a network of slave poisoners. It was caused by one professional plantation manager who specialized in running multiple estates for absentee owners. The Carré and Dupaty plantations were managed by the same estate agent. A horse that had lived on the Carré plantation was taken to Dupaty, where it died. The illness then spread through the Dupaty herd, killing eighty mules, not counting horses and oxen. From there, the disease spread to Dupaty's neighbors, including the Laplaigne, Sacanville, and Macarty estates. Eventually, the Noé estate was infected.[14]

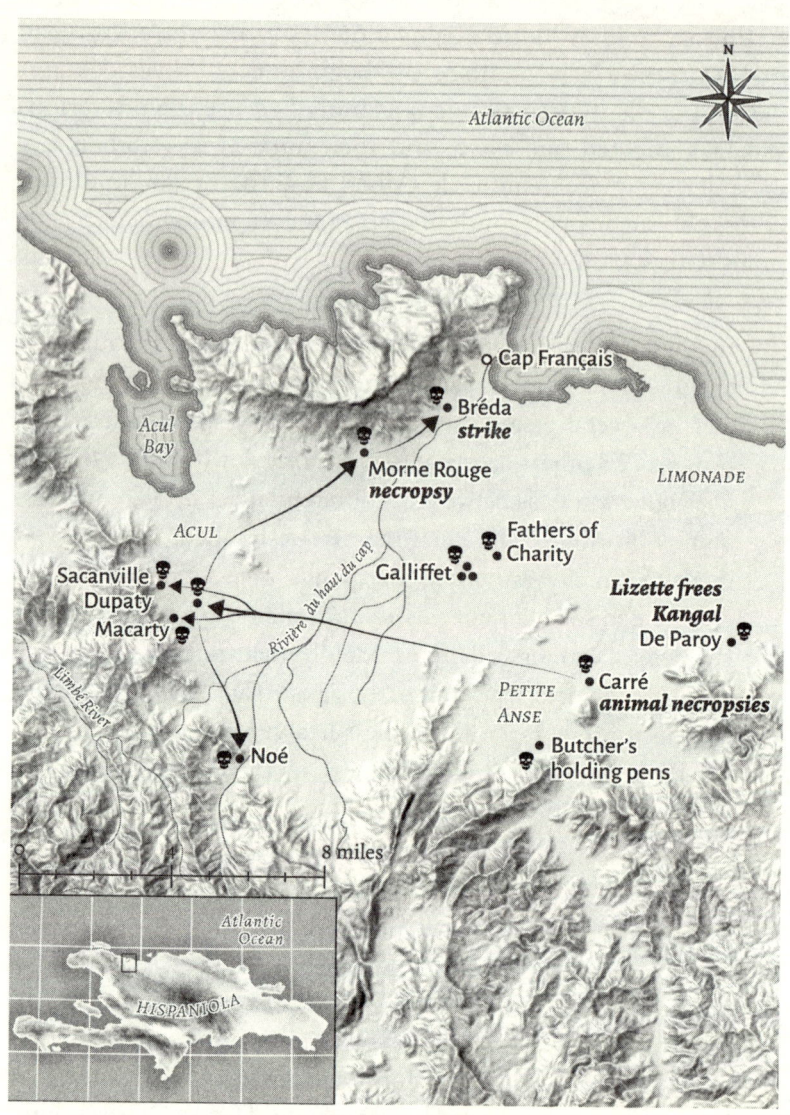

MAP 5.1 Doctors Diagnose Anthrax and Describe Its Spread, 1770s

In the early 1770s, attitudes about disease and medicine were changing among some Saint-Domingue colonists. After a long history of smallpox epidemics, some colonists began to inoculate themselves and their enslaved workers. In 1745 and again in 1757, colonists in Cap experimented with inoculation, but the method did not spread. Then, in 1767, Charles Fournier de la Chapelle, who had interrogated Makandal, inoculated ninety-six people enslaved on his plantation.[15] Those who were inoculated, including Polony and his family, survived a devastating smallpox epidemic that killed twelve hundred people in the colony in 1771 and 1772. Growing demand for inoculation convinced Simeon Worlock to migrate from Antigua to Saint-Domingue. Starting in 1774, Worlock immunized thousands of people in the North Province, some thirty years before Napoleon launched France's first mass inoculations.[16]

In the same year, 1774, Polony performed necropsies on 150 animals over six months. He wrote a detailed report that convinced Saint-Domingue's administrators that a contagious disease, not poison, was killing the province's livestock.[17] It was against this backdrop of growing interest in inoculation and new French veterinary and medical discoveries that Saint-Domingue's colonial doctors began to take steps toward a medical explanation of mysterious animal and human deaths in the North Province.

Planters were slow to accept the disease explanation, and they continued to conduct brutal poison inquisitions that were resisted by enslaved people. When the outbreak that Polony diagnosed on the Carré estate spread to the Bréda sugar plantation at Haut-du-Cap, the estate agent, Delribal, blamed poison and asked his employer for permission to kill one slave to terrorize others into confessing. Before receiving an answer, Delribal arrested three men and asked three neighbors to come and interrogate them. The neighbors refused because they believed the deaths were due to animal disease.[18] Delribal tortured the men and jailed the livestock foreman as a poisoner in Cap Français.

The foreman slashed his own throat with a broken bottle, and another accused man, Jean-Baptiste, attempted suicide on the plantation. Although Delribal reported that all the reasonable slaves "were reduced to the greatest despair,"[19] a number of them considered their options and decided to resist him.

Twenty-five of the roughly one hundred enslaved people on the Bréda estate left the property for days. If dying mules had not shuttered the sugar refinery, these striking workers likely did. They appealed to Bréda's nephews, who owned and lived on the Noé plantation in Acul.[20] On the advice of his nephews, Bréda fired Delribal and brought back a former manager, Bayon de Libertat. The striking workers returned. Toussaint Louverture may have been involved in resolving this standoff because he was enslaved as a coachman on the Bréda estate until around this time and was well known for his skill in healing animals. Delribal did not mention him, but Toussaint's family still lived there, and he knew both Bayon and the enslaved livestock keepers well. In 1776, as a free Black man, Toussaint purchased Jean-Baptiste and freed him from slavery.[21]

As to the cause of the deaths, Bayon wrote his employer that "after 23 years in Saint-Domingue, what I know about slaves' maliciousness, their ability to kill whites, slaves and animals with poison, as they have in the past, makes it difficult to persuade myself that this sickness is natural, especially because it is not affecting everyone." But because "it does not suit me to think differently from all the planters who generally think that an epidemic has struck the animals," he abandoned Delribal's poison investigation.[22]

To deal with the livestock crisis, the Naval Ministry in 1774 asked the royal veterinary schools to send two or three graduates to Saint-Domingue.[23] The colony's first veterinarian, Jean Lapole, arrived in Cap Français with firsthand experience combating a terrible livestock epidemic in southern France.[24] He remembered his early encounters with Saint-Domingue's planters: "In 1777 I debarked on these shores; something deadly was ravaging the animal population in the most devastating way; these cruel and unforeseen deaths led to the most inconsistent interpretations. Preconceptions made everything look like malefice ... a crowd of planters, trying to make me support their prejudices ... demanded that I, as a veterinarian, confirm their charges in writing, as proof of the slaves' wickedness."[25]

The livestock disease most fatal to humans is anthrax, and this was prevalent in France in 1757–1763, 1774–1780, and 1786–1793. Unlike livestock diseases that must spread from animal to animal, anthrax bacteria can live as spores in the soil. Animals contract the disease when they eat plants or soil containing the spores. In an animal's digestive tract, the spores become active bacteria, cloning themselves and killing the host in twenty-four to forty-eight hours. As the victim decomposes, millions of bacteria sink into the soil and become spores. This creates a spot that may be deadly to grazing animals for years. Anthrax outbreaks often follow a drought, because hungry animals paw at the ground to expose and eat edible roots. Flooding can also bring spores back to the surface.[26]

Anthrax can attack humans in at least three ways. In cutaneous anthrax, the most common form of the disease, patients develop coal-black pustules, which look like benign skin infections but can quickly cause swelling of the lymph glands, high fever, and death. Gastrointestinal anthrax can kill in a single day, with few distinctive symptoms: nausea, headache, abdominal pain, and swelling in the neck and throat. This form of the disease most often killed people who ate infected meat. A third form, a pneumonic variety, was largely unknown until the mid-1800s, when it began killing workers who sorted wool in textile factories. These types present very different symptoms, but all are deadly.[27]

Livestock diseases had so badly undermined France's economy in the eighteenth century that the kingdom's agricultural reformers mobilized. They coined a new word—*epizootic*—to describe epidemic animal disease. In 1762, Louis XV chartered

Europe's first veterinary school in Lyon; four years later, a second school opened in Alfort, just outside Paris.[28] Anthrax attracted early attention.

In 1769, a physician in France named Jean Fournier published a description of how anthrax infects the skin after contact with a sick animal. This lethal infection caused "a surprise tumor, emerging within an hour." Fournier also discovered that people who ate meat from infected animals developed infections in their digestive system, explaining that "its violence and rapidity is unbelievable; the most terrible failures occur almost simultaneously, and the organism collapses all at once." Gastrointestinal anthrax, he noted, occurs "in those unfortunate and cruel years of drought and famine, when the poor and indigent eat anything they can find, and in long and stubborn sieges, when troops ... are forced to eat unusual meats, which disgust them even as they calm their hunger."[29]

French advances in understanding virulent livestock diseases did not stop planters from hunting for poisoners. Sugar planters with the money to hire doctors could graft elements of medicine onto investigations that were nonetheless founded in rumor and coerced testimony. This happened in 1774 when livestock began to die on one of three adjacent Galliffet sugar plantations. An estate manager ordered an investigation, and rounds of interrogation led one captive to claim that a Black woman had made chocolate and fed it to the animals.[30] Searchers went looking for this chocolate, which is a food product that enslaved people made by roasting the seeds of a cacao gourd and grinding them into a paste. Sometimes makers added herbs for additional flavors. Dissolved in hot water, the paste became drinking chocolate. This was a common pleasure among all residents of the colony, so it is not surprising that the searchers found chocolate paste in the living quarters of one of the estate drivers, named Dau, and on the farm of a man named Laurin and his wife, Marie-Louise, who were probably free people of color.[31]

Judge Estève asked Antoine Baradat to test the seized chocolate. Baradat and his team administered ordinary chocolate to dogs with no ill effects, then fed Laurin's chocolate to a dog that died four days later, showing "livid and gangrenous spots" throughout its digestive canal, kidneys, liver, lungs, and heart. Dogs wouldn't eat Dau's chocolate, so the investigators force-fed it to a mule. It died after several days, showing livid gangrenous spots in its lungs, heart, and digestive canal. Another mule survived ordinary chocolate with no ill effects until it was dosed with Dau's chocolate, and then it died. All the dead animals had heavily coagulated blood. Baradat, who had been deeply involved in poison trials since Médor's time, concluded that the seized chocolate pastes were poison.[32]

An enslaved man named Jean-Pierre and his free Black aunt were imprisoned on another claim of poison chocolate when many animals died on the estate across the road from Galliffet. The Fathers of Charity were a Catholic order of priests who operated a sugar plantation in Petite Anse and a hospital in Cap Français. In 1774, the Father Superior requested a criminal investigation into the deaths.[33] Nicolas Odelucq, Galliffet's agent, reported to his employer that "they have discovered that the sickness of horses and mules came from a poison and that the slaves grated it into the trough where they fed [the animals] crushed sugarcane. A slave of the Fathers of Charity declared that by doing this he had killed more than 100 mules belonging to these priests."[34] His free Black aunt was accused of passing him poison in prison.

The chocolate poison cases are examples of the fifteen-year pattern of blaming enslaved people for mass death among previously healthy animals. Searching for and seizing a substance, testing it, and conducting necropsies lent empirical credibility to a roundup that began in coercion. It is not likely that Dau, Laurin, Marie-Louise, or Jean-Pierre killed hundreds of mules by force-feeding them chocolate. However, the fact that mixtures intended for human consumption were toxic does raise questions about their purpose.

Enslaved people were probably the first to observe anthrax in Saint-Domingue's animals and be killed by it. Those who tended sick livestock or worked with their hides would have contracted cutaneous anthrax and likely would have died. Baradat's work suggests that enslaved people, after seeing an animal eat a plant and then die, might have collected anthrax-tainted leaves to use as medicine or as a weapon. In 1757, Baradat found anthrax symptoms in dogs killed by leaves from Médor's supplier Daouin. Another supplier, Gaou, might have deliberately consumed anthrax when he knew constables were coming to arrest him.

Some people probably did use anthrax intentionally. As a form of resistance, they might have sabotaged an estate by feeding anthrax-laden leaves to draft animals. This could slow the pace of work or undermine a hated plantation agent who had promised vast profits to an absentee owner. Although planters claimed that enslaved people poisoned other enslaved people as a form of sabotage, mass death among the enslaved more likely came from eating anthrax-tainted food in a time of starvation.[35] It is also conceivable that captives used anthrax to kill their enslavers, although that was unlikely to bring their freedom. Anthrax would not have been the substance used in any case where an enslaver lingered ill for months.

Anthrax in Saint-Domingue should primarily be understood not as a poison but as the deadly legacy of an overseas livestock trade that supported plantation agriculture by supplying hundreds of thousands of draft animals to be systematically worked to death. By 1776, Antoine Baradat concluded as much under the guidance of French anatomist Félix Vicq d'Azyr, who had published a detailed account of an anthrax outbreak in Bordeaux. He found that leather made from the skin of infected animals, as well as tainted meat, carried the disease. Correspondence with Vicq d'Azyr ultimately convinced Baradat that anthrax was killing mules and oxen in Saint-Domingue.

Writing about anthrax, Baradat described dissections he performed in the 1770s on the Morne Rouge estate owned by Makandal's enslaver. The carcasses showed the telltale signs of gastrointestinal anthrax that Baradat had earlier interpreted as poison: livid internal gangrenous spots and blood so thick that it would not flow. He also described slaves who had worked with the sickened animals and then died of cutaneous anthrax. Many of those animals would have come from the Soufrière livestock corral, still in operation, where Makandal had been enslaved thirty years earlier. In a ringing indictment of the poison mindset, Vicq d'Azyr noted the injustice of blaming slaves for poisoning these animals. "We take away from an enslaved man, in effect, all means and all reasons to do good, but, on the other hand, we imagine he is much better supplied than he actually is, to do evil."[36]

Although cases of human anthrax were rare in France, they were common in Saint-Domingue because the colony was designed to produce famine among the enslaved. To save labor and land, planters and their agents routinely decided to buy food rather than produce their own. This maximized sugar profits and made their workers' food supply vulnerable. Plantation life exposed enslaved people to anthrax in many ways. Despite a growing awareness of the disease in Saint-Domingue, there were no measures in place to contain it, and there was no cure. Over the next twenty years, the epidemic would be aggravated by a recurrence of drought and war as had devastated the region in Médor's and Makandal's time.[37]

El Niño events in the early 1770s caused a series of severe Caribbean hurricanes and droughts. Although Saint-Domingue's North Province escaped the worst hurricanes, it did not escape the ensuing droughts. Drought became "a catastrophe for enslaved peoples throughout large sections of the Caribbean"[38] because it devastated local food production. In the winter between 1775 and 1776, ports in France froze over, depriving the colony of imported food. By law, the colony could only import food from France.[39]

In the spring of 1776, the British blockaded rebel ports in North America, heading off smugglers who were Saint-Domingue's best source of emergency food. Drought combined with wartime trade disruptions left slaves starving throughout the Caribbean.[40]

By August, administrators in Saint-Domingue had to order estates to plant food for their slaves, noting that "generally here planters sacrifice even their slaves' subsistence for the temporary increase of their revenue."[41] As the British blockade and the drought worsened, doctors told of slaves so hungry that they dug up cattle buried in shallow graves, fished carcasses out of rivers, or ate the charred remains of diseased animals.[42] A plantation surgeon wrote that "in [1776] four slaves on a sugar plantation in Terrier Rouge dug up a sheep and ate it. One of these slaves suffered an anthrax tumor on his face and died; another was affected in his stomach and died in four hours, with terrible convulsions. Having seen several slaves die of anthrax on the Brethoux plantation I told the manager that his workers must have eaten oxen who died on the estate; he investigated and found rotten meat in almost all the slave huts."[43]

To survive, enslaved people on the Galliffet estate and elsewhere bought sundried beef jerky from peddlers.[44] Pelissot, the estate surgeon, reported this practice to authorities, who temporarily outlawed the sale of *tassau* in Cap Français and the surrounding plain. They determined that the meat "mostly came from animals dead of the epidemic sickness which has caused and continues to wreak cruel havoc, and that these meats caused the most deadly accidents in the slaves who ate them." As early as 1776, police inspectors seized peddlers' stores of tassau and burned them.[45] Yet starving people were desperate, even for tainted meat. In 1780, officials in Cap Français again ordered constables to confiscate and destroy tassau. Free trade advocates later estimated that tassau had killed fifteen hundred slaves and hunger had killed another fifteen hundred during the war.[46]

Pelissot described the grim picture in Petite Anse: "When I treated slaves for anthrax . . . I almost always discovered that oxen had died suddenly on their plantation or the neighboring one; that they had dug up these oxen and had eaten them, or that they had bought [such meat] from slaves on neighboring estates, or from butchers, or from Spanish merchants."[47] Nicolas Odelucq, the Galliffet plantation agent who had levied poison charges, now acknowledged how anthrax came to afflict enslaved people and animals on the estate. "Their symptoms resembled those of the animals who died in the epizootic. . . . The Spanish ranches are depopulating, they made dried meat with animals that died of the sickness, which harmed the slaves who bought it. . . . They have prohibited this trade."[48]

Anthrax was able to kill thousands of people in Saint-Domingue because the French colonial system was structured to produce the very hunger that drove Galliffet's workers to eat bad meat. To funnel profits back to French producers and merchants, the monarchy's laws prohibited colonists from trading with foreign merchants. Colonists generally ignored the national monopoly and bought imported cheap slave food from any available source, and so put minimal effort into growing their own slave provisions. When a severe drought occurred during a wartime blockade, colonists and slaves alike turned for sustenance to draft animals and meat from Santo Domingo.

Engineering the conditions that favored an epidemic was not the empire's only contribution. It was an imported French strain of the bacteria that arrived to afflict the colony sometime in the late 1740s. Genetic evidence suggests that it arrived from French Louisiana, probably with livestock.[49] It was an epidemic of the empire's own making that caused the deaths Médor blamed on himself and that killed Assam's swollen patients on the Valette estate around the same time. The six thousand to seven thousand slaves and "great many whites" described as Makandal's victims likely also fell to the same strain of anthrax, which has since become endemic in Haiti.[50]

Unsurprisingly, hunting for poisoners across the North Province from 1757 until the Haitian Revolution did not curtail mass sickness and death. Nonetheless, planters in poison inquisitions used torture, threats, and intimidation to divide enslaved communities that were struggling against starvation and illness. They subjected family, friends, and neighbors to interrogation, exploiting the confusion and suspicion that would naturally occur in a community afflicted by mysterious deaths. In some communities that resisted their enslavers, poison trials and other litigation created a record of resistance. This is what happened in the early 1770s on the de Paroy sugar estate in a case involving dead mules, a newly freed man named Kangal, and his freed mother and enslaved father. In their story, we see how a complex pattern of resistance by free and enslaved Black people unfolded during six years of legal and political process.

Kangal was enslaved on the sugar estate of the Marquis le Gentil de Paroy, an absentee owner of two such plantations in the Limonade parish.[51] Kangal lived and worked as a coachman; his enslavers called him Antoine. A coachman was responsible for taking care of horses and mules that pulled the owner's coach and for driving the owner on trips away from the estate. This would involve regular travel to Cap Français and neighboring plantations. Personal access to an enslaver and the possibility of earning his favor was one benefit of being a coachman. Building a network of acquaintances with other coachmen, people living on other plantations, and people living in the city, including free Black people, was another.

The marquis relied on his brother to manage the estate in his absence. In 1762, the brother freed Kangal's mother, Lizette, but Kangal and his father remained enslaved. When the marquis's brother died, he hired an estate agent who in 1774 oversaw the manumission of Kangal and three other men who were domestic slaves.⁵² An enslaver or his agent usually paid for and managed the multiple steps required to formalize manumission.⁵³ An enslaver with a personal interest in the freed party would ensure that all these steps were taken; otherwise, the freed person could be re-enslaved.

Kangal's manumission was not a result of his enslaver's affection. Later reports explained that he and three others were freed because they were unsuitable for fieldwork and of "defiant character." The estate agent wanted them gone, and he viewed their manumission as a business opportunity for his employer. He insisted that each of the four men buy himself from de Paroy.⁵⁴ In February and March 1774, Kangal's mother, Lizette, paid the enormous sum of three thousand livres for her son's freedom. It was, she said, "all the fortune she had accumulated."⁵⁵ She was a freed person but had no land and lived on the village commons in Limonade. She turned over eighteen hundred livres in gold and silver coins and two mules, each worth six hundred livres. After taking her payment, the plantation agent let Kangal go, but did not complete the official paperwork confirming his manumission.

A year or two later, the marquis hired a new agent named Marc-Antoine Avalle, who developed a dangerous antipathy to Kangal. This was manifested on September 10, 1776, when Kangal returned to the plantation to visit his father, who was ill in the plantation hospital, a locked shed where sickened slaves were confined. By this time, livestock epidemics had begun to affect the marquis's properties, though we don't know what illness Kangal's father had. In June or July, in a week's time, ninety-nine mules on the estate grew strange tumors on their chests and stomachs. None died, but in July, three healthy mules died suddenly. Avalle suspected poisoning and told the livestock guards not to let any unknown slave into the pasture.

When Kangal arrived at the plantation to see his father, he went to the plantation house to ask permission, as was required by Avalle. The marquis and Avalle were both there. Avalle told

Kangal to come back during the workday; he said the hospital was locked at night, and no one was allowed in or out. He knew Kangal and thought he was a troublemaker. He was irritated that Kangal and other former house slaves kept coming back to the estate. Avalle complained that they came "on the pretext of seeing their relatives" but really returned on "business that was prejudicial to de Paroy."[56]

Kangal was angry and insisted on seeing his father. Avalle claimed that Kangal spoke rudely and "continued to insult me to the point where I could no longer doubt that he had some plans underway." When Avalle threatened to put him in the stocks, Kangal continued to speak in an insulting tone. Avalle told nearby servants to call the sugar refiner, perhaps to have Kangal whipped, but they pretended not to hear him. Eventually, Kangal left, calling out "impertinences" to Avalle. The next day, September 11, the marquis wrote to the local commander of the Cap district and asked him to punish Kangal and forbid him from returning to the plantation. The commander replied that he would not intervene.[57]

On September 15, two more mules died in the middle of the sugar harvest. Avalle assembled all the slaves, intimidated them, and threatened to hold the slave driver responsible for any "un-natural" events. When another two mules died, Avalle oversaw a dissection. Their stomachs were inflamed and corroded. Avalle later admitted that he knew that the driver, himself, was not responsible. His threat was designed to generate leads.[58]

Avalle arrested a relative of the slave driver, pressuring the driver to find a poisoner. As more mules died, Avalle arrested more slaves until suspicion fell on one of the livestock guards. One of the mules had died after being left in the pasture all night; its stomach was badly inflamed and its intestine had perforated. The guard denied any knowledge of the dead mules until, after being whipped, he said that he saw Kangal go into Jupiter's hut.[59] Jupiter, who worked in the sugar mill, denied what the guard had said. After Avalle had him whipped, Jupiter escaped, was captured, and was whipped again; he still denied the accusation. When one of the white people seized Jupiter's young son, Amboise, and Jupiter's wife, Mariejeanne, and subjected them to interrogation, a highly detailed poison narrative emerged.

Unusually, the statements included verbatim transcriptions of the Creole language ostensibly uttered by Kangal and the others. The statements described how Kangal came several times to Jupiter's home, including the night before the mules died. Kangal ostensibly showed Jupiter a powder, saying it was "to fuck with the whites. Put it in the pasture to torment everyone . . . they tormented me, they argued, now today we have something to use on them."[60] Kangal also purportedly asked where Avalle was, and Jupiter told him he was in Cap Français, then Kangal gave Jupiter a powder that they put into a small broken kettle with water. Jupiter's son purportedly watched Kangal and his father mix powder and water, heat it on a fire, and pour it into a small container, then leave. Under interrogation, Jupiter's wife confirmed this account.

Interrogators then returned to Jupiter bearing a paper they said contained testimony against him. They said it was Kangal's confession. Jupiter then gave up his denials. He said that Kangal had done everything. The colonists wrote up a confession that included his eyewitness description of how and where Kangal fed poison to a mule. The document refers to Kangal by his slave name, Antoine. According to Jupiter's testimony, the poisoning happened the night of September 10, 1776, immediately following Kangal's run-in with Avalle.[61]

According to Avalle's notes, it had taken a month of arrests and whippings before he found enslaved people willing to blame Kangal. On September 11, the day after the run-in, de Paroy asked the Cap commander to ban Kangal from the plantation not for being a poisoner but for being insolent. The core of Kangal's offense surely was being a freed man who kept returning to the plantation. When the commandant refused to ban Kangal from the plantation, Avalle bypassed him, writing directly to both the governor and the intendant in Port-au-Prince. Then the rationale became poison. Avalle included the testimony of Jupiter and his family and complained to the high administrators "that the scourge of a supernatural mortality that he just experienced on the plantations of Monsieur the Marquis de Paroy had obliged him to take just measures to avoid the total ruin of the said plantations." The authors of the deaths, he claimed, were de Paroy's freed slaves, who had caused a "general revolt" on the plantation.[62]

Avalle no longer sought to exclude Kangal from the plantation; he wanted to re-enslave him. He had realized that the manumissions of Kangal and the other three men were never ratified by the administration, so he asked the governor and intendant to let him "return the said slaves into slavery to avoid the misfortunes with which they have threatened him and . . . to stop the progress of the evil that such individuals will spread throughout the colony, which is unfortunately already too afflicted with this scourge."[63] The governor and the intendant acceded to Avalle's request, which nullified Kangal's freedom based on a poisoning claim. The formerly free man was arrested, jailed at Cap Français for three months, then transferred to the de Paroy plantation.

In November 1777, Kangal's mother, Lizette, intervened. In an extraordinary act of resistance, she asserted Kangal's freedom using the colonial courts.[64] As a free woman, she had the right to bring a lawsuit, but this required hiring willing lawyers and scribes and paying court costs. In the roughly ten months after Kangal's arrest, Lizette must have assembled a community of supporters. This group could have included the handful of wealthy free people of color in Limonade parish, including the family of the future revolutionary Jean-Baptiste Chavanne.[65] She also could have recruited the support of colonists who disliked Avalle and de Paroy enough to break with powerful conventions of white solidarity.⁶⁶ Lizette's attorney LaRoque filed a motion with the court in Cap Français accusing Avalle of treating Kangal like a slave after de Paroy had freed him and accepted her payment. She accused Avalle of holding her son in solitary confinement and subjecting him to the "cruelest punishments." She said Kangal had the right to know the charges against him, and she convinced the court to make her Kangal's legal guardian so she could defend him against Avalle's claims. The court had constables transfer Kangal from de Paroy's plantation back to the jail in Cap Français, at Lizette's expense, and hold him there, again, at Lizette's expense.⁶⁷

Avalle's lawyer filed a counter motion insisting that Kangal was a poisoner. He made a list of all the animals and humans who had died on the estate in 1776. This included twenty mules, twelve of which were poisoned, he claimed. A few died in July 1776, but most died in September and October, after Kangal visited Jupiter. He also claimed that poisoners had killed two of eleven dead oxen and three of eight dead sheep. Twenty-five enslaved workers on the estate had died in this period. He claimed that poison had killed five of them. Four of these victims died of a mysterious swelling around the time of the mule deaths.⁶⁸

Lizette fought back in the courts. She produced the receipts de Paroy had given her for Kangal's freedom price and wrote that Kangal was working to pay for additional liberty papers when Avalle had him arrested. In February 1779, the Cap Council decided in Kangal's favor.⁶⁹ De Paroy again superseded local authority by using his connections at Versailles. In October 1778, as Lizette began to fight him in the courts, Avalle signed a long memorandum to Louis XVI's State Council describing the case in dire terms. The document was written by one of de Paroy's lawyers in France.⁷⁰ A year later, the royal Council of Dispatches overruled the colonial court.⁷¹

When Avalle suddenly had Kangal arrested and taken to the de Paroy plantation, Lizette again petitioned the Cap Français court.⁷² Defending his actions, Avalle argued that Kangal posed too great a flight risk and too great a danger to the colony to remain at liberty. On the strength of a poisoning allegation, Avalle planned to hold Kangal in chains and in solitary confinement for the rest of his life.⁷³

Lizette persisted in her son's defense. On June 9, a notary, scribe, and royal surgeon traveled to the de Paroy estate to officially observe Kangal's condition.⁷⁴ Avalle described this as an attack on the property rights of any master: "If the slaves ever persuaded themselves that their masters' conduct over them was subordinate to the judges, all is lost! The hope of having protectors always nearby to prevent or check punishment that is frequently well deserved will encourage all kinds of disorder." Nonetheless, on June 26, 1780, a team of constables and a bailiff appeared at the de Paroy plantation with a locksmith to transfer Kangal back to the Cap Français jail.⁷⁵

The record of this case suggests that Avalle's predecessor intended to remove Kangal and other men from the community through manumission and to see the cost of that borne by the men and their families. When Kangal remained a part of the plantation community after being freed and resisted Avalle's control, Avalle tried to re-enslave him and the three others to put an end to their plans.⁷⁶ Over years of litigation, Lizette created a rich record of resistance on the de Paroy estate. Kangal and free Black people conducted "business" on the estate that the agents didn't like. Kangal insisted on seeing his father and insulted Avalle when the agent refused to allow this. Jupiter endured a month of whipping and other torture before saying what Avalle wanted him to say. Lizette paid to have Kangal jailed in Cap Français to get him out of de Paroy's plantation dungeon. She almost defeated one of Saint-Domingue's wealthiest planters in court until de Paroy got the royal council to overturn the Cap Français high court.

Lizette also revealed how planters cynically abused legal process to extort, control, and destroy slave communities. What

Avalle feared was the community that Kangal and the other ex-slaves maintained with enslaved people on the plantation. Avalle might have associated free Black visits with resistance activities or feared that Kangal's "insolence" might spread to others. Or Avalle might have suspected Kangal of commercial business, of helping enslaved people sell their produce or handicrafts, or even fencing stolen property for them. All these would have created bonds of community that could play an important role in an enslaved person's decision as to whether and how to oppose domination.

Lizette and Kangal believed that resisting through legal action was possible on the merits of their case, and they were right. They convinced judges in Cap Français, most of whom were planters, that de Paroy had no right to rescind Kangal's liberty simply because the freedman insisted on visiting his father. Nor was Avalle's poisoning evidence convincing to the colonial bench, perhaps because of the mounting evidence of the anthrax epidemic. Their battle was only lost when de Paroy convinced the king's advisors in France that masters retained their property rights even after manumitting someone; those property rights lasted until the colonial government ratified the slave's freedom. In other words, until the official paperwork was completed, "a master whose slave has rendered himself unworthy of this favor can revoke his consent and make the slave return [to bondage]."[77]

Lizette's attempt to protect Kangal by appealing to the French ideals expressed in the Code Noir could not prevail over de Paroy's appeal to high-ranking royal officials. The Crown ordered that Kangal be returned to de Paroy's plantation and it rebuked the Cap Council for not attending to the "larger issues" involved in this case—an allusion to the problem of holding enslaved people in check.[78]

By the 1780s, enslaved people across the North Province had formed communities in response to years of environmental, material, and spiritual threats. They fought these forces and the slave system that created them in ways as various as the lands they came from and the colonial situations they encountered. Médor resisted by using medicines he hoped would soften the hearts of his enslavers and lead them to free him. He joined others who imagined a future Saint-Domingue where free Black people could confront the white people and demand changes. Makandal and his Congo-inspired community harnessed the power of the spirit world in Saint-Domingue, using rituals and concepts from their homelands. The slaves at Bréda Haut-du-Cap mounted a strike to defeat Delribal. The two from Cassarouy, the ten from Dessources, and Kangal's mother, Lizette, all resisted by recruiting French law to their own ends. Although colonists like Courtin, Fournier, Delribal, and Avalle did their best to destroy these communities, they did not succeed in erasing them from the archive.

Resistance would continue in the mountains of Plaisance and Marmelade, where coffee planters were among the last colonists to accept that anthrax was Saint-Domingue's mysterious killer. There, free and enslaved men and women were haunted by Makandal's ghost up to the eve of the Haitian Revolution.

6

Makandal's Ghost

MANY AFRICAN CAPTIVES took their first measure of Saint-Domingue in Cap Français, then were forced to walk to their enslaver's estate. Heading south from the port city, newly arrived people bound for coffee slavery walked past cane fields where other enslaved Africans toiled. The flat land gave way to foothills, then mountains. This was the coffee frontier, where slaves labored to fulfill the dreams of colonists too poor or too poorly married to become sugar planters. A whole generation of Congo captives walked on, past the farthest limits of Soufrière, where Makandal made his own freedom. In the 1770s, colonists forced slaves to cut a road still deeper into the mountains, widening a curved and twisting mule path. Closer to Cap, the mountains channeled travelers south through river valleys. Deeper in the interior, the mountain chains ran from east to west, so newcomers had to climb and descend ridges, one after the other, until they entered the isolated parish of Marmelade.

Coffee work in Marmelade in the 1770s still functioned much as it had done in Makandal's Soufrière and Médor's Les Perches twenty years before. Enslaved people were forced to clear the land using axes and machetes, plant coffee bushes in rows along the slopes, and harvest the fruit that their enslavers hoped would make a fortune. It was cold and wet on the high slopes, and people's clothes turned quickly to rags, but because coffee does not rot, coffee work was less pressured than sugar work during the harvest season. In a small holding, a few enslaved people could be made to supply all the needed labor, and berries could be picked, washed, and sold locally. A quarter of Saint-Domingue's coffee operations had fewer than eighteen slaves. It was more profitable to sell coffee beans than coffee berries. On an estate with lean financial backing, slaves would crank a hand mill to grate away the pulp and then spread the beans on the ground to dry. A wealthy planter might build a series of water- or mule-driven mills to clean the beans and then dry them on a masonry platform. Depending on the number of coffee bushes under cultivation, a coffee plantation could demand the labor of as few as ten captives or as many as two hundred.[1]

Coffee crews had fewer specialized workers than sugar crews, but both types of planters relied on drivers. They were enslaved men who stood over the other slaves and directed their work, hour by hour, punishing them if necessary to accomplish a planter's goals. They were central figures in the life of the estate. Their work for their enslaver, their good judgment, and their authority over an enslaved community were critical to an estate's profitability. A manual for coffee planters described drivers as "the soul of the plantation. . . . They ought to possess fidelity, affection, intelligence, sobriety, discretion, justice, and severity. They should know to preserve distance and authority, make themselves acquainted with all that the negroes do or intend to do, chiefly during night, keep an eye upon the nocturnal visits and excursions; observe, while at work, if any are indisposed, give attention to everything, and render account of every thing to the master. Lastly, to be perfectly skilled in work of every kind."[2]

On coffee estates, drivers walked behind workers as they pruned bushes, spread manure, and harvested berries. They trained, corrected, and disciplined them. They were allowed to whip fellow slaves. Enslavers gave drivers more food, double rations of cloth, and often better housing than other enslaved people. They had to earn workers' loyalty and respect while also enforcing standards of productivity and discipline. Colonists also held drivers responsible for what enslaved workers did during their time off. On smaller estates, a driver reported directly to the planter. On medium or large plantations, a driver might report to a white overseer or bookkeeper, who was accountable to the owner.

In 1776 and 1783, doctors diagnosed anthrax in the Artibonite Plain to Marmelade's west; the two were linked by a road. In 1785, Marmelade's eastern neighbor Grande-Rivière reported undiagnosed epizootics.[3] Estates in Marmelade reported terrible mortality without describing its cause. In 1784 and 1785, one hundred enslaved people died on the Marmelade estate of the Chevalier de la Rivière, an expert on the Santo Domingo cattle trade.[4] If those outbreaks went undiagnosed, it was probably because physicians and veterinarians rarely ventured into the mountains. Enslaved people fighting for their lives on the frontier of this new anthrax battle got medical care from so-called plantation surgeons, men whose clinical experience came from amputating limbs on battleships.

Isolated coffee planters were not without medical advice. Although most could not afford to bring French doctors to their estates, in 1778, physician Julien-François Duchemin de l'Etang began publishing the *Gazette de Médecine* to guide colonists who had to do their own doctoring. In the first issue, he described the autopsy of an ox belonging to a planter who had lost many animals. He related that, while some suspected poison had killed the ox, an examination of its stomach using a magnifying loupe showed that the ravenous animal had eaten a plant with tiny needles that destroyed its stomach.[5]

The *Gazette*'s second issue described the epizootic that still raged around Cap Français. It criticized medical experts who observed obvious symptoms of anthrax yet blamed poison: "Even members of the [medical] profession have publicly maintained that the pestilential carbuncles seen in these illnesses, which are transmitted to the men who open these animals' carcasses, can only be the effect of a coagulating poison, something unheard-of in the annals of medicine."[6] Duchemin's diatribes against poison may have cost him subscribers, for the *Gazette* folded in 1779 after only eight issues. Even as the anthrax diagnosis came to replace accusations of poison across the sugar plain, coffee planters in the mountains still ignored or rejected it. They instead pursued Makandal's ghost in what one official called a "theater of masters' barbarity and slaves' vengeance."[7]

Enslaved people within the reach of colonist Pierre Cappé knew this to be true. Cappé was a retired military man, not high ranking, and he was erratic and irascible, sometimes violently so. His land was the hilliest in his district, so mountainous that it was not surveyed. On a 1779 map, it was labeled as an area where pigs were raised.[8] He likely traded in livestock, acquiring animals from Santo Domingo, fattening them up, and reselling them in Saint-Domingue. He may have hoped to grow coffee, but he depended on market farming. He forced his captives to raise root crops that were considered slave food, and he sold those in the coastal market. His slaves would have been the last to eat. To survive, they could have resorted to eating fallen animals or buying *tassau* from the Spanish side of the border. At one point, Cappé was reduced to selling homemade sugar syrup to cover his expenses.[9]

To sell his crops, Cappé could travel for a day to reach Cap Français or spend a little more time heading westward to Gonaïves, a port town of sixty-seven houses.[10] Cappé chose Gonaïves, where scarce supply drove up the value of his products and sheltered him from the competition at the bustling market in Cap Français. To reach the mule path that crossed to Gonaïves, Cappé drove animals loaded with produce across his neighbor's land. Trouble erupted when his neighbor, a widow, took steps to stop him. She asked her white overseer to stop Cappé from crossing through, and the overseer ordered the estate's enslaved driver

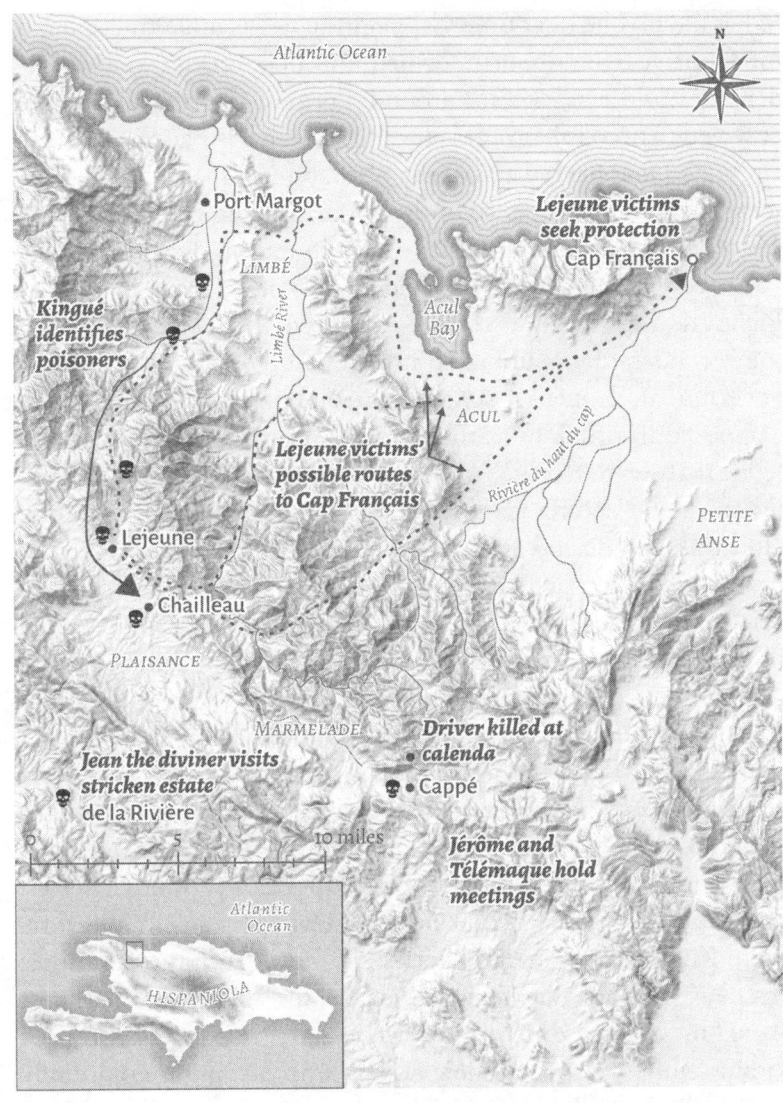

MAP 6.1 Resisting Anthrax and Poison Accusations in the Coffee Zones, 1780s

to handle it. The next time Cappé brought his mule train bound for Gonaïves, the driver informed him that, on the widow's order, he would need to turn around. Furious, Cappé knocked the enslaved man to the ground and shot at him with his musket. He continued undeterred across the plantation and later returned to search the main house, room by room, looking to confront the widow or her overseer, neither of whom was on the estate.[11]

A year or two later, the widow married Charles-François Pichot de Kerdisien de Trémais, a retired official who had been the second-ranking administrator in Saint-Domingue's civilian government. Trémais assumed control of her plantation. When Cappé confronted him about stray animals, Trémais built a fence that separated the two properties, containing each owner's livestock and ending Cappé's transit across the estate. Not long after this, people and animals on Cappé's estate experienced the deadly epidemic that was all around them. The Trémais plantation was untouched. Seeing that the losses were his alone, Cappé became convinced that a poisoner was attacking him. He suspected the Trémais driver who had tried to block his passage.[12]

Trémais was generally skeptical about claims of poisoning. As a member of the Superior Councils of Cap Français and Port-au-Prince from 1769 to 1784, he had seen a number of poisoning trials. When slaves did use poison, he claimed, it was most frequently to commit suicide, not to kill planters or other slaves. He also believed that when slaves did use poisons, they resorted to European chemicals like arsenic, not African preparations. Trémais asserted that unexplained deaths among the enslaved were "most often due to [owners'] culpable negligence in providing enough food to their slaves, who are quite commonly very badly nourished."[13]

Cappé asked Trémais to put the driver in chains and bring him to a meeting. Trémais complied, accompanied by his overseer and three friends, as witnesses. When they entered the building that Cappé used as a prison, they saw a Black man lying on a board wearing a heavy neck collar with a thick iron chain shackled to the ceiling. This was the driver who ran crews on Cappé's estate. He was in great pain, for Cappé had burned his legs to make him confess, and his injuries had been untreated for so long that a terrible infection had set in. The witnesses interviewed the torture victim, and the overseer took notes.[14]

At Cappé's urging, the mutilated driver confessed that he had given poisons supplied by the Trémais driver to people and animals on the Cappé estate. Trémais advised that, by the smell of his wounds, he probably did not have long to live and asked whether he wanted to "face God" with lies on his conscience. The man recanted, saying that the Trémais driver was innocent of any deaths; he had not supplied any poisons. The dying man said he had only made the claim because Cappé tortured him. The delegation left, and Trémais freed his driver from chains the following day after Cappé sent a message acknowledging his innocence.

When Cappé's losses continued, he blamed another neighbor's driver. Cappé convinced the young and inexperienced planter to turn over his driver, who was presumably killed. Cappé also continued to torture his own slaves to make them confirm his suspicions. He accused the enslaved woman who cared for sick workers and locked her in a plantation dungeon. After three or four months, she said that the Trémais driver had supplied poisons. Cappé sent a vial of the alleged poison to the court in Cap Français and had the Trémais driver imprisoned there for over a month. The poison was found to be harmless, and when the court questioned the accused, she recanted. The driver was released to Trémais.[15]

On Christmas Eve, when Trémais and his wife were away on a holiday visit, Cappé saw his chance. The Trémais driver and many enslaved workers were attending a holiday calenda in the coffee warehouse of the neighboring Julbin estate. Around nine o'clock in the evening, four parish constables appeared at the door. The constables said they were responding to a noise complaint, likely a pretext because the celebrants were not playing drums; they were playing a much smaller and quieter calabash gourd. Soon after entering the warehouse, the constables stabbed the Trémais driver with their swords, killing him. Despite constables' claims that some slaves resisted, no one was arrested, and the constables left, uninjured, carrying the gourd. Trémais maintained that Cappé arranged to have the constables attend the calenda to kill the driver.[16]

The outcomes for these three drivers, whose names were never recorded, illustrate how men in their position were forced to negotiate painful and dangerous dilemmas of leadership and responsibility.[17] Colonists like Cappé were isolated, outnumbered, and unable to do the work they demanded of others. They relied on drivers who could create community among the enslaved, influence them to work, and repress their dissent. Enslavers also relied on information from drivers to make decisions about plantation work and to weigh the likelihood of disruptions or resistance. To maintain control over a plantation, planters rationed oppression and tolerance; for example, outlawing calendas but permitting them informally. Inside information helped planters strike their balance. If an enslaved person was absent from the plantation, knowing whether they were seeking medicine, visiting family, engaging in commerce, or gone to seek freedom would help a planter measure out forbearance or punishment.

Forging the communities that enslavers exploited could be deadly to drivers. When bad land, drought, or epidemics pressured an unsuccessful planter, drivers were held responsible for delivering results well beyond their control. When Cappé decided that poison was tipping the precarious balance of his operation, he tortured and killed his driver. When that didn't work, he killed enslaved leaders on two neighboring estates. Trémais did not believe Cappé's charges, and he knew that his estate's profits stemmed from the skill and judgment of his driver, yet he was unable to protect him from persecution.[18] That driver's importance likely contributed to his demise; taking him from the midst of a calenda would have been a highly effective form of terrorism conducted by Cappé against a community he had no authority to control. If he could not root out a poisoner on someone else's estate, he might scare the community into submission by reaching past an absent owner to strike at its heart.

Enslaved communities in Marmelade had their own ways of understanding the evil that was killing animals and people around them. Some feared a poisoner. Others feared malevolent spirits operating in the world. Many believed that humans could manipulate spirits to cause harm. In West Central Africa, many cultures believed that an imbalance in society could cause mass deaths and epidemics.[19] Congo diviners living in Marmelade met threats to a community by convening ritual meetings and providing weapons endowed with spiritual power.[20] One of them, named Julien, visited the Trémais estate to hold meetings.

The most active of the organizers was a man named Jean, enslaved by a colonist named Molliers in the Soufrière canton of Marmelade, only a few miles from where Makandal had lived. Although he was enslaved, Jean moved between many plantations and found ways to hold meetings on them and in Marmelade's forests and deep valleys. On the Estève estate, an overseer saw Jean enter the hut of an enslaved man named Jean Ladot. Peering through holes in the wall, he glimpsed the two men and possibly others sitting before a covered table that held two burning candles. On the ground nearby were two machetes, placed with their blades crossed. At other meetings, called *mayombe* or *bila*, Jean charged an entrance fee and conducted rituals that he promised would protect participants from punishments. He gave out raspberry, avocado, or orange leaves and fed rum mixed with pepper, garlic, and white chalk dust to kneeling people. When the drink made them fall over, Jean struck them with a machete to make them get up. He carried a little bag containing a crucifix, garlic, gunpowder, pebbles, nails, and a small box.[21]

Jean also visited a man named Jérôme who was enslaved on the Béliers estate.[22] The two led ritual meetings together. On the Lalanne plantation, they led mayombe gatherings, and Jean sprinkled people with rum and poured gunpowder in their hands, then lit it. Jean carried small limestone rocks in a sack called a *fonda* and placed them into rum that he blew into followers' eyes and also gave them to drink. He carried pepper and white chalk dust for people to drink if they had a fever. And he carried cannon powder that he dissolved into rum, which made people fierce or wild (*furieux*) when they drank it. Jérôme also carried small black and red seeds that he called *poto*, which were used for divining. He claimed he could use them to reveal chicken thieves and to detect *makandals*, meaning poisoners.[23]

A neighboring planter named Desplas told officials that he frequently saw large slave meetings on the Béliers plantation. One meeting was so tumultuous, Desplas said, that he went to see what was happening. The participants fled when he approached, and he found coins on the ground. Desplas sought out the estate's driver, Télémaque, and criticized him for holding these meetings. Télémaque turned to Desplas's valet and told him, "You think you are still in Gonaïves, but you will soon know the power of the slaves here." The next day, Desplas said, his valet had violent stomach pains and died.[24]

A former bookkeeper of Pierre Cappé claimed that Jérôme and Télémaque held meetings at night in slave cabins, banana groves, and other out-of-the-way places.[25] The employee believed enslaved people attended to buy and sell special fighting sticks. These were wooden staffs equipped with small pouches called *mazombo* that were filled with a mixture of white powder and pepper. Makers would drill a hole in the staff, fill it with the powder, and seal the powder in by driving a nail into the hole. This would make the weapon more effective against an opponent. Sticks were used as weapons in many African cultures, but in the French Caribbean stick fighting was associated with West Central Africans.

Fighting sticks could be inhabited by spirits who were fed and otherwise tended by the fighter who possessed the weapon. The stick was also likely a sign of membership in a community.[26]

Trouble arose when Jean the diviner traveled to a rapidly expanding coffee plantation owned by a man who boasted that he would build Saint-Domingue's largest coffee operation. Located close to the high plateau where Santo Domingo ranchers grazed their cattle, this estate had suffered the deaths of a hundred workers in 1784–1785, close to a third of all the people enslaved there.[27] Jean likely came to the estate because its people were looking for protection from the terrible dangers that surrounded them, which included an epidemic of mortality compounded by the risk of a brutal poison inquisition.

By 1786, some colonists had entirely dispensed with the need to allege poison and began to punish slaves merely for associating with one another in ritual communities. This is what happened to Jean, Jérôme, and Télémaque. Jean's work on the high plateau near Santo Domingo was interrupted by Judge Estève's brother, Henry, who had pursued him. There, Jean was arrested for meetings held on the Estève estate and on the plantation of Jean-Baptiste-Bernard de Saint Martin, a judge on the Superior Council. Jean claimed that his master had given him permission to live freely, but Henry Estève said the permission paper Jean carried was for "Simon Lafleur" signed by "Brûle," who was not Jean's enslaver. Imprisoned at Cap Français, Jean refused to say anything to the council interrogators.

Jean's prosecutor argued that he should be hanged for holding disorderly slave meetings at night and for selling ritual objects to slaves. The council also charged Jérôme and Télémaque with disturbing the public and holding disorderly slave meetings at night. Neither had been arrested, but the prosecutor said they should be sentenced, in absentia, to life on the chain gang. Julien, who was convicted of holding meetings on the Trémais plantation, was sentenced to watch Jean's execution.

Significantly, none of these men was charged with poisoning or harming anyone. In recommending punishment, the prosecutor told the council judges that Jean and the other organizers were not much different from charlatans in other parts of the world who assembled naive people and fleeced them of money. But in Saint-Domingue, these meetings were feared.[28] Between the time of Makandal and the time of Jean, Jérôme, and Télémaque, the Congo population in Saint-Domingue had expanded by tens of thousands of people, particularly in the coffee areas of the North Province. As many as two hundred people—which represented about 4 percent of the parish's enslaved population—gathered at some of the Marmelade meetings.[29] Attendees may have been seeking spiritual leadership, material protection, commerce, or bonds of kinship and support, each of these a raw material from which resistance could be fashioned.

One Congo diviner's practice was so significant that Nicolas Louis François de Neufchâteau, the attorney general of the Cap Superior Council, described her as Makandal's second act.[30] He likely meant to imply that she was the leader of a conspiracy against the colony, as Makandal had been portrayed. Her name was Kingué, and her work as a diviner carried her from plantation to plantation, moving up the Port Margot valley and into Plaisance, a coffee parish west of Marmelade where the headwaters of the Limbé River form. In the early days of the Haitian Revolution, along the same path, enslaved communities would rise in resistance to burn hundreds of estates.

Kingué left Port Margot for the coffee-growing mountains of Plaisance in the mid-1780s. She was a Congo woman in her late thirties and had been enslaved for some time under the name Marie Catherine to an unnamed "girl" who lived with a white man named Belhumeur. This arrangement suggests that Kingué was enslaved by a free woman of color.[31]

In 1784 and 1785, Kingué performed divination, healed people, made spiritually powerful objects, and created a community around her practices. She channeled spirits, speaking sometimes in the voice of a weak woman and sometimes in a man's voice.[32] She also made and sold *gardes de corps*, objects with protective spiritual powers, that were worn by people throughout Plaisance. West Central Africans there could view epidemics, droughts, and other far-reaching troubles as symptoms of collective problems, including "social tension, arguments, and rampant selfishness."[33] A village in West Central Africa might consult a spirit medium, who, if possessed by a spirit, could diagnose the problem. Congo diviners in Saint-Domingue might blame illness and death on witches. Congo speakers on one coffee plantation translated the French phrase "you are a poisoner" as *guéïé n'doki*; the word *n'doki* means witch or witchcraft.[34]

By 1785, Kingué was living like a free woman and paying a monthly fee to Belhumeur. She had a rapidly growing following, attracted by her ability to identify poisoners, whom colonists labeled makandals. She likely did this first for Africans, perhaps other people enslaved by Belhumeur or his companion. One colonist complained that when she revealed poisoners to Belhumeur, he "kill[ed] these unfortunates, with no other form of trial than the verdict of this négresse."[35] The diversity of people who wanted Kingué's services increased, suggesting that many people were seeking to remedy an ill, whether that meant divining a poisoner or healing a sickness. She had followers on plantations all over the parish; her enemies said that she knew everything that was happening among the enslaved population.[36] Kingué also had a following among free people of color. At least three free colored households in Plaisance asked her to perform divination. They were Jean and Bernard Lérice, Pironneau, and L'Herissé. They did not kill the people Kingué identified as poisoners.[37]

As a ritual leader engaged with communities across the parish, Kingué may have resembled Makandal to the attorney general, but she differed in that she was able to gain the favor of colonists. Some coffee planters who were haunted by the specter of poison invited her to search their estates for a poisoner. One of these was Antoine Chailleau, commander of the parish militia. Chailleau had come to Saint-Domingue at the height of the Makandal affair, and when he felt unwell in 1785, he was convinced that his slaves were poisoning him. Belhumeur brought Kingué to Chailleau's Plaisance estate, which stood at the top of a mountain on the only road from Cap Français to the island's west coast.[38]

After examining the commander, Kingué told him that he had been given poisons but was in no danger of dying; someone had given him a substance to make him more agreeable.[39] What happened next, according to the attorney general, was known by everyone in Plaisance: Kingué pulled a toad out of Chailleau's head and another out of his side. She told him she had removed the poisons, and he said he felt better. He arranged for her to stay on his plantation and identify which of his slaves were poisoners. She named seven or eight people, and Chailleau burned one at the stake, had three or four whipped to death, and sold three to a slave merchant for shipment overseas. He sent Kingué away but took her back when she convinced him that there were still enslaved poisoners on his plantation who had targeted his life.[40]

Chailleau was well known in Plaisance for lending his draft animals, carriages, and enslaved workers to colonists traveling from Cap Français.[41] As Kingué's reputation grew, Chailleau provided her with transportation and slaves to help her reach plantations throughout the parish. She found poisoners for Vazou, a planter at Ravine à Bodin, and for Saulmier, a planter located in La Trouble, the canton in Plaisance where Chailleau was based. In Pilatte, a neighboring canton, Kingué identified a poisoner on the Marsan estate, and that person was put to death in front of the slaves there.[42] Once, on Chailleau's plantation, François Dudemaine, the parish's leading surgeon, expressed skepticism about whether poisoners were really causing the deaths. Kingué was confident enough to threaten him before a group of white people.[43] She called on Dame Chailleau, a planter unrelated to the militia commander, and boldly accused her driver of poison.[44]

In her work, Kingué created community among enslaved people by conducting protective rituals and identifying a poisoner or witch they all feared, but she also harmed the enslaved people she named as poisoners. One badly injured man who escaped from Belhumeur presented himself before the local judge in Cap Français, presumably asking for protection from torture or execution. Echoing the Cassarouy and Dessources cases, this happened in 1785, when new legal provisions, hotly contested by colonists, arrived from France to enhance slaves' ability to report abusive masters.[45] There are no records describing the outcome of the unnamed man's act of resistance, but by then, Kingué was beginning to lose favor among some colonists.

Kingué's closest ally (perhaps her husband) was a man named Polidor, who had similar spiritual or healing skills. He was enslaved in Pilatte, on the Labauche plantation, where the estate manager initially supported Kingué but later decided to detain her. She resisted and fled. Showing loyalty to Kingué or perhaps fearing her powers, none of the hundred enslaved people on the Labauche estate would stop her. By that time, it was said that enslaved people throughout Plaisance regarded Kingué as a kind of god who had the power to kill, revive the dead, and cure all kinds of sicknesses. They saved and even stole money to give her and to buy her protective charms.[46]

On September 3, 1785, an anonymous informant complained to the attorney general about Kingué. Two weeks later, a notary called LeMay also wrote about her. Both informants were worried that their neighbors would spread bad rumors about them if they were known to have denounced Kingué.[47] The letter writers nonetheless demonized Kingué and her supporters, calling her a charlatan and "a monster" because of the deaths she caused.

Her Black and white followers were "gullible imbeciles." The attorney general lamented that "at her urging, many innocent slaves have been sacrificed inhumanely and burned alive."[48] LeMay speculated that Kingué's goal was to earn money from other slaves, who bribed her to accuse their enemies of poisoning.

In late September, the attorney general ordered the arrest of Kingué and Polidor. He wrote that the parish was on the verge of a slave uprising because planters' "revolting injustices" at her urging left slaves with no alternative but rebellion.[49] His informants may have been offended by Kingué's leverage over Chailleau and other white people. We do not know what happened to Kingué and Polidor after their arrest.

Roughly two miles from where Kingué worked for Chailleau, the Lejeune estate was a large and established coffee plantation where a hundred or more enslaved Africans lived under the control of their enslaver, Nicolas Lejeune, his family members, and an overseer.[50] By 1781, waves of human and livestock deaths had devastated this estate, and other plantations in Plaisance. The Lejeunes were in a position to know about the growing consensus of experts around the anthrax diagnosis, but they nonetheless unleashed a brutal tide of repression, investigation, and torture. The Lejeunes justified their actions by claiming that poisoners had killed more than four hundred enslaved workers over a decade.

Enslaved people across the North Province were in a double bind, threatened by epidemic anthrax and subjected to deadly poisoning interrogations. Many fled the Lejeune estate between successive and unrelenting episodes of epidemic and abuse. In 1781, when an enslaved man called Jean-Baptiste escaped, Lejeune described him as a makandal.[51] In November 1782, an enslaved man named Pierre escaped, as did Jean-Pierre, Zinga, and Vinba, also enslaved by the Lejeunes.[52] All were later imprisoned. The planters and their overseers claimed to have been sickened many times by poison, but no white people ever died of it on the estate. Enslaved people were the ones dying, including many on a neighboring plantation, where the owner blamed Lejeune's captives.[53]

In 1782 or 1783, Lejeune hired his nephew as overseer, and conditions grew so bad that three people—the "leaders of the slaves," according to Lejeune—traveled thirty miles to Cap Français and informed authorities about abuses on the estate. The judge refused to investigate their charges and returned them to the plantation as escaped slaves. In 1783, other Lejeune resisters left seeking freedom, not legal relief. Many were captured and returned to bondage. Men named Jean-Pierre, Toussaint, and Jacques escaped to Spanish territory before they were returned to their captor.[54] Jacob, a Mondongue man with an iron collar around his neck, left in the same direction and made it as far as Marmelade parish.[55] Rosette, a twenty-eight-year-old woman born on the island, went to Cap Français, where she might have passed as a free Black woman but was instead imprisoned.[56]

Oppression escalated to repression when Lejeune's nephew brought in armed men to patrol while slaves worked.[57] His authority ended when he was killed in a remote coffee field. We do not know what he was doing to the enslaved people in that field when he was killed; it could have been a heated murder, or enslaved people could have resolved to eliminate an intolerable manager, as had been done peacefully on the Bréda estate. In October 1783, the Cap Français Council convicted two enslaved men of his murder. To crush any further resistance, an executioner broke them on the rack in Plaisance and placed their heads on pikes in the town.[58]

In the following six months, fifty-two Lejeune slaves, most of them newly arrived, died of the epidemic, and a great drought occurred. A son of Lejeune, also named Nicolas, assumed management of the plantation, and deaths continued. Though Lejeune claimed to have made great expenditures on food for enslaved people, in less than two years, the estate lost forty-seven more slaves and thirty mules. The son, like his father, blamed enslaved people, complaining that "like ferocious beasts they breathed only blood and the most implacable hatred of the whites."[59]

A twenty-eight-year-old biracial man named Jeannot made his attempt for freedom in 1784 but was retaken before he could leave Plaisance.[60] A Congo man named Macaya escaped the Lejeune estate in 1786 and reached a wooded area, but he was so sick and swollen that he was captured and taken to the prison in Cap Français.[61] A man "so newly arrived that he couldn't say his name or that of his master" accomplished the thirty-mile journey to Cap before he was captured there in 1787.[62]

In 1787, Lejeune killed two enslaved people on his estate: Goma, a man from the Congo, and Zabeth, an Arada woman, born in West Africa.[63] Pierre Darius, an enslaved African cook, explained that Lejeune had purchased six young women in Cap Français and brought them to the plantation.[64] Zabeth, who occupied a solo room on the plantation, was ordered to introduce them to slavery. Lejeune and an overseer named Tranquille accused Zabeth of poisoning the women by giving them dirt to eat. They tortured Zabeth with burning pine branches until "in the grip of suffering and after the different torture sessions done to her," she confessed that Goma had helped her. She said that he fed the slaves callaloo, a stew, implying that it was poisoned. Lejeune and Tranquille tortured Goma. Zabeth died of her burns a few days later, and Goma died the following day.

In the first three months of 1788, twelve more slaves died on the plantation.[65] Lejeune hired a man named Jean Magre to treat eight sick slaves, but he was "profoundly ignorant of the surgical arts."[66] In the same period, Lejeune and his new overseer suffered terrible stomach pains and were convinced they had been poisoned.

Shortly after, an enslaved woman named Julie died.[67] Julie had given birth near the beginning of the year and was still weak from loss of blood. When she experienced terrible stomach pains, Lejeune rushed to her side and held her in her final moments. Unaware of her postpartum bleeding, Lejeune suspected poison and ordered Magre, who had just come from a rum shop in the town, to do an autopsy.[68] Magre found leaves of a plant called *quebec* in Julie's stomach. The surgeon claimed quebec was poison, though contemporary doctors and veterinarians disputed that.[69] A day later, Lejeune buried three slaves and then three more, two days after that.[70]

Next, Lejeune took aim at the two oldest women on the estate, Marie Rose, from the Mesurade nation, and Zabeth, from the Congo. Lejeune and Magre burned their feet and legs with pine branches and forced Darius the cook and Nicolas the driver to watch. Lejeune claimed that the women confessed,[71] but Darius told the judge their admissions only came when they were "in the grip of their suffering."[72] An enslaved African named Paul described hearing an enraged Lejeune threaten to "burn all the slaves on his plantation who spoke French" because "he only wanted to have new slaves."[73] This undoubtedly expressed Lejeune's desire to destroy leaders among enslaved people and exploit vulnerable newly arrived slaves who might be isolated by their language differences.

The next day, Nicolas the driver led twenty enslaved people away from the plantation toward Cap Français to denounce Lejeune to the judge. They were the core of the estate's workforce, according to Lejeune. One of the resisters, Charlot, testified, "I would rather die in prison than return to the Lejeune plantation."[74] Fourteen made it to Cap: Nicolas the driver, and men named Charlot, Jean, Bruno, Jasmin, Charles, Michel, Paul, Alexis, and Louis, with women named Barbe, Marie Noëlle, Catherine, and Geneviève. None of them was born into slavery on the island. All were African.

This was the second Lejeune crew to brave the long walk to Cap Français seeking protection. They traveled at night, hiding in the woods during the day to avoid the constabulary. They had to choose one of three routes to Cap Français. If they descended the Port Margot River valley, they would pass through communities that had worked with Kingué only a few years earlier. If they descended the Limbé River valley, they would meet enslaved people who in three years would lead the great slave uprising that launched the Haitian Revolution. Their third option was the most direct: to cross Makandal's and Assam's Soufrière River valley and skirt the Acul foothills, where an equal number of future revolutionaries lived. On their way, they must have depended on communities like these for food, shelter, and directions. It was a trip three petitioners from the Lejeune plantation made five years earlier to no avail. That the new group was willing to try shows their bravery, their desperation, and their optimism about the power of French law to protect them.

The group sought protection under a controversial 1785 law from France that was designed to prevent colonists' cruelties from provoking revolt. The law was controversial because it gave the governor and the intendant authority over all questions of plantation order, including "complaints by slaves unjustly treated." The law also gave local militia commanders the right to inspect plantation conditions and established punishments for plantation managers or owners who violated existing Code Noir regulations, including prosecution for murder when they killed a slave.[75]

These provisions enraged many colonists. In 1785 and 1786, servants attending their enslavers in colonial dining rooms and on front porches throughout the North Province would have heard heated discussion of the laws and how to defeat them. Nicolas, the Lejeune driver, and the men and women who followed him to Cap Français in 1788 understood that colonists had strong disagreements with the far-off French monarchy about how to best sustain the slave system. Although earlier groups of resisters had failed to obtain relief under provisions of the Code Noir, enslaved people in Nicolas's time would have witnessed the Crown's renewed intent to curtail planters' ability to abuse slaves. They acted on this avenue of resistance.

What Nicolas and the others could not predict was the outcome of the contest between French officials and colonial powers over the law's enforcement. A plantation manager named Morange wrote, "If the ordinance is upheld, it would be better to be a good slave than to be a manager, a plantation attorney, or even a proprietor, I would say.... The more I see, the more I understand that they want to free the slaves and put whites under the yoke."[76] Acceding to opinions like this, the Cap Français Superior Council in 1785 illegally refused to accept the law.[77]

In 1786, Versailles sent a second law that made minor concessions to planters but reiterated that militia commanders were "to ensure that slaves are not abused by owners, managers, or overseers."[78] It specified that slaves "unjustly mistreated, undernourished or otherwise treated badly" could not be regarded as insubordinate, unless their complaints were proven false. The Cap Council ultimately promulgated both laws in May 1786.[79]

Nicolas the driver and his group convinced the Cap Français court to send an investigator and constables to the Lejeune plantation. They found the two suffering women and took their testimony, as well as statements from Nicolas Lejeune, Jean Magre, the overseer Jean Chaussepied, and Pierre Darius, the enslaved cook. They called a trained surgeon, Dudemaine, to care for the two wounded women and to describe their condition. Dudemaine removed the two women from Lejeune's dungeon to his own property. Marie Rose died a day later, and Zabeth died a few days after that.[80]

According to the terms of the 1785 law, the younger Lejeune and Magre were now liable for murder. The Cap Français court ordered their arrest, but the two men ran away. None of the Lejeune neighbors, the former overseer, or other white witnesses would implicate Lejeune in the killings. The former overseer, for example, claimed that both victims had died of poison. Without appearing, the Lejeunes wrote memoranda arguing that planters had to conduct their own investigations and that some violence would always be necessary. They and their neighbors claimed that poisoners were about to launch a revolution in Saint-Domingue. Two dozen Plaisance colonists wrote a memorandum to the governor-general and the intendant claiming that Lejeune's slaves had stirred up trouble in the region and had tried to revolt ten times.[81]

Although the corps of resisters had succeeded in generating an investigation, when the facts were returned, the court in Cap Français buckled under public pressure and ruled that the court's investigator had violated procedure. Colonial officials appealed to the Superior Council to prosecute the case, but the Council absolved Lejeune of the charges.[82] Nicolas the driver and the thirteen people who had followed him were returned to Lejeune's control.

That people enslaved on the Lejeune coffee estate and elsewhere appealed to French courts for protection defeats the idea that Saint-Domingue's enslaved people passively accepted slavery. The Lejeune petitioners exercised their awareness of the divide between French legal ideals and planters' practices, much like Lizette did in her litigation against her son's enslaver. Where Lizette likely recruited de Paroy's wealthy rivals for financial support in her extended litigation, the Lejeune crew throughout their travel relied on communities of enslaved people who had organized under the dual threat of anthrax and poison persecution.

Opportunities to leverage the gap between local enslavers and powers in France were not limited to legal reforms. People enslaved on absentee estates understood that the estate agents they saw every day answered to owners in France. Striking slaves at the Bréda estate in 1773 unseated a reviled estate agent by shuttering operations and outflanking him with an appeal to Noé, their enslaver's nephew. Resistance strategies varied between communities and according to people's means. Some communities made, distributed, and administered African-inspired medicines in a plan to exercise influence over their enslavers, to sweeten an angry disposition, or to befuddle or confuse. At least a handful of people discerned how to use anthrax-tainted plants to make poisons to kill quickly. As would be shown in 1791, after years of building diverse communities of resistance, enslaved people could mobilize swiftly and violently.

7

The Haitian Revolution Begins

WHEN ENSLAVED COMMUNITIES in Saint-Domingue rose to the call of revolt, they did so prepared by over thirty years of practice. In case after case of resistance, enslaved people and their communities were forced to determine their needs and abilities and resolve to make change against terrible odds. Over time, diverse cultures of resistance emerged, but in the early hours of the revolt that launched the Haitian Revolution, many well-practiced resistance communities found common cause and mobilized to stunning effect. On the Noé sugar plantation, enslaved drivers named Jean-Jacques and Hippolyte had, over years, led enslaved workers through epidemic disease, escalating industrial sugar production, wartime deprivations, and unfulfilled promises of manumission. When they mounted an effective labor strike, the absentee owner's agent schemed to marginalize the community's two leaders. The agent's campaign looked likely to succeed, but on August 22, 1791, the night workers at the Noé sugar refinery struck the first successful blows of the Haitian Revolution.

With over 350 workers in 1791, the Noé plantation was at the intersection of the Acul sugar plain and the Soufrière foothills. Soufrière, where enslaved people had been battling anthrax and poison accusations for decades, connected half a dozen parishes, including Acul with its sugar plain, the river valleys of Limbé and Port Margot, and the coffee mountains of Plaisance and Marmelade. People enslaved in this region had built connections that allowed them to plan and launch a massive uprising. The first days of the revolt revealed a network of communities that linked Plaisance, Acul, Limbé, and Port Margot. It spanned the route that Lejeune slaves probably took in 1783 and again in 1788 when they traveled secretly to the court in Cap Français. This resistance network was largely invisible to colonists, but in 1791, revolutionary fires revealed its contours.

A driver named Jean-Jacques directed work in the Noé sugar refinery throughout the 1780s.[1] Jean-Jacques is known to history because an estate agent described his actions in multiple letters to Count Louis-Pantaléon de Noé, the absentee landlord. We don't know when Jean-Jacques arrived on the Noé estate or even whether he was born in Africa or the Caribbean. It does seem likely that he was present in 1775 when anthrax struck the Noé estate, killing at least forty mules. An estate agent described the speed of these Noé deaths to the Count de Bréda: "It's truly frightening; you have to see it to believe it."[2]

Anthrax had been diagnosed in western Acul in 1773; for three years, it had killed people and livestock on estates all along the foothills that separated Acul and Limbé, starting with the Dupaty, Sacanville, and Laplaigne plantations.[3] It spread all the way to Bréda's plantation in Haut-du-Cap, where Delribal's brutal poison investigation had prompted workers to mount a strike. Western Acul's history of livestock disease and poison accusations suggests that enslaved people all along the border between Acul and Limbé responded like their counterparts in Soufrière, Marmelade, Plaisance, and Port Margot: by creating ritual communities or strengthening existing ones.

Such communities would have surely existed on the estate where Jean-Jacques lived, which was about three miles from the

MAP 7.1 Enslaved Labor Strikes on Sugar Estates, 1770s and 1780s

livestock pen where Makandal had escaped slavery and about six miles from the Dufresne coffee estate where he was arrested. Jérôme and Télémaque gathered hundreds of followers about ten miles from the Noé estate. Their colleague Jean was enslaved much closer, about five miles away from Noé. Kingué built her communities about fifteen miles from where Jean-Jacques lived.

For his enslavers, Jean-Jacques was the most important of the more than three hundred people bound to labor on the Noé estate. He was a key driver, directing work at the cane-crushing mill, in the adjacent boiling house, and in the drying house. One estate agent described him to Louis-Pantaléon de Noé as "your master sugar maker."[4] In this position, Jean-Jacques also collaborated with the estate's ox drivers, whose heavy carts carried harvested cane to the mill and barrels of sugar to a wharf on a nearby river.

Like drivers on other estates, Jean-Jacques worked closely with the colonists who owned or managed the plantation. In the late 1770s, he would have spoken daily about the pace of sugar making with one of the estate's co-owners, the Chevalier d'Héricourt. Noé, the other co-owner, returned to France in 1775, and d'Héricourt stayed on to manage the property in 1778. He relied heavily on Jean-Jacques and on Hippolyte, the estate's main field driver, giving them money and more authority than he gave his white employees. When d'Héricourt died in 1779, he left a testamentary request that Noé free Jean-Jacques, Hippolyte, Hippolyte's wife, Fanchette, and their children.[5]

Two years later, the estate agent Bayon de Libertat told Jean-Jacques and Hippolyte that Noé was considering manumitting them. The news came in a letter from Noé that Bayon read to the two men. Jean-Jacques knew at least one man who had won his freedom from an absentee master. This was Toussaint Louverture, enslaved on the Bréda Haut-du-Cap plantation, who became a free man sometime before 1776 and would become the leading figure of the Haitian Revolution. Historians don't know how Louverture obtained his freedom, but Jean-Jacques probably did. Some scholars believe that Noé had a role in Toussaint's liberty.[6] If this was true, Noé's letter would have persuaded Jean-Jacques that his own freedom was almost guaranteed. Bayon told Noé that announcing the prospect of their manumission "made a good impression on the whole workforce." He described Jean-Jacques and Hippolyte as "very grateful for your good intentions towards them and [they] have expressed their gratitude to me. They have promised me that they will always be attached to you."[7]

Their good news came at a difficult time for the enslaved workers, because in 1781, the American Revolutionary War was still disrupting trade. Bayon informed Noé's slaves that he could not provide their annual supply of clothing because of the British blockade. In addition, drought had dried up the river that powered Noé's sugar mill. To save the harvested cane, Bayon revived an older animal-powered mill, buying fifty-three mules for nearly forty thousand livres, which was enough to buy at least twenty African captives. He claimed that Jean-Jacques and Hippolyte were pleased to see the mules arrive.[8] Perhaps the two drivers hoped that Noé would sign their emancipation papers if his sugar refinery became more profitable.

In 1782, conditions had not improved. The war continued, so at the beginning of the year, there was no annual allotment of cloth or imported food, like salted cod. In April of that year, news from Guadeloupe crushed the morale of enslaved and free people alike. A British naval squadron had defeated a much larger French fleet in the so-called Battle of the Saintes. The loss destroyed Saint-Domingue's hopes for peace. It also left forty thousand Spanish and French soldiers stranded in Cap Français, men who had been gradually massing for an attack on

British Jamaica. That plan was now canceled, but it took months to evacuate the invasion force. Food prices were sky-high, and feeding the soldiers exhausted even Santo Domingo's massive cattle herds. In May, Bayon complained, "You cannot imagine the high cost of living here. If we don't receive a convoy soon, we will die of hunger."[9] What Bayon meant was that colonists couldn't buy imported flour to make wheat bread, a staple of the French diet.

Incredibly, as he worried about "dying of hunger," Bayon claimed that enslaved people were practically tripping over crops on the plantation. "Every day for the past four months we have harvested 150 bunches of plantains and still more is rotting in the fields."[10] He fumed about the fact that Jean-Jacques and Hippolyte, presumably with the help of their work crews, were selling some of these provisions to merchants at the estate's river wharf.[11] He forbade them from doing this, likely because he did not want their advantages on the estate to be so obvious.

In curtailing the commerce of his drivers and their crews, Bayon struck the wrong balance between tolerance and oppression. In 1782, the Noé slaves were seething about how much sugar he was ordering them to plant, harvest, and manufacture. The two drivers told their crews that Bayon was pushing too hard. Jean-Jacques was furious when Bayon's on-site manager, a white man named Pascault, rebuked him for being too lax in the sugar refinery.[12] Tensions were plain enough that Bayon later said the workers were plotting to make him fire Pascault.[13]

As drivers, Jean-Jacques and Hippolyte had forged communities that allowed them to fight Bayon's ambitious production schedule. A decade earlier, workers on Bréda's Haut-du-Cap estate had resisted a brutal poison investigation by walking off the estate in protest. Now, in May 1782, workers at Noé launched a strike that shut down the plantation for over a week. Hippolyte led his field crews off the estate. On a plantation with roughly 350 slaves, this meant that about 140 people left the estate, likely in small groups. Some might have headed to other plantations in the Acul sugar plain, where they had friends or family. Most of them probably walked south into the mountainous Soufrière region where Makandal and Assam had lived three decades earlier. There were many places where Noé's striking workers—technically runaways—could hide for the night. After twenty-four hours, the field crew did return.[14]

Jean-Jacques engineered a longer and more aggressive strike among the skilled workers, whom Bayon could not easily replace. These men may have had tight bonds. Sugar manufacturing required close coordination, especially in the refinery, where workers had to move the boiling syrup through a series of cauldrons from early morning until late in the night. Night work during harvest was especially onerous because workers had to report to the boiling house after long, exhausting days in the fields.

For nine days, Jean-Jacques shut down the sugar factory, taking sixty-four sugar refiners, barrel makers, cart drivers, and others off the estate.[15] The artisans probably split into small groups, taking refuge with friends and family. In a week's time, some might have crossed the mountains west into Limbé or south into Soufrière. Bayon was about to hire slave hunters when Jean-Jacques and his workers returned.[16] In a later letter, Bayon told Noé that Jean-Jacques had led all the enslaved men off the plantation, suggesting it was Jean-Jacques who controlled both strikes.[17]

Over the next few years, enslaved workers struck in at least eight more sugar plantations between Acul and Petite Anse. Nearly all the work stoppages occurred on plantations owned by absentee colonists and run by managers who enslaved workers regarded as too harsh. In most of these cases, the strikers appealed to authorities above the manager to fire him or asked for pardons. Managers and owners cited these episodes as examples of how the plantation management laws of 1785 and 1786 could destroy plantation discipline, but the strike that Jean-Jacques mounted at Noé came two years before the controversial law. It seems more likely that the strikers faced intolerable conditions, for they understood that managers would inflict severe punishments on them, including branding and flogging to near death in some cases. In June 1789, the Galliffet agent, Nicolas Odelucq, described the work stoppages as insurrections and said, "One could fill a book with examples of these sorts of disturbances."[18]

In one instance, workers on the Cabeuil sugar estate refused to go to the cane fields because of overwork and a lack of meat and decent food. The manager found some of the strikers digging up sweet potatoes. They threatened to report his abuses to the estate agents in Cap Français. One of the agents came out from the city and, after several days of working with the rural police, was able to round up most of the strikers. After savagely flogging them, he informed his colleague back in Cap, "I haven't killed anyone but I aimed close."[19]

When slaves on the Lombard plantation walked off, they told white employees that they had the right to choose their manager. On the Mentor plantation, laborers refused to work at night in the sugar mill. The Chastenoy slaves walked off their estate to complain to the Vicomte de Choiseul. Forty skilled slaves on the Walsh estate walked away for two months because the agent had demoted the head cooper, sending him into the cane fields. When twenty-three workers walked off the La Gossette estate in the Galliffet sugar complex, the manager punished the top driver, who then claimed that the second driver had organized the strike as a way of getting the manager fired. The second driver was given one hundred lashes. The strikers eventually returned and accepted harsh conditions, which included being branded and working on Sundays until they made up the days they were absent. The letter describing the end of the strike noted that the plantation was still experiencing drought and animal disease but that the "new Negroes are doing well." Most of those captives would be dead in the next few years, and mules continued to die.[20]

For the community of enslaved workers on the Noé estate, Jean-Jacques's strike succeeded, since in later years, Bayon seems to have understood there were limits to how far he could push his workers. When Jean-Jacques brought his factory crew back to the refinery, Bayon gave him 120 livres, enough to buy an ox in less inflated times.[21] However, the strike had a steep personal cost for the two leaders. Bayon's letters to Noé described the drivers as a liability to the estate. "I can assure you that your plantation will run much better when you have gotten rid of Jean-Jacques and Hippolyte; they are doing much more damage to your interests than you think. Give them freedom like the Chevalier [d'Héricourt] promised them; you will be better off; these people will always stir up trouble and dissension."[22] Bayon may have hoped that manumitting Jean-Jacques and Hippolyte would isolate them from their community and curb their influence.

Within three months of the strike, Bayon removed Hippolyte from his driver's position, allowing him to remain at his cabin and not work. "This slave is of no use to you; on the contrary. He produces only discontent," he wrote.[23] This was punishment for Hippolyte because he was still consigned to the estate. He lost his official status on the plantation but was not a free man. Without manumission papers, as far as the outside world was concerned, he was still enslaved to Noé.

It took Bayon much longer to marginalize Jean-Jacques—eighteen months—because his skills made him hard to replace. In October 1783, Bayon forced him into the same internal exile as Hippolyte, stripped of his authority but without formal freedom papers. Jean-Jacques could not travel as a free man or hire himself out to another plantation as a sugar refiner. He could not lease or buy property or free an enslaved woman by marrying her. The American Revolutionary War was over, and the plantation was shipping record amounts of sugar without him, which meant that Noé was unlikely to ever manumit him. Bayon wrote, "Jean-Jacques is very bad. He wants to be free. I let him act as if he were, [since I] can do without him. What angers me is that he stirs up the other slaves with his bad advice. . . . Hippolyte is less dangerous than him, he is very quiet in his house with his wife."[24]

Because Jean-Jacques was with Boukman at the outbreak of the 1791 uprising, it seems likely that around 1783, deeply frustrated at still being enslaved, Jean-Jacques became more involved with Boukman's resistance work. Boukman was a coachman on the adjacent Dutilh plantation (likely pronounced *Dutty* by the people enslaved there).[25] Historians credit Boukman Dutty with leading one and perhaps two meetings in August 1791 that united Congo, West African, and Creole slaves into the force that launched the Haitian Revolution.[26] A colonist's account of the first night of that uprising, examined later in this chapter, illustrates that Boukman and Jean-Jacques knew and trusted each other. They lived less than a mile apart, and both were members of the mostly male cadre of skilled workers who had special privileges and greater freedom of movement than most field slaves. Each of them had spent weeks exploring the Limbé hills. When Boukman was enslaved in Limbé, he often left the plantation, returning to steal food. His enslaver's relative remembered him as a "bad slave." In one episode, Boukman was shot and soon after was sold to Jean Dutilh in Acul.[27]

Stripped of his leadership role but not manumitted, Jean-Jacques probably continued to challenge Bayon. The Noé refinery crew was working harder than ever because Bayon kept ramping up sugar production without buying new captives. In 1786, the sugar workers and cart drivers stood up to Bayon, showing the same kind of resistance leadership Jean-Jacques had once displayed.[28] As was the case during the strike Jean-Jacques led, Bayon was pushing workers to meet his production goals. In April, he ordered workers to crush canes using both the water mill and the mule mill. Each mill was attached to its own refinery, so the workers had to run two refineries as well.[29] Environmental problems resolved the standoff when a drought shut down the water mill, but this made mules even more essential to the plantation.[30]

The following year, 1787, Noé's mules began dying. No one on the plantation blamed slave poisoners. Doctors had diagnosed an epizootic that was killing hundreds of animals on other estates.[31] To his employer, Bayon denied that contagion was killing mules at Noé. He insisted the cause was "ordinary disease and old age," but the count fired him soon after. In 1789, the estate experienced an unnamed human epidemic. The new estate agent said that the plantation hospital treated fifty enslaved people; he did not say if any died. Around the same time, drought returned with a vengeance.

Writing of that time, the Count de Bréda's agent explained, "A winter without rain is not bearable in Saint-Domingue, especially in Haut-du-Cap where illnesses have again begun to take their toll."[32] Although some rain fell in March 1790, drought returned in June, and with it, more illness. "The illnesses continue still, and many whites and slaves are dying."[33] From 1779 to 1791, Bayon and his successor had increased sugar acreage by two-thirds, while there is no evidence that they bought new workers.[34] Enslaved people in Acul, Soufrière, and Limbé had been through this cycle many times before. They needed to continuously reinvigorate their communities to fight drought, disease, and the abuse from enslavers that arose in these conditions. Within a year, the Noé workers would destroy the plantation that held them in slavery.

Against this backdrop of colonial suffering, momentous changes were taking place in France. King Louis XVI had convened representatives of the clergy, nobility, and commoners to resolve the government's long-standing tax problems. Selecting these delegates led to a passionate debate about why commoners were underrepresented in this important gathering, when they formed the vast majority of the French population. In the summer of 1789, several weeks into the meeting, an alliance of commoners, radical priests, and nobles split off, declaring themselves the French National Assembly. After crowds in Paris captured the royal fortress known as the Bastille, Louis XVI reluctantly accepted the legitimacy of the new group. In August, the Assembly adopted a Declaration of the Rights of Man and Citizen as the preamble for the kingdom's first written constitution. Revolution was underway in France, and two of Saint-Domingue's wealthiest free men of color, Julien Raimond and Vincent Ogé, were in Paris arguing that people like themselves should be allowed to vote in the colony.

Free Black men and men of color in the parish of Grande-Rivière, who outnumbered white men by 50 percent, were aware that the terms of French citizenship were being redefined. When white colonists excluded them from a meeting to elect a local representative, free colored militiamen from the parish objected. On October 30, 1789, about fifty of them assembled in the pasture outside the town. Their leader was Jean-Baptiste Chavanne, a free-born biracial man and militia sergeant, the highest rank a man of color could hold. He owned property in Grande-Rivière and was involved in the animal trade as well, probably bringing Spanish cattle down the river valley to the butcher's pasture in Petite Anse.[35]

In 1789, Chavanne appears to have understood that revolutionary changes in Paris were creating political opportunities for colonial men of color, especially in districts where they outnumbered white people. Thirty years earlier, in 1757, Médor revealed that free Black people in Cap Français hoped to build their numbers to confront white people, if needed. In Paris, in 1789, Raimond and Ogé engaged in a different form of confrontation: trying to convince the National Assembly to grant civil rights to colonial free people of color.

Within a year, Chavanne became a key figure in what colonists called the "Ogé revolt."[36] He was the first person Vincent

Ogé went to see when he returned from Paris, reporting that a new French law could be construed to allow propertied men of color to vote in the colony. Ogé was a wealthy biracial merchant based in Cap Français whose family owned a coffee plantation. Like many light-skinned free people of color, he held himself apart from free Black people, who were often former slaves. He later told interrogators that he didn't even know any free Black people.[37] Chavanne's network brought roughly three hundred armed men of color from Grande-Rivière and the surrounding parishes to support Ogé's demand that wealthy men of color be allowed to vote in upcoming elections. Many free Black people, who would not be qualified to vote even if Ogé succeeded, appeared unexpectedly. A delegation of free Black men from Cap Français came to Grande-Rivière to read Ogé a message welcoming him. Over half of the supporters who rallied around Ogé on the Chavanne farm were free Black men. They understood that his success would erode white supremacy and ultimately benefit them.

The colonial military scattered this armed gathering, and authorities arrested hundreds who were rumored to be involved.[38] Most of the 226 people they detained were members of free families of color who owned land and slaves. They were propertied residents who could not easily evade arrest. The court ordered brutal and humiliating executions of the men convicted of leading the rebellion. Ogé and Chavanne were broken on the rack in Cap Français, and their heads were displayed on pikes, a punishment given to rebel slaves. Colonial judges wanted free men of color to know that their demands for equality were equivalent to a slave insurrection. The government hanged twenty-one other men and branded fifteen people, sentencing them to life on the chain gang. The court eventually released 188 people it considered innocent.

The court condemned forty-four Ogé participants in absentia. Half of these were free Black men; the other half were either free biracial men or enslaved men, including Chavanne's brother Marc. Few of these forty-four men left records in the surviving parish registers of Grande-Rivière or the surrounding parishes.[39] This indicated that they were too poor or lived too remotely to take part in baptisms, marriages, and burials recorded by the local priest. They were able to evade arrest.

Of the group of forty-four, the court ordered effigies erected of two free Black residents of Grande-Rivière to receive the punishment meted out in Cap Français to Ogé and Chavanne. The figures, representing Amboise Déclain, known as Yamé, and his brother-in-law Quiquo Lapeyre, were to be broken on the rack in the town of Grande-Rivière and the executioner was to display their severed heads on the road leading to Cormier, a nearby valley that was home to free Black coffee planters.[40] This treatment suggests that they were not merely following Ogé but were principals in their own right. Three other Déclain family members and seven other men were sentenced in absentia to be hanged.[41]

Colonists' refusal to share political rights left free biracial men who wanted equality with few alternatives to violence, which meant mobilizing enslaved people into revolt. Men like Marc Chavanne, Yamé Déclain, and Quiquo Lapeyre likely alerted the leaders of existing resistance communities in Acul and Limbé to the fact that the time for action was imminent. In January 1791, colonists described how people "fleeing from the Ogé revolt are gathering in Limbé, Acul, and Plaisance where they are committing attacks. . . . A letter from the Assembly warns us to keep our guard up." In February, fourteen Ogé supporters who eluded arrest in Grande-Rivière were arrested in Limbé.[42] The Acul and Limbé gatherings were confirmed by Ogé's brother Jacques, by then a prisoner in Cap Français, who implicated Marc Chavanne, and the free Blacks Déclain and Lapeyre.[43] They likely gathered in the mountains of Acul and Limbé because Marc Chavanne and his sister Marie-Marthe had each married natives of Soufrière and settled there; Marie-Marthe's husband was an Ogé supporter.⁴⁴ They would have been well aware of the potential for alliances with resistance communities in the region.

In May 1791, France passed new voting regulations for the colony that explicitly enfranchised propertied free-born men of color. When colonial white people refused to accept the law, free men of color took up arms in the area surrounding Port-au-Prince. Free people of color in the North Province were too intimidated by the bloody aftermath of the Ogé affair to join this movement, but people everywhere noticed when rioters burned Port-au-Prince. Cap Français seemed a likely site for political unrest at summer's end, because a Colonial Assembly elected only by white people was scheduled to meet there on August 25.⁴⁵ For free people of color and resistance leaders in Acul and Limbé, the Assembly represented an unprecedented opportunity: a gathering of the entire white leadership of the colony only a few miles away.

On the night of Sunday, August 14, 1791, around two hundred drivers and other elite slaves gathered four miles from Cap Français to plan an uprising. Boukman, of the Dutilh estate, led the pivotal meeting, which took place on the large LeNormant de Mezy sugar plantation at Morne Rouge. Like so many of the estates where resistance communities formed, the Morne Rouge sugar estate had suffered anthrax, and it was easily accessible over major roads to people from the western mountains of Limbé and Port Margot and from the eastern sugar plain. Jean-Jacques likely attended the Morne Rouge meeting, possibly walking or riding with Boukman. Within two days of the Morne Rouge gathering, its message of coordinated insurrection was conveyed to resistance communities across the North Province.⁴⁶

The details of the Morne Rouge meeting come from an eighteen-year-old revolutionary named Jacques Cautant who

MAP 7.2 Prelude to Revolution

was detained for starting a fire on the Chabaud plantation on Tuesday, August 16.[47] Cautant was a driver on the Grieux coffee plantation, probably in Limbé's southern mountains.[48] He said that people there were planning to set fire to their estates and kill their masters, then come down the valley to join other rebels at the coast. When he lit the fire, he was halfway between Morne Rouge and his enslaver's plantation.

Cautant said that one of the Morne Rouge leaders was Paul, of the Belin (or Blin) plantation, likely one of several estates with this name in lower Limbé. Cautant also named several Black people planning a rebellion in upper Limbé. He named four leaders on the Héron de la Filière estate in Acul, which was less than two miles north of the Noé estate and directly adjacent to Boukman's Dutilh plantation.[49] His testimony shows that there was a resistance network that extended the length of the Limbé valley, from the coastal plain to the high mountains. It also included plantations on the Acul side of the foothills; the Héron and Dutilh estates were located on a major road through those hills. Cautant must have left the meeting expecting an imminent start to the fighting because he told interrogators that "he was astonished that the revolt had not started that night; he didn't understand what had caused the delay, but it was certainly pushed back only a few days."[50]

Cautant said that a biracial man spoke to the drivers assembled at Morne Rouge and read them a letter that was supposedly written by royal officials. The speaker, possibly one of Ogé veterans, claimed that Louis XVI had given slaves three free days a week to work in their gardens but that colonists were keeping this a secret.[51] It was not true, but using the king in a call to revolution showed that discrepancies between French ideals and colonial practice were important to enslaved people. Though their appeals to French judges had too often failed, the speaker hoped that reluctant rebels in Saint-Domingue could be provoked by this injustice.

THE HAITIAN REVOLUTION BEGINS

The Morne Rouge meeting was critical because the drivers who attended represented thousands of people from Limbé and Acul parishes. When communities from these two parishes joined forces to fight eight days later, they created a mass that could not be stopped. The Ogé veterans likely mobilized communities in Acul and Limbé that had been proving grounds for many types of resistance.

On August 20, 1791, a free Black man who was an Ogé veteran from Grande-Rivière instigated an uprising on Galliffet's La Gossette sugar estate in Petite Anse, where twenty enslaved workers had launched a strike in 1789. The estate was one of three adjoining plantations in a complex that held over eight hundred people in bondage. The man met with Ignace, who, like Jean-Jacques, had been freed from work without being freed from slavery. The Ogé veteran urged resistance leaders to kill the resident white manager, burn the estate, and start the uprising. The next night, Blaise, the driver, sent three men with knives to the manager's apartment in an attempt to kill him. Rebels set fires and rang an alarm bell to call slaves out to join the uprising, but the estate agent, Odelucq, foiled the assassination attempt and succeeded in locking everyone down.[52]

That same night, Sunday, August 21, less than a mile away, resistance leaders led a ceremony in a swampy woods known as Bois Caïman. This would prove to be a defining moment in the Haitian Revolution. The location of Bois Caïman, which means caiman woods, has long been in doubt, but evidence suggests that the ceremony took place on the Choiseul plantation, directly north of Galliffet.[53] Three enslaved people from the Galliffet plantation attended the ceremony and were later arrested. A witness to their interrogation described the meeting:

> They celebrated a kind of feast or sacrifice in the middle of an uncultivated wooded plot on the Choiseul plantation, called *le Caïman*, where a very large number of slaves

gathered. A black pig, surrounded by spirit objects, each loaded with offerings more bizarre than the next, was the offering made to the all powerful spirit of the black race. The religious ceremonies that the slaves practiced in slaughtering it, their greed to drink its blood, their eagerness to have some of its bristles as a kind of talisman that, according to them, would make them invulnerable, are all characteristics of the African.[54]

Scholars have explained that these men and women were adapting a West African ritual that created a bond of loyalty to a community's purpose. Many people believe that Boukman led the ceremony. The celebrants made an oath when they took the drink, and if they later broke the oath, they would die.[55] If Morne Rouge gathered the commanders of the coming uprising, Bois Caïman rallied its soldiers from resistance communities that had been growing since at least the time of Makandal.

The night after Bois Caïman, on Monday, August 22, a group of rebels from the Héron estate arrived at the Dutilh plantation in Acul at about ten o'clock in the evening.[56] Boukman received them, and he was one of two men the group elected to lead the revolt.[57] After an initial foray to a warehouse on the river, where they may have joined workers from the troubled Trémais coffee plantation in Marmelade, they made their way to the Noé sugar refinery.[58]

With a history of organized resistance and a leader who still lived on the estate, Noé's slaves were ready to fight. About a dozen rebels stabbed the apprentice refiner, who was likely supervising night work. They dragged him into the courtyard. When Dumenil, the estate agent, rushed out of the house to investigate the apprentice's cries, they shot him. Jean-Jacques was probably part of this group. The rebels then found the head sugar refiner in his rooms and killed him. They stabbed another white employee and

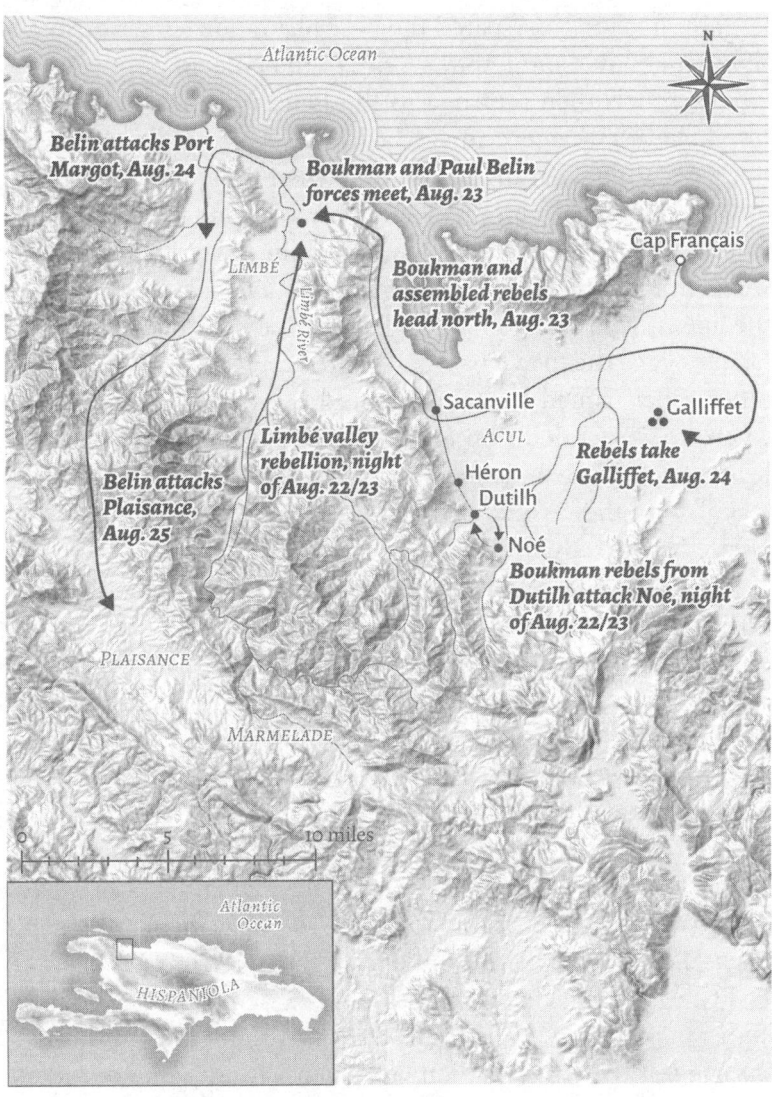

MAP 7.3 Early Days of the Revolution

left him for dead but spared the Noé plantation surgeon. Sometime around midnight, they set fire to the Noé estate.[59]

The rebels then returned to the Dutilh plantation and captured the estate agent in his bedroom. A group of men were hotly debating what to do with him when Boukman arrived and told them to hold him prisoner. He was taken to the courtyard where a crowd gathered, menacing him. They calmed down when Boukman arrived, carrying a vest and some trousers for the agent, who had complained about the cold night air. Jean-Jacques gave the man a battered white hat. Jean-Jacques and another rebel named Vincent removed the estate agent to Noé, where they guarded him and other prisoners for hours. Jean-Jacques and Vincent assured the agent that if other rebels tried to kill him, they would "talk to them and persuade them that justice had already been meted out on this plantation."[60]

Years after the event, the agent claimed that by the time the sun rose, Jean-Jacques and Vincent were drinking wine and answering his questions about who started the revolt and what their goals were. The rebel plan, he claimed, aimed for "nothing less than the destruction of all the white people except some who didn't own property, some priests, some surgeons, and some women, and of setting fire to all the plantations and making themselves masters of the country."[61] This was a scenario that colonists had invoked since at least Makandal's time. It may have been true, but it also served to justify colonists' harsh treatment of enslaved people before and during the uprising.

The agent also claimed that the rebels acted on the orders of high-ranking white people in France. Although some historians suggest that the rebellion was prompted by white outsiders, there is no conclusive evidence of that.[62] The speed with which the rebellion spread from the Noé and Dutilh estates suggests that resistance networks connected thousands of enslaved people in this region and that their leaders did the difficult work of mobilizing them in the early insurrection. On the Dutilh plantation, Boukman went from hut to hut, urging workers to carry the rebellion to other estates.⁶³

On the first full day of the revolt, Tuesday, August 23, Boukman's forces left Noé and headed north, picking up recruits from communities that may have been organized and resisting for years. Many of Boukman's fighters were from the Dutilh and Héron estates; they passed back through those and into neighboring sugar estates that had been hit hard by anthrax since the 1770s: Molines, Laplaigne, Sacanville, and Pillat.⁶⁴ When they reached the coast, perhaps fifteen hundred strong, the rebels streamed through the Saint-Michel plantation and crossed into Limbé. There, they learned that Paul, the Belin driver who spoke at the Morne Rouge meeting, was raising a revolt against the coastal sugar plantations. And as Jacques Cautant had predicted, enslaved coffee workers in Limbé rebelled and were descending the valley to join Belin's forces.⁶⁵

Once Boukman's warriors met Belin's rebels, the revolt reached a critical mass. They must have recognized that the oaths given at Bois Caïman were being honored and the plans made at Morne Rouge were within reach.

At the Limbé coast, the insurgent army split back into two wings, eastern and western. Boukman led his force toward the east, to raise the enslaved sugar workers of the plain. Gathering more fighters as they moved, they burned cane fields and destroyed sugar works, pushing fifteen miles east toward Petite Anse, home to the poisoned chocolate controversies of the 1770s. On Wednesday night, August 23, they arrived at the Choiseul plantation, where the Bois Caïman meeting was held three nights before. They burned the plantation house and attacked the neighboring Fathers of Charity estate, which had a long history of poison accusations and deadly animal disease. From there, the fighters moved east, setting fire to the Bongars and Cléricy plantations. They then circled back to the massive Galliffet sugar complex, to succeed where Blaise and his resistance network had failed Sunday night.⁶⁶

At Gallifet, Boukman's army found Nicolas Odelucq with twenty or so white militia men from Cap Français. Most fled when the rebels approached, but Odelucq remained. Confronted by Philibert, whom he enslaved as a coachman, Odelucq reproached him, saying, "You wretch, I was only ever good to you; why do you want to kill me?" Driving a knife into his enslaver, Philibert replied, "That is true, but I promised to kill you."[67] This exchange shows the power of Philibert's oath to his community. Despite the fact that enslavers plied coachmen, drivers, and other elite workers with threats, promises, and privilege, Philibert honored his vow. A man who captured his enslaver had to weigh his tormentor's fate. Jean-Jacques and Boukman chose to protect the estate agent at Dutilh. Paul Belin, the leader of the Limbé army, gave his enslavers a boat so they could escape their coastal sugar estate, and he was killed by other rebel leaders who saw this as a betrayal.[68] Toussaint Louverture helped Bayon de Libertat and his family hide in the Limbé woods during the uprising.[69]

While the east wing pushed out into the flat sugar plain, Paul Belin's western force burned plantations in Limbé and headed to Port Margot, which had been the boundary of Makandal's influence thirty-four years before and was only six years removed from Kingué's enterprise. The rebels attacked Port Margot Wednesday evening and destroyed all the plantations in the Port Margot plain by Thursday. They moved on, tracing the same route Kingué had used to ascend to Plaisance, which was still home to the torturer Nicolas Lejeune. Colonists there repelled the rebels and drove them temporarily back down into the Limbé plain.[70] But the next day, the insurgents returned to burn dozens of plantations and set up an armed camp in the mountains.[71] Cycles of drought, disease, and poisonous accusations in those remote coffee fields had forged powerful connections that transformed enslaved workers into rebels.

As the sky filled with cinders from burning cane fields, thousands of colonists streamed to Cap Français to take refuge. Rebel armies suffered massive casualties, but the uprising was all but unstoppable. Within the first eight to ten days of the revolution, fifteen thousand people escaped their enslavers and destroyed 184 sugar plantations. By the end of September, they had burned all plantations within a fifty-mile radius of Cap Français, including twelve hundred coffee estates.[72]

The first fortified rebel camps were in the areas that launched the rebellion: Morne Rouge, Galliffet, and Limbé. After a month, colonial troops captured the Galliffet camp, but nearly all of the six thousand rebels escaped. The Limbé camp fell shortly after, but rebels moved into the mountains where they could better defend themselves against colonial soldiers. By November, rebel forces had extended their territory eastward, almost to the Spanish colonial border.

Boukman was killed in a battle in mid-November, and colonists captured Jean-Jacques. They executed him in Cap Français for murders on the Noé estate.[73] Rebels named Georges Biassou and Jean-François commanded camps in Dondon and Grande-Rivière, where Toussaint Louverture served as their advisor. With the help of priests and captured colonists, rebel leaders sought to negotiate an end to the fighting. One of their offers was to return their followers to plantation slavery in exchange for amnesty for all and freedom for hundreds of enslaved leaders.[74] Their offer was refused. Colonial society was built on white supremacy, and colonists in the North would not negotiate it.

The French Revolutionary government sent commissioners and some six thousand troops to restore order, but the new soldiers were unable to dislodge the rebels from their camps. In Paris, in 1792, influential politicians in the National Assembly began to insist that colonists would never defeat the uprising unless they incorporated free men of color into their forces. This would require the reform that Ogé and Chavanne had wanted. On April

4, 1792, Louis XVI signed a law permitting propertied free men of color and free Black people in the colony to vote and run for office, with no distinction of color.[75] By August 1792, the Black generals understood the power of their position, and they established a new negotiating stance, arguing that French Revolutionary ideology condemned both slavery and racial discrimination. No longer would they seek freedom only for leaders. Now they insisted on freedom and amnesty for all rebels and promised that the rebels would return to the fields to work as wage laborers.[76]

In September 1792, a second Revolutionary Commission arrived from France to enforce this law. Its leaders, Léger Sonthonax and Etienne Polverel, set about enrolling free men of color in military units and promoting them to positions of leadership despite colonists' opposition. They eventually replaced the former Colonial Assembly with a body made up of equal numbers of white men and free men of color.[77]

In January 1793, Parisian revolutionaries executed Louis XVI. Spain and England declared war against France, and both kingdoms eventually opened military fronts in Saint-Domingue. Santo Domingo had been informally supporting rebel armies in the North Province since 1791. Now Spanish officials commissioned Jean-François, Georges Biassou, and Toussaint as officers in the Royal Spanish Army.

By June 1793, Sonthonax and Polverel had achieved some military success against rebels in various colonial provinces. In the North, their troops drove Jean-François, Biassou, and Toussaint out of their camps and re-enslaved thousands of their supporters.[78] Many white colonists in Cap Français were deeply unhappy about the commission's racial reforms. They rallied to newly arrived French military governor Etienne Galbaud and appealed to him to roll back the new policies. For three days in June, Galbaud and his backers fought Sonthonax and his soldiers for control of the city. When more than a thousand French sailors from Galbaud's fleet stepped ashore to fight on behalf of the new governor, Sonthonax appealed to Black rebel forces outside the city. He offered them amnesty and freedom if they would help him hold Cap Français and join the French Revolutionary Army.[79]

Galbaud's forces panicked when they heard of this offer and evacuated the city as fires broke out. With Cap Français destroyed by the fighting, Galbaud and thousands of colonists fled Saint-Domingue. Confirmed in their power, Sonthonax and Polverel gradually extended freedom to rebels and enslaved people. On October 31, 1793, they issued a decree of general emancipation. On February 4, 1794, the French National Assembly extended it to all territories under French control. Saint-Domingue's people, regardless of their status in the era of slavery, were citizens of the French Republic.

After three years of fighting, the Haitian Revolution would last another ten. In 1802, Napoleon attempted to take control of the territory administered by Toussaint Louverture. An earlier French regime had appointed him governor-general of the colony, and in this role, the Black general did his best to revive the plantation system. His army administered many abandoned estates and forced ex-slaves to return to work. When Napoleon promulgated a new constitution that did not apply to France's overseas territories, a committee handpicked by Louverture wrote a new constitution for Saint-Domingue that named him governor-general for life and gave him the power to name his own successor.

Louverture's attempt to force Bonaparte to accept his authority failed. When a treaty lifted a British naval blockade, Bonaparte sent a massive fleet to Saint-Domingue. Saint-Domingue's former slaves, who resented Louverture's policies, did little to protect him from the French expeditionary force that forced him from power. After promising to let him retire in peace, French troops kidnapped Louverture, and he died in a cold French prison cell a year later.

In some ways, Louverture's downfall evoked the scenario that Médor's free Black friends described in the 1750s. If Saint-Domingue had enough free Black people, they could confront white people and force them to end the colony. What Médor's friends did not anticipate was just how much power it would take to force colonists to negotiate. Like colonists throughout the revolution, Bonaparte would not compromise.

Bonaparte's attempt to reassert control over Saint-Domingue provoked massive resistance in the months after Louverture's arrest. Armies led by rival Black and biracial generals united to defeat a French force that was badly weakened by malaria and yellow fever. On January 1, 1804, the Black general Jean-Jacques Dessalines, formerly enslaved on a coffee plantation in Grande-Rivière, declared that Saint-Domingue would henceforth be known as Haiti, an independent and sovereign state.

Conclusion

A MANAGER NAMED PIERRE MOSSUT who survived Boukman Dutty's assault on the Galliffet plantation would later write, "How could we ever have known that there reigned among these men, so numerous and formerly so passive, such a concerted accord that everything was carried exactly as was declared?"[1] Knowing so little, if Mossut is to be believed, colonists nonetheless had their say. Many colonial narratives about the Haitian Revolution persist today. Colonists insisted that the enslaved people who launched the rebellion had no political goals or vision; they were driven only by a violent desire for revenge. Colonists also told and retold the Makandal poisoning myth, which writers and people across Haiti adopted a century later as evidence of an organized rebellion. Historians have abandoned many misleading colonial narratives; this book has challenged a few more.

Enslaved people resisted slavery by forming communities and acting in their own interests. Mossut himself was the target of a work stoppage organized by nearly two dozen slaves that lasted over two weeks. For at least three decades, conditions in the North Province led men and women to forge communities to alleviate the suffering colonists inflicted on them. Resistance communities arose from a particular set of conditions that afflicted enslaved people on sugar and coffee plantations; dangerous food instability was chief among them.

Saint-Domingue's economy was designed to force enslaved people to depend on an unstable food supply. They survived on produce from the gardens they tended in their scarce free time and on imported grains, low-quality salted fish and beef, and meat from imported draft animals. Some enslavers grew provision crops for the estate, but many did not. Hunger was a given, and when wars halted food imports, enslaved people died. Malnutrition combined with overwork was deadly for the weakest, but anthrax could take the strongest in a community. Doctors eventually diagnosed the fast-acting and deadly disease, which came to Saint-Domingue during the 1740s or 1750s in French livestock imported through Louisiana. When starving animals foraged deeply in dry soil during cycles of drought, they consumed dormant anthrax spores that rapidly killed them. A combination of drought and wartime blockades led starving slaves to consume the meat of those downed animals.

When anthrax swiftly cut down both healthy livestock and strong men and women, survivors searched for explanations. Deaths came so quickly that they seemed supernatural, the work of witches, poisoners, or spirits. Then came brutal poison inquisitions by planters who enjoyed free rein from colonial courts. To many African people and their descendants, these terrible events exposed the malevolent forces at the core of colonial society. Some turned to leaders like Makandal, Kingué, Jérôme, or Jean and formed spiritual communities seeking protection and insight. Others created different kinds of resistance communities, organizing strikes, seeking legal protection, or distributing African-inspired medicines. There was no single culture of resistance that pervaded Saint-Domingue.

Randy Browne vividly evokes enslaved people in Berbice, Guyana, for whom "the daunting challenge of staying alive shaped a wide range of social relationships, cultural practices, and political strategies." In Saint-Domingue, the challenge of staying alive provoked a wide range of resistance strategies.

Carolyn Fick writes about how resistance in Saint-Domingue "was expressed or carried out by the slaves in many ways." She documents partial revolts, conspiracies, plots to kill the master, suicide, infanticide, voodoo, poisonings, and *marronage*. David Geggus has unearthed evidence of religious divination, legal activism, labor strikes, marronage, theft, insolent speech, and satirical songs.[2]

The conditions that drove some to resistance were a crucible that could destroy or strengthen relationships among enslaved people. Confessions produced during poison investigations revealed that people had built communities around shared spirituality, ethnicity, and bonds of friendship and kinship. Interrogation and torture tested those communities and destroyed many of them. The interrogation records at the heart of this book often show desperate people revealing secrets that would cause terrible trouble for their friends. Médor and Assam exposed their communities in confessions. Kingué's divinations helped define communities but also targeted individuals in them. Some relationships held. Venus and Daouin burned at the stake without revealing the location of André Carbon's daughter, Marie Jeanne.

In forming communities, individuals chose leaders, built trust in their methods and in each other, and developed a sense of group identity. This was an enormous challenge in Saint-Domingue and elsewhere. As Randy Browne writes, plantations "were not only sites of exploitation but complex social worlds inhabited ... by Kongolese, Igbo, and Coromantee immigrants, husbands and wives, drivers, carpenters, sugar-boilers and 'domestics,' parents, children, and shipmates, obeah practitioners and clients—in short, communities of individuals and groups from diverse backgrounds who had a range of concerns and faced different challenges."[3]

Competition for authority, power, and material resources created complex relationships among enslaved people. Enslavers understood this competition and used it to their own advantage.

Trevor Burnard describes how a Jamaican enslaver manipulated his captives using sadistic punishments, sexual domination, and food scarcity. Enslaved people had divergent interests, including gardens and other property they did not want to risk losing. Burnard argues that "slaves came and went so frequently that it is misleading to even describe groups of slaves as communities."[4]

Nevertheless, communities did emerge. Makandal, Kingué, and Jérôme built their communities around Congo-inspired practices. West Africans had their own ways to affiliate. In the 1780s, Moreau de Saint-Méry reported how vodou groups gathered privately under the authority of a king and queen, whom they also called master and mistress and father and mother. Followers repeated vows of secrecy sealed by a West African blood oath, like the oath that closed the Bois Caïman meeting. Moreau described a vodou ceremony in which the king, possessed by a spirit, received requests from members of the group who wanted help from the spirit world. According to Moreau, "Most asked for the ability to direct the mind of their masters." A spirit then possessed the queen; under its influence, anything she said would be decreed as law.[5]

A leading historian of the Haitian Revolution, David Geggus, concludes that "as long as [vodou] promoted magical rather than political remedies to real-world problems, its revolutionary potential was limited."[6] This book argues the contrary: that some African and African-influenced practices in Saint-Domingue created powerfully bonded communities that were essential to the uprising of 1791. As Geggus notes, nothing about vodou is inherently revolutionary. However, the revolutionary potential of a community in Saint-Domingue did not depend on whether it voiced an overarching ideology of revolution. Instead, resistance communities' revolutionary potential derived from bonds within them that were later recruited to a striking new purpose. Workers on the Noé estate and the Galliffet complex who organized work stoppages, for example, turned rapidly to the task of revolt in 1791.

Resistance could involve direct confrontation. Some people insulted, assaulted, or killed their tormentors. Kangal argued with his enslavers when they would not let him visit his sick father. Daouin, Gaou, Laurin, his wife, Marie-Louise, and the driver named Dau made toxic potions and pastes using the leaves that carried anthrax bacteria. Two men killed their enslaver's nephew on the Lejeune estate.

Many others were willing to negotiate. As Trevor Burnard observes, "Slavery was not maintained by force alone (though, of course, force was what sustained it). It was a negotiated relationship subject to continual renegotiation and redefinition. That negotiation, moreover, was done at the level of individual relations because, although the state mandated and supported masters' control over slaves, masters' control was bolstered only through a complex web of continuing interactions between two unequal parties. . . . Although the playing field was uneven, slaves did not always lose, and masters did not always win."[7]

Those who dosed their enslavers with African-style medicines to hasten manumission were evening out the playing field. They tried to gain an advantage in their freedom negotiations. Work stoppages were another form of negotiation, as employed on the Bréda Haut-du-Cap plantation, on the Noé estate where Jean-Jacques was enslaved, at one of the Galliffet estates, and on at least seven other sugar plantations. Enslaved people seeking legal protection from torture attempted to provoke a negotiation that would benefit them between colonial legal administrators and local planters.

Negotiation was at the heart of the political vision Médor revealed when he described how ex-slaves were building a free Black population that might someday confront French colonists.[8] This was a long-term project, aiming for a future in which free Black people would be able to negotiate political and social changes by threatening violence. Médor expected that this negotiation would "necessarily end the colony." That phrase terrified his enslavers, who assumed this meant killing all the white people, an interpretation that obscured the political imagination of Saint-Domingue's free and enslaved people of African descent.

An end to the colony might have meant many different things to African captives. People from societies that practiced forms of slavery might not have aimed for the kind of general emancipation that Léger Sonthonax decreed in 1793. They might have imagined a framework to restrain colonists' cruelty or improve the lot of field-workers. They might have envisioned pathways for ex-slaves to become part of Saint-Domingue's military, economic, and social elite.

Dismantling white supremacy was a goal many Black people and free people of color shared, but alliances among these groups have been difficult to see. Vincent Ogé and Jean-Baptiste Chavanne were the third-generation descendants of Black women and French colonists. For years, they were accepted by other wealthy colonists. After 1770, however, colonial society began defining biracial people as ex-slaves rather than as a kind of colonist.[9] Free people of color described themselves as humiliated by a new requirement that they carry proof of their free status. They also experienced formal segregation from white people in public settings. These conditions drove Ogé and another wealthy man of color, Julien Raimond, to lobby colonial officials in France about reforms in the 1780s. A need to distinguish themselves from ex-slaves made the idea of a public alliance between free people of color and enslaved or free Black people unacceptable to many biracial people.

In the lead-up to the rebellion, members of these groups tried to negotiate with colonists to redefine the colony's racial hierarchy. Ogé and Raimond were enslavers; they opposed a Black revolution. But some of Ogé's followers suggested that invoking the power of the massive enslaved population could force white people to compromise on the issue of voting rights. When colonial troops attacked the Ogé camp, at least one of his followers, Jacques Lucas, reportedly suggested recruiting slaves to help fend them off.[10] Later, with Ogé and Chavanne broken on the rack, the prospect of negotiating for reform was nonexistent. But survivors of the movement may have hoped to regain leverage by provoking a slave revolt.

Historians have been critical of colonists' claims that free people of color incited or organized the revolution, which Marlene Daut calls the "mulatto/a vengeance narrative."[11] But evidence concerning the outbreak of the uprising in Acul and Limbé suggests that Ogé veterans were there, pushing enslaved leaders to seize the moment. Theirs was not a driving force; it was one influence on resistance communities whose leaders were working to assess priorities and meet opportunities.

Enslaved people in the time of the uprising would have seen free Black people as the very incarnation of successful negotiation. A small minority of enslaved people successfully navigated the manumission process. Another path to liberty for enslaved people was serving in the military. Expeditions docked in Cap Français after they concluded, and many who held new freedom papers made their home in the port city. Other veterans settled in Grande-Rivière, which grew into a free Black population center. In and around Cap, there were also many artisans and small merchants who had purchased their freedom.

Some free Black people directly supported enslaved people, such as those who urged Médor and Assam to dose their masters to obtain manumission. According to Médor, at least some free Black people believed that each manumission brought the free Black population one step closer to being strong enough to confront the white people. The case of Lizette and Kangal demonstrates another reason why free Black people and enslaved people worked together: freed former slaves wanted their families released from slavery. Perhaps the most important engagement between free Black people and enslaved people occurred in the aftermath of the Ogé episode. More than half of Ogé's men who eluded arrest were free Black people, so that group was probably well represented among those who encouraged the August 1791 slave uprising in Acul, Limbé, and Petite Anse.

Saint-Domingue had hundreds of resistance communities fighting local problems and practicing different forms of resistance. The diversity of their interests may explain why the colony had no tradition of violent uprising. Even in 1791, rebel leaders who gathered to plan the uprising were a heterogenous group. They may have known each other, but they had no reason to trust one another. It took enormous energy to forge a movement out of these groups, to overcome distrust, and to accept different perspectives. That process began at the Morne Rouge meeting, expanded at Bois Caïman, and was revealed when the Limbé and Acul rebel armies met at the Belin plantation.

Many currents converged when enslaved people launched the Haitian Revolution. The headwaters of the revolution rose in the North Province like the Soufrière and Limbé Rivers. They surfaced amid widespread hunger, drought, death, and persecution. After the slave trade doubled and then doubled again in the 1780s, other wellsprings of revolution emerged. Enslaved Congo war veterans flooded the region. The French revolution brought political instability to white society. The Declaration of the Rights of Man and Citizen inspired free men of color to push colonists toward negotiation over voting rights and then fight when colonists were intransigent. Enslaved Africans who supported Louis XVI may have opposed revolution in France, but they were revolutionaries in Saint-Domingue.[12] Rebels with different motivations could all agree that colonial society had never been more vulnerable than it was in 1791.

As scholars have shown, the fight against plantation slavery did not end with Dessalines's Declaration of Independence in 1804.[13] The new Haitian state did its best to maintain the export economy, and rural people continued to fight forced plantation labor. Resistance from 1804 to the 1840s, like earlier resistance, took many forms and had very few outright rebellions. Little is known about the communities that fought the plantations of the national era because the fledgling Haitian state created few records of its attempts at repression.

Features of Haiti's nineteenth-century peasant society, which Jean Casimir has dubbed "the counter-plantation," may reflect resistance strategies from the colonial era. These include extended family housing known as *lacou*, vibrant rural markets and the networks that produced them, spiritual practices that eventually coalesced into Haitian Vodou, and secret societies that emerged as protectors of rural communities. As Johnhenry Gonzalez has written, these institutions did not emerge spontaneously or accidentally.[14] Using traditions that predated 1791, rural Haitians constructed a new society devoted to self-sufficiency. They wanted to stave off some of the same threats that created North Province resistance communities at least sixty years earlier: forced labor, dependence on imported food, constraints on their ability to buy and sell produce, and surveillance of their religious and communal life.

The stories told here of African people and their descendants resisting slavery in Saint-Domingue's North Province show that modern-day Haiti is not newly afflicted with environmental disaster, global dislocation, and industrial capitalism; it was born of them. French colonial plantations were voracious factories in the field that relied on forced migration to replace dying and dead workers. At first, West African people were the majority of Saint-Domingue's population, drawn through the Cap Français port and out across the sugar plain. Later, a growing stream of

Congo captives from Central Africa traveled that path and beyond into mountainous coffee territory. At the end of a journey that for many would be their last, some people formed communities to access the power of an African spiritual world that surrounded them even away from their homelands. When dislocated people began to earn, worship, heal, and defend themselves, white fear produced intense persecution across racial and religious lines. When thousands of enslaved Africans, hundreds of colonists, and tens of thousands of livestock animals perished in recurring outbreaks of anthrax, French colonists blamed Africans for the devastating consequences of their own actions. Enslaved people who lived where the first fires of the Haitian Revolution burned knew how to make the costly personal decision to resist. They were ready when revolution called, and a tide of thousands who had been siphoned from distant homelands surged from fields, factories, and dwellings to make a new world for themselves.

Notes

INTRODUCTION

1. The exception is Jean Fouchard, *Les marrons de la liberté* (Port-au-Prince: H. Deschamps, [1972] 1988). On slave resistance in the French historiography, see Jean-Pierre Le Glaunec, "Résister à l'esclavage dans l'Atlantique français: aperçu historiographique, hypothèses et pistes de recherche," *Revue d'histoire de l'Amérique française* 71, nos. 1–2 (2017): 13–33. In the 1970s, Gabriel Debien, the most important French historian of slavery in his generation, famously said it was too early to write the history of slave resistance in the French Caribbean. *Les esclaves aux Antilles françaises, XVII–XVIII siècles* (Basse-Terre: Société d'histoire de la Guadeloupe, 1974), 394. See also Pierre de Vaissière, *Saint-Domingue: La société et la vie créoles sous l'ancien régime (1629–1789)* (Paris: Perrin, 1909), 232; C. L. R. James, *The Black Jacobins: Toussaint L'ouverture and the San Domingo Revolution* (New York: Vintage, 1963), 21. Lucien Peytraud, *L'esclavage aux antilles françaises avant 1789, d'après des documents inédits des archives coloniales* (Paris: Hachette, 1897), 370, incredibly, does not mention Saint-Domingue in his discussion of slave revolts.

2. Tiya Miles, *All That She Carried: The Journey of Ashley's Sack, a Black Family Keepsake* (New York: Random House, 2021), 300.

3. See James H. Sweet, *Domingos Álvares, African Healing, and the Intellectual History of the Atlantic World* (Chapel Hill: University of North Carolina Press, 2011); Kristen Block, *Ordinary Lives in the Early Caribbean: Religion, Colonial Competition, and the Politics of Profit* (Athens: University of Georgia Press, 2012); and Pablo F. Gómez, *The Experiential Caribbean: Creating Knowledge and Healing in the Early Modern Atlantic* (Chapel Hill: University of North Carolina Press, 2017).

4. Médéric-Louis-Elie Moreau de Saint-Méry, *Description topographique, physique, civile, politique et historique de la partie française de l'isle Saint-Domingue,*

2 vols. (Philadelphia: Chez l'auteur, 1797), 1:382; Marie Houllemare, "Vers la centralisation des archives coloniales françaises au XVIIIe siècle: Destruction et conservation des papiers judiciaires," in *Pratiques d'archives à l'époque moderne—Europe, mondes coloniaux*, ed. Marie-Pia Donato and Anne Saada (Paris: Classiques Garnier, 2019), 349–367, 658.

5. See León Vignols, "La destruction d'archives coloniales," *Revue d'histoire des colonies françaises* 22 (1929): 45–52, and Houllemare, "Vers la centralisation des archives coloniales, 349–367.

6. On Léogane, see Houllemare, "Vers la centralisation des archives coloniales," 359; for Cap Français, Vignols, "La destruction d'archives coloniales," 46.

7. *Le code noir ou Edit du roy, servant de reglement . . . pour la discipline & le commerce des negres & esclaves dans ledit pays. Donné à Versailles au mois de mars 1685* (Paris: Claude Girard, 1735), 6, 9; these are articles 22 [food], 26 [slaves' ability to file a legal complaint], 42 [whipping], and 43 [criminal persecution for murder and torture]. Sala-Molins notes the contradiction between the letter of the Code Noir and conditions in Saint-Domingue. Louis Sala-Molins, *Le Code noir, ou, Le calvaire de Canaan* (Paris: Presses universitaires de France, 1987), 174–177.

8. Malick W. Ghachem, "Prosecuting Torture: The Strategic Ethics of Slavery in Pre-Revolutionary Saint-Domingue (Haiti)," *Law and History Review* 29, no. 4 (November 2011): 995n31. See M. L. E. Moreau de Saint-Méry, *Loix et constitutions des colonies françoises de l'Amérique sous le Vent* (Paris: l'Auteur, 1784), 3:674.

9. See Yvan Debbasch, "Le Marronage: Essai sur la désertion de l'esclave antillais, première partie," *L'Année Sociologique* 11 (1961): 2–4.

10. Fouchard, *Les marrons*, 138.

11. Carolyn Fick, *The Making of Haiti* (Knoxville: University of Tennessee Press, 1990), 49.

12. Debbasch, "Le Marronnage," 195.

13. David Geggus, "Saint-Domingue, le marronnage et la révolution haïtienne," in *Sociétés marronnes des Amériques: Mémoires, patrimoines, identités et histoire du XVIIe au XXe siècles*, ed. Jean Moomou (Matoury, French Guiana: Ibis Rouge Editions, 2015), 132.

14. Crystal Nicole Eddins, "Runaways, Repertoires, and Repression: Marronnage and the Haitian Revolution, 1766–1791," *Journal of Haitian Studies* 25, no. 1 (2019): 5.

15. Crystal Nicole Eddins, *Rituals, Runaways, and the Haitian Revolution: Collective Action in the African Diaspora* (Cambridge, UK: Cambridge University Press, 2021), 298.

16. James, *Black Jacobins*, 16, 21.

17. [Anonymous], *Relation d'une conspiration tramée par les nègres dans l'Isle de S. Domingue* (S.l.: s.n., 1758), 2–3. This letter fragment described a failed uprising in Cap Français, months after Makandal's execution, but no official correspondence mentions it, which suggests it was merely a rumor.

18. The author was identified as "M. de C." in 1787 and "Larival" in a 1788 republication, according to Rachel Danon, *Les Voix du marronnage dans la littérature française du xviiie siècle* (Paris: Classiques Garnier, 2015), 109–110. Nothing more is known of this person. M. de C. [Larival], "Makandal: Histoire véritable," *Le Mercure de France*, September 15, 1787.

19. Justin Girod-Chantrans, *Voyage d'un Suisse dans différentes colonies d'Amérique pendant la dernière guerre* (Neuchatel, Switzerland: Société typographique, 1785), 155–157.

20. Anonymous, "Account of a Remarkable Conspiracy in St. Domingo," *Literary Magazine and British Review* 2 (January 1789): 22–27; Duncan Faherty, Ed White, and Toni Wall Jaudon, "Introduction: 'Account of a Remarkable Conspiracy (1787),'" Just Teach One (blog), Spring 2016, http://jto.common-place.org/just-teach-one-homepage/account-of-a-remarkable-conspiracy-makandal/.

21. For the publication history, see Faherty, White, and Jaudon, "Introduction." Matt Clavin, "Race, Revolution, and the Sublime: The Gothicization of the Haitian Revolution in the New Republic and Atlantic World," *Early American Studies: An Interdisciplinary Journal* 5, no. 1 (Spring 2007): 1–29. Marie-Joséphine Augustin, *Le Makandal: Épisode de l'insurrection des noirs à St-Domingue*, ed. Lindsey Monds (Shreveport, LA: Les Cahiers du Tintamarre, 1892) is a novel about the outbreak of the Haitian Revolution that invents a "son of Makandal" to lead the Black rebellion.

22. Civique de Gastine, *Histoire de la république d'Haïti ou Saint-Domingue, l'esclavage et les colons* (Paris: Plancher, 1819), 35–36.

23. James, *Black Jacobins*, 16.

24. Alejo Carpentier, *El reino de este mundo* (Habana: Biblioteca Nacional José Marti, 1948), translated into English as *The Kingdom of This World*, trans. Harriet de Onís (New York: Farrar, Straus and Giroux, 1957).

25. See Évelyne Trouillot, *The Infamous Rosalie*, trans. Marjorie Attignol Salvodon (Lincoln: University of Nebraska Press, 2013).

26. Sarah Juliet Lauro, "Digital Saint-Domingue: Playing Haiti in Videogames," *Small Axe: A Caribbean Journal of Criticism*, no. 2 (July 2017): 1–21, and Alyssa Goldstein Sepinwall, *Slave Revolt on Screen: The Haitian Revolution in Film and Video Games* (Jackson: University Press of Mississippi, 2021), 194–196.

27. Annette Gordon-Reed, "Rebellious History [Review of Saidiya Hartman, Wayward Lives]," *New York Review of Books* 67, no. 16 (October 22, 2020): 4.

28. Vincent Brown, *Tacky's Revolt: The Story of an Atlantic Slave War* (Cambridge, MA: Belknap Press of Harvard University Press, 2020), 107.
29. Brown, *Tacky's Revolt*, 128.
30. Brown, *Tacky's Revolt*, 131.
31. Le Glaunec, "Résister à l'esclavage," and James Sidbury, "Resistance," in *The Routledge History of Slavery*, ed. Gad J. Heuman and Trevor Burnard (Routledge, 2010), 204–219.
32. Frédéric Régent, *La France et ses esclaves: De la colonisation aux abolitions (1620–1848)* (Paris: Grasset & Fasquelle, 2007), 156.
33. Régent, *La France et ses esclaves*, 155, 156, 162.
34. Randy M. Browne, *Surviving Slavery in the British Caribbean* (Philadelphia: University of Pennsylvania Press, 2017), 4.
35. Browne, *Surviving Slavery*, 2–4.
36. Browne, *Surviving Slavery*, 3.
37. Brown, *Tacky's Revolt*, 74.

1. MÉDOR'S TOWN AND COUNTRY LIVES

1. "Recensement général de l'île St. Domingue pour l'année mil sept cent trente-neuf," 1739, ANOM DPPC G1/509.
2. Pierre Pluchon, *Histoire de la colonisation française* ([Paris]: Fayard, 1991), 422.
3. "Transatlantic Slave Trade Disembarkations, 1700–1790," Transatlantic Slave Trade Database, https://slavevoyages.org/voyages/qfdGjYNy.
4. On the relative size of labor forces, see David P. Geggus, "Indigo and Slavery in Saint Domingue," *Plantation Society in the Americas* 5 (1998): 200–201.
5. Information about the Delavaud household comes from Louis Auguste Aymard et al., "Extrait des déclarations de Médor," May 1757, ANOM, F3 88, folios 212–214, except for this *marronage* notice, identifying a Congo man as the Delavauds' cook: Charles-Philippe Delavaud, "[Marronage notice]," *Affiches américaines*, October 22, 1774, sec. parution 42; see also Delavaud, "[Marronage notice]," *Affiches américaines*, April 1780, sec. parution 14. Delavaud family members spelled their name in some documents as Lavaud.
6. See Jessica Marie Johnson, *Wicked Flesh: Black Women, Intimacy, and Freedom in the Atlantic World* (Philadelphia: University of Pennsylvania Press, 2020), 130–131.
7. On the Dahomey association for "Gaou," see Philippe R. Girard and Jean-Louis Donnadieu, "Toussaint before Louverture: New Archival Findings on the Early Life of Toussaint Louverture," *William and Mary Quarterly* 70, no. 1 (2013): 44–46; for Venus's claim, see Louis Auguste Aymard et al., "Extrait des pièces déposées en le procès criminel instruite au siège royal du

Fort Dauphin contre les nommés Daouin et Venus," May 1757, ANOM C⁹A Correspondance générale St Domingue, vol. 102, microfilm 5345, reel 91.

8. Robin Law, "Slave-Raiders and Middlemen, Monopolists and Free-Traders: The Supply of Slaves for the Atlantic Trade in Dahomey c. 1715–1850," *Journal of African History* 30, no. 1 (1989): 46–50.

9. "Regions of Embarcation, Saint-Domingue, 1713–1756," Transatlantic Slave Trade Database, https://www.slavevoyages.org/voyages/MdCkyPm5.

10. J. Cameron Monroe, "Urbanism on West Africa's Slave Coast: Archaeology Sheds New Light on Cities in the Era of the Atlantic Slave Trade," *American Scientist* 99, no. 5 (2011): 402, 405.

11. "Recensement général, 1739"; Médéric-Louis-Elie Moreau de Saint-Méry, *Description topographique, physique, civile, politique et historique de la partie française de l'isle Saint-Domingue*, vol. 1 (Philadelphia: Chez l'auteur, 1797), 300, 314, 491; see also David P. Geggus, "The Slaves and Free People of Color of Cap Français," in *The Black Urban Atlantic in the Age of the Slave Trade*, ed. Jorge Cañizares-Esguerra, Matt Childs, and James Sidbury (Philadelphia: University of Pennsylvania Press, 2013), 101–121.

12. "Recensement général de la colonie de St. Domingue pour l'année 1754 joint à la lettre de Mr de Vaudreuil et de Lalanne du 10 juin 1755," 1754, ANOM 5DPPC63.

13. For free people of color in this region, see Geggus, "Slaves and Free People of Color"; Stewart R. King, *Blue Coat or Powdered Wig: Free People of Color in Pre-Revolutionary Saint Domingue* (Athens: University of Georgia, 2001); and Dominique Rogers, "Les nègres libres de la plaine du Nord à la veille de la révolution," in *La révolution et l'indépendance haïtiennes: Autour du bicentenaire de 1804, histoire et mémoire*, ed. Jean Casimir, Michel Hector, and Danielle Bégot (Gourbeyre: Archives départementales de la Guadeloupe, 2006), 47–69.

14. Geggus, "Slaves and Free People of Color," 112, explains how slaves were auctioned aboard ships in the Cap harbor until 1784.

15. M. L. E. Moreau de Saint-Méry, *Loix et constitutions des colonies françoises de l'Amérique sous le Vent*, vol. 3 (Paris: l'Auteur, 1784), 451.

16. Jean-Baptiste René Pouppé-Desportes, *Histoire des maladies de S. Domingue*, vol. 1 (Paris: Lejay, 1747), 40, 66, 69, 122, 166; Moreau de Saint-Méry, *Loix*, 3:451; Karen Bourdier, "Vie quotidienne et conditions sanitaires sur les grandes habitations sucrières du nord de Saint-Domingue à la veille de l'insurrection d'août 1791" (Université de Pau, 2005), 187.

17. Pouppé-Desportes, *Histoire des maladies*, 1:89–90, 2:114; Bourdier, "Vie quotidienne," 186; James E. McClellan III, *Colonialism and Science: Saint Domingue in the Old Regime* (Baltimore: Johns Hopkins University Press, 1992), 144.

18. Moreau de Saint-Méry, *Loix*, 3:574–577.

19. Moreau de Saint-Méry, *Description topographique*, 1:317.

20. Médor described these sums as nineteen and thirty piastres, respectively. John McCusker describes a conversion rate of 8.25 piastres per colonial livre in *Money and Exchange in Europe and America, 1600–1775: A Handbook* (Chapel Hill: University of North Carolina Press, 1978), 286n90. For slave prices, see Anonyme, "Saint-Domingue. Prix des terres, des noirs, des denrées, des mulets et cours des especes," 1785, ANOM DFC SDOM, 3 #206, which says an adult slave would cost fifteen hundred livres in 1755.

21. M. L. E. Moreau de Saint-Méry, *Loix*, 2:272.

22. *Le code noir ou Edit du roy, servant de règlement . . . pour la* discipline *& le commerce des nègres & esclaves dans ledit pays* (Paris: Claude Girard, 1735).

23. Moreau de Saint-Méry, *Loix*, 2:398, 3:343, 3:703.

24. Moreau de Saint-Méry, *Loix*, 3:96.

25. Moreau de Saint-Méry, *Loix*, 1784, 3:885.

26. Rogers, "Les nègres libres," 62; on the houses, see David P. Geggus, "Jean-Baptiste Belley: France's First Black Legislator," in *Unexpected Voices in Imperial Parliaments*, ed. Josep Fradera, José Maria Portilla, and Teresa Segura-Garcia (London: Bloomsbury Academic, 2021), 28.

27. Rogers, "Les nègres libres," 51–55; for a free Black master who branded others, see Geggus, "Jean-Baptiste Belley," 29.

28. Moreau de Saint-Méry, *Description topographique*, 1:426.

29. For complaints about free Black criminality, see Claude-François Borthon, "Mémoire [on free Blacks]," n.d. 1763, ANOM C9A v120.

30. Louis Auguste Aymard et al., "Extrait des déclarations de Médor," May 1757, ANOM, F3 88, folio 212, r.

31. Moreau de Saint-Méry, *Description topographique*, 1:370–374.

32. Moreau de Saint-Méry, *Loix*, 4:352–355. The ordonnance is dated February 1761 but makes clear that this behavior had been going on for years.

33. Moreau de Saint-Méry, *Loix*, 4:353.

34. Moreau de Saint-Méry, *Loix*, 4:354.

35. Margat, "Du Père Margat [au Cap ce 20 juillet 1743]," in *Lettres édifiantes et curieuses, écrites des missions étrangères*, ed. Charles Le Gobien et al. (Lyon: J. Vernarel, 1743), 398–404; Moreau de Saint-Méry, *Loix*, 3:457.

36. Moreau de Saint-Méry, *Loix*, 3:478–480.

37. They owned a profitable sugar plantation in the North Province of Saint-Domingue, worked by hundreds of slaves; see Moreau de Saint-Méry, *Description topographique*, 1:157.

38. Moreau de Saint-Méry, *Loix*, 3:251, 453.

39. Justin Girod-Chantrans, *Voyage d'un Suisse dans différentes colonies d'Amérique pendant la dernière guerre* (Neuchatel, Switzerland: Société typographique, 1785), 199.

40. James H. Sweet, "The Evolution of Ritual in the African Diaspora: Central African Kilundu in Brazil, St. Domingue, and the United States, Seventeenth–Nineteenth Centuries," in *Diasporic Africa: A Reader*, ed. Michael Angelo Gomez (New York: New York University Press, 2006), 64.

41. Moreau de Saint-Méry, *Description topographique*, 1:44; Sweet, "Evolution of Ritual," 74.

42. Aymard et al., "Extrait des pièces déposées."

43. The 1739 census lists sixty-nine white sugar refineries in the entire North Province, twenty-three in the West, and three in the South; see "Recensement général de l'île St. Domingue pour l'année mil sept cent trente-neuf," 1739, ANOM DPPC63.

44. Bernadette Rossignol, Phillipe Rossignol, and Pierre Bardin, "Incendie du Cap en 1734, note de la rédaction," *Compléments à Généalogie et Histoire de la Caraibe*, nouvelle, no. 26 (2017): 15; Moreau de Saint-Méry, *Description topographique*, 1:201; on Carbon's appointment to the Superior Council in 1724, see Gille-Charles Des Nos (Comte de Champmeslin), ANOM E 62. Carbon's plantation is shown in Carte topographique de la région du Cap-Français et du Fort-Dauphin, au Nord-est de la colonie française ou St. Domingue, ([s.n.][s.n.], 1760). Bibliothèque nationale de France, département Cartes et plans, GE SH 18 PF 150 DIV 2 P 8.

45. Bourdier, "Vie quotidienne," 92.

46. Natacha Bonnet, "L'organisation du travail servile sur la sucrerie domingoise au XVIIIe siècle," in *L'esclave et les plantations: De l'établissement de la servitude à son abolition*, ed. Philippe Hrodĕj (Rennes, France: Presses universitaires de Rennes, 2008), 125–160, 150–152.

47. Jean Thoret and Gérard Carbon, "[Investment agreement, signed in Nantes]," August 1, 1740, 41-APC Carbon dossier 6; image 1553–1555.

48. Delampe, "[Letter to Gérard Carbon, written from Camp de Louise, Saint-Domingue]," December 7, 1734, ANOM 41APC-1-dossier 6. img1533; on the land grant, see Rossignol, Rossignol, and Bardin, "Incendie du Cap en 1734, note de la rédaction."

49. Moreau de Saint-Méry, *Description topographique*, 1:278–282.

50. At age sixty-four, Carbon married Anne de Trudaine, a thirty-three-year-old French noblewoman. She gave birth to a daughter, Marie-Charlotte, three years after the wedding and died a few months later. "Habitation Carbon-Leroux," 1813 1692, ANOM 41 APC 1-2; Rossignol, Rossignol, and Bardin, "Incendie du Cap en 1734, note de la rédaction." On Carbon's purchase of an ennobling office, see Pierre Jean Jacques Guillaume Guyot, *Traité des droits, fonctions, franchises, exemptions, prérogatives et privilèges*, vol. 4 (Visse: Guyot . . . & Merlin, 1788), 255; Marie-Charlotte Carbon married François, Duc de Crillon, a high-born aristocrat, whose father was trying unsuccessfully to establish his

own slave plantations in Puerto Rico and Saint-Domingue. See Jorge Chinea, "Francophobia and Interimperial Politics in Late Bourbon Puerto Rico: The Duke of Crillón y Mahón's Failed Negotiations with the Spanish Crown, 1776–1796," *Nieuwe West-Indische Gids* 81, nos. 1–2 (2007): 37–54.

51. Randy M. Browne, *Surviving Slavery in the British Caribbean* (Philadelphia: University of Pennsylvania Press, 2017), 73.

52. Gabriel Debien, *Les esclaves aux Antilles françaises, XVII-XVIII siècles* (Basse-Terre: Société d'histoire de la Guadeloupe, 1974), 131–133. Browne, *Surviving Slavery*, notes that "drivers' power derived at least as much from their peers' respect as it did from their official rank," 98. But he also says that in Berbice "very few drivers were rebels," 100.

53. For Colas, see Moreau de Saint-Méry, *Loix*, 3:48–49; for Polydor, Moreau de Saint-Méry, *Loix*, 3:399.

54. Brevet, *Essai sur la culture du café, avec l'histoire naturelle de cette plante* (Port-au-Prince: Imprimerie Royale, 1768), 71.

55. Aymard et al., "Extrait des pièces déposées"; on the inheritance and slave numbers, see Lavaud, "Condamnation de la somme de 51,977 ... en faveur de la Dame Veuve Lavaud," 1767, ANOM E263, ark:/61561/up424bvvowvo.

56. Moreau de Saint-Méry, *Description topographique*, 1:175; see the maps in CARAN, "Fonds Rochambeau; IV-Fonds de documentation cartographique. 135AP/4."

57. Delavaud likely had no extra funds for emergency food or supplies. A master surgeon could expect to save between three thousand and seven thousand livres per year, one-tenth of a modest sugar planter's income. Pierre Pluchon, "La santé dans les colonies de l'Ancien Régime," in *Histoire des médecins et pharmaciens de marine et des colonies*, ed. Pierre Pluchon (Toulouse: Privat, 1985), 105, 107. The coffee boom had driven up slave and mule prices considerably. See Anonyme, "Saint-Domingue. Prix des terres, des noires, des denrées, des mulets et cours des especes." Delavaud spent at least 32,800 livres to buy twenty-four enslaved people at twelve hundred apiece and ten mules at four hundred apiece.

58. Thomas M. Truxes, *Defying Empire: Trading with the Enemy in Colonial New York* (New Haven, CT: Yale University Press, 2008), 66–69.

59. Lafarge, "Dernière lettre de Mr Lafarge [à Gérard Carbon, à Paris] qui instruit de cequi se passe et de l'état de l'habon," March 29, 1758, ANOM 41APC-1, dossier 6.

60. Pierre Force, *Wealth and Disaster: Atlantic Migrations from a Pyrenean Town in the Eighteenth and Nineteenth Centuries* (Baltimore: Johns Hopkins University Press, 2016), 10.

61. McClellan III, *Colonialism and Science*, 90.

62. *Carte topographique de la région du Cap-Français et du Fort-Dauphin, au Nord-est de la colonie française ou St. Domingue* ([s.n.][s.n.], 1760), Bibliothèque

nationale de France, département Cartes et plans, GE SH 18 PF 150 DIV 2 P 8.

63. Pouppé-Desportes, *Histoire des maladies*, 1:179; on drought in Trou parish, see Moreau de Saint-Méry, *Description topographique*, 1:173–176; on the 1756 drought in the North Province, see Richard Pares, *War and Trade in the West Indies, 1739–1763* (London: Cass, 1936), 387.

64. On the cattle shortage of the 1740s, see Simon-Pierre Maillart, "Maillart to naval secretary" (Petit Goave, Saint-Domingue, June 24, 1745), ANOM C9A 67; Charles de Brunier marquis de Larnage and Simon-Pierre Maillart, "Lettre des adrs au ministre sur le commerce des mulets avec la cote d'espagne; les bateaux achetés de l'etranger etc.," October 9, 1746, *r* 81, ANOM F3 79, folios 178–187; Sanson, "[Letter to naval minister]," March 1746, Colonies C9A Correspondance générale St. Domingue, microfilm 5345, reel 68.

65. Pouppé-Desportes, *Histoire des maladies*, 1:75, 92, 115–116, 130, 141, 145–146; Brevet, "Suite du mémoire sur les hattes," *Affiches américaines*, March 30, 1768, 113.

66. Moreau de Saint-Méry, *Description topographique*, 2:285; Moreau de Saint-Méry, *Loix*, 4:37–38.

67. Moreau de Saint-Méry, *Loix*, 4:176, 187, 287, 290.

68. See David P. Geggus, "Sugar and Coffee Production and the Shaping of Slavery in Saint Domingue," in *Cultivation and Culture: Labor and the Shaping of Slave Life in the Americas*, ed. Ira Berlin and Philip D. Morgan (Charlottesville: University of Virginia Press, 1993), 73–100, 90; Madame Delavaud inherited eighty-four carreaux (268 acres), but in the 1750s, her husband cleared and planted only half of this property. See David Lanoue, "Biens et effets à vendre," *Affiches américaines*, May 22, 1769, Supplément edition; Bellevue-Delavaud, "À vendre ou à affermer," *Affiches américaines*, September 7, 1776, sec. Supplément; Delavaud, "Avis divers," *Affiches américaines*, January 30, 1789, sec. Supplément.

69. See Pierre Joseph Laborie, *The Coffee Planter of Saint Domingo* (London: T. Cadell and W. Davies, 1798), 15.

70. Raymond Delaborde, "Effet dangereux de l'erreur et de la superstition dans les colonies françaises de l'Amérique" (Cayenne, January 31, 1775), *v* 3, ANOM C 8B, 14.

71. Nicolas-Louis Bourgeois and Pierre-Jean-Baptiste Nougaret, *Voyages intéressants dans différentes colonies . . . et un mémoire sur les maladies les plus communes à Saint-Domingue* (Londres: J.-F. Bastien, 1788), 470.

2. MÉDOR'S MEDICINES

1. Louis Auguste Aymard et al., "Extrait des pièces déposées en le procès criminel instruite au siège royale du Fort Dauphin contre les nommés

Daouin et Venus," May 26, 1757, ANOM C⁹A Correspondance générale St Domingue, vol. 102, microfilm 5345, reel 91.

2. Jean-Baptiste de Laporte Lalanne, "Lettre de Mr De Laporte Lalanne au ministre sur les empoisonnements," letter, December 12, 1757, folios 249–250, ANOM, F3 88, folios 224–227.

3. See Aymard et al., "Extrait des pièces déposées." "Gaou" was a name and military title associated with the eighteenth-century Fon-speaking kingdom of Dahomey. Boniface I. Obichere, "Change and Innovation in the Administration of the Kingdom of Dahomey," *Journal of African Studies* 1, no. 3 (Fall 1974): 243. On "*atin*," see B. (Basilio) Segurola, *Dictionnaire fon-français* (Madrid: SMA Société des Missions Africaines, 2009), 76–77; Suzanne Preston Blier, *African Vodun: Art, Psychology, and Power* (Chicago: University of Chicago Press, 1995), 212, 240.

4. G. I. Jones, "A Boundary to Accusations," in *Witchcraft Confessions and Accusations*, ed. Mary Douglas (London: Routledge, 1972), 323.

5. Lynn Wood Mollenauer, *Strange Revelations: Magic, Poison, and Sacrilege in Louis XIV's France* (University Park: Pennsylvania State University Press, 2007), 129–131.

6. Matthew Ramsey, *Professional and Popular Medicine in France, 1770–1830: The Social World of Medical Practice* (New York: Cambridge University Press, 1988), 22.

7. Pierre Pluchon, "La santé dans les colonies de l'Ancien Régime," in *Histoire des médecins et pharmaciens de marine et des colonies*, ed. Pierre Pluchon (Toulouse: Privat, 1985), 109–110.

8. Augustine's maiden name was Richer de Bellevue, and she described herself as the sole heir of her mother, Marie Anne Naudin. If Augustin Richer was related to Augustine, he was probably her half brother by her father, Jérôme Richer de Bellevue. She spelled out her ancestry in Lavaud, "Condamnation de la somme de 51,977 . . . en faveur de la Dame Veuve Lavaud," 1767, ANOM Col E263.

9. "Le nègre Gao appartenant à Monsieur de Juchereau et Bonnement." Aymard et al., "Extrait des pièces déposées."

10. Their text survived because Saint-Domingue's top civilian administrator sent a copy to the Naval Ministry in Versailles. See "Lettre de Mr De Laporte Lalanne au ministre sur les empoisonnements," December 12, 1757. The longest version of the text is found in the Naval Ministry archives. Aymard et al., "Extrait des pièces déposées." Another manuscript copy, written in a different hand and collected by Moreau de Saint-Méry, is abridged in some ways, but it contains additional information, such as slaves' names; see Louis Auguste Aymard et al., "Extrait des déclarations de Médor," May 26, 1757, ANOM Col., F3 88, folios 212–214.

11. Jason T. Sharples, "Discovering Slave Conspiracies: New Fears of Rebellion and Old Paradigms of Plotting in Seventeenth-Century Barbados," *American Historical Review* 120, no. 3 (June 2015): 811–843.

12. On the improvised nature of enslaved peoples' testimony, see Sophie White, *Voices of the Enslaved: Love, Labor, and Longing in French Louisiana* (Chapel Hill: University of North Carolina Press, 2019), 14.

13. For example, Médor might have known about how Gérard Carbon damaged his neighbors' irrigation works, presumably using his slaves. See Chevalier de Conflans and Simon Pierre Maillart, "Extrait du jugement rendu par Messieurs de Conflans et Maillart" (Léogane, février 1749), ANOM Col. E 62. I'm assuming Carbon's slaves did the demolition work, based on Paul Cheney's account of a similar "water war" in *Cul de Sac: Patrimony, Capitalism, and Slavery in French Saint-Domingue* (Chicago: University of Chicago Press, 2017), 57.

14. On French judicial torture, see White, *Voices of the Enslaved*, 36–38. The powerlessness that Marisa Fuentes documents for slaves in Barbados courts was also true in Saint-Domingue. See her *Dispossessed Lives: Enslaved Women, Violence, and the Archive* (Philadelphia: University of Pennsylvania Press, 2016), 101–103.

15. James H. Sweet, *Domingos Álvares, African Healing, and the Intellectual History of the Atlantic World* (Chapel Hill: University of North Carolina Press, 2011), 93.

16. M. L. E. Moreau de Saint-Méry, *Loix et constitutions des colonies françoises de l'Amérique sous le Vent* (Paris: l'Auteur, 1784), 6:801.

17. Moreau de Saint-Méry, *Loix*, 2:398–399.

18. Moreau de Saint-Méry, *Loix*, 2:398–399, 5:152.

19. John D. Garrigus, *Before Haiti: Race and Citizenship in Saint-Domingue* (New York: Palgrave Macmillan, 2006), 85–86.

20. Moreau de Saint-Méry, *Loix*, 3:589–590.

21. Moreau de Saint-Méry, *Loix*, 3:703.

22. These three names are given only in the copy of the document collected by Moreau de Saint-Méry, not the one that is part of administrative correspondence. Aymard et al., "Extrait des déclarations de Médor," folio 212.

23. Gallica, the website of the French National Library, lists 120 titles from the eighteenth century that mention Brinvilliers.

24. Nicolas-Toussaint Des Essarts, *Essai sur l'histoire générale des tribunaux des peuples tant anciens que modernes, ou Dictionnaire historique et judiciaire*, vol. 3 (Paris: Durand, neveu, 1778), 77.

25. Etienne Rufz, *Recherches sur les empoisonnemens pratiqués par les nègres à la Martinique* (Paris: J.-B. Baillière, 1844), 19–20n1, cites Charles Lacretelle, *Histoire de France pendant le 18e siècle* (Paris: Buisson, 1808), 1:14–23.

26. "Qu'il y a aussi un secret parmi eux qui ne tend qu'à faire périr la colonie, que les blancs ignorent et dont les nègres libres sont la cause principale faisant jouer tous ces ressorts pour augmenter leurs nombres afin d'être en état de faire face aux blancs en cas de besoin." Aymard et al., "Extrait des déclarations de Médor," folio 212.

27. Pablo F. Gómez, *The Experiential Caribbean: Creating Knowledge and Healing in the Early Modern Atlantic* (Chapel Hill: University of North Carolina Press, 2017), 166–183.

28. Aymard et al., "Extrait des déclarations de Médor," folio 212.

29. The family name alternated between the spellings "Lavaud" and "Delavaud." Lavaud, "Avis divers," *Supplément aux Affiches américaines* (January 30, 1789), 679. On the family dispute, see Augustin Claude Lavaud, "Extrait des minutes du Conseil Supérieur" (Cap Français, February 10, 1774), ANOM Col E263; [Agreement between Widow Lavaud and her children]" (May 1, 1775), ANOM Col. E263; Charles-Philippe Delavaud, "Declaration," April 30, 1776, ANOM Col E263; and Lavaud and Cassaignard, "Declaration de huissier," February 29, 1777, ANOM Col E263.

30. Delaviviaud lived in Limonade parish and in 1751 he endorsed this book: Élie Monnereau, *Le parfait indigotier ou, Description de l'indigo . . . ensemble un traité sur la culture de café*, Nouv. éd, rev.cor.augm. par l'auteur. (Amsterdam: Marseille: J. Mossey, 1765), 210. Delavivaud's plantation is shown in René Gabriel Rabié, *Carte de la plaine du nord de l'isle St. Domingue, depuis le Limbé jusques au Fort Dauphin*, 1770, manuscript, 1:36, 300; 1770, Cartographic Items Maps K.Top.123.37.2 TAB., The British Library, St Pancras.

31. Aymard et al., "Extrait des déclarations," fol. 214 recto describes Angélique's previous enslaver as a M. Diion, a plantation surgeon.

32. A woman named Angélique was one of five people Hilliard d'Auberteuil described as having been burned at the stake after conviction for poisoning. See his *Considérations sur l'état présent de la colonie française de Saint-Domingue* (Paris: Grangé, 1776), 1:137.

33. Fort Dauphin's royal prosecutor described this pattern in different terms: "These poisons were made by the most simple field slaves, sold [to and] administered by those, in contrast, who were both the most talented and had their master's greatest confidence." Marie François L'Huillier de Marigny, "Mémoire sur les poisons qui règnent à Saint-Domingue," 1762, ANOM, F3 88, folios 260–264.

34. Fredrik Thomasson, "Black Healers, Surgeons and 'Witches': Medicine, Mobility and Knowledge Exchange in Swedish St Barthélemy 1785–1815," *Social History of Medicine* 35, no. 1 (August 2021): 49–71, 66–67; João José Reis, *Divining Slavery and Freedom: The Story of Domingos Sodré, an African Priest in Nineteenth-Century Brazil*, trans. Sabrina Gledhill (New York: Cambridge University Press, 2015), 134–136.

35. Pierre-François-Xavier de Charlevoix and Jean-Baptiste Le Pers, Histoire de l'isle espagnole ou de S. Domingue: écrite particulièrement sur des mémoires manuscrits du P. Jean-Baptiste Le Pers, jésuite, vol. 4 (Amsterdam: François L'Honoré, 1733), 366–368.

36. Lebrun de la Fortière, "[Letter to Gérard Carbon in Paris]," November 4, 1758, ANOM 41APC-1, dossier 6, folio 6, describes Marie Jeanne as a "griffe," meaning one parent was biracial and the other was Black.

37. Laporte Lalanne, "Lettre de Mr De Laporte Lalanne au ministre sur les empoisonnements," December 12, 1757.

38. Laporte Lalanne, "Lettre de Mr De Laporte Lalanne"; Antoine Baradat, Jean Cruon, and Etienne Lhèr, "Raport de Mrs Médicin et Chirurgien, extraits des minutes de greffe criminal du siege royal de Fort Dauphin" (Fort Dauphin, July 8, 1757), ANOM, F3 88, folios 215–217.

39. Jean-Barthélemy-Maximilien Nicolson, *Essai sur l'histoire naturelle de l'isle de Saint-Domingue avec des figures en taille-douce* (Paris: Gobreau, 1776), 133.

40. L'Huillier de Marigny, "Mémoire sur les poisons" (1762), 260–264.

41. See Baradat's 1774 letter in Félix Vicq d'Azyr, *Exposé des moyens curatifs & préservatifs qui peuvent être employés contre les maladies pestilentielles des bêtes à cornes* (Paris: Merigot l'aîné, 1776), 178.

42. For Daouin's former home, see Millot, Friou & Compagnie, "Biens et effets à vendre," *Supplément aux Affiches américaines*, August 20, 1774. In 1784, the estate where Gaou lived had no crops, but there were 123 cows, goats, and sheep and eighteen horses or mules. Worlock, "Biens et effets à vendre," *Supplément aux Affiches américaines*, January 7, 1784.

43. Jean-Baptiste Pouppé-Desportes, *Histoire des maladies de S. Domingue*, vol. 2 (Paris: Lejay, 1747); Pierre Poissonnier Desperrieres, *Traité des fièvres de l'isle de S. Domingue*, 2nd ed. (Paris: Chez Vallat Lachapelle, 1766); Jean-Barthélémy Dazille, *Observations sur les maladies des nègres: leurs causes, leurs traitemens et les moyens de les prévenir* (Paris: Chez Didot le jeune, 1776); Julien-François Duchemin de L'Étang, *Gazette de médecine pour les colonies* (Cap Français, Saint-Domingue: Imprimerie royale du Cap, 1778); M. E. (Michel Etienne) Descourtilz, *Voyages d'un naturaliste, et ses observations . . . à St.-Domingue*, vol. 3 (Paris: Dufart, père, 1809); Nicolson, *Essai sur l'histoire naturelle*.

3. POISON AND PANIC

1. Louis Auguste Aymard et al., "Extrait des pièces déposées en le procès criminel instruite au siège royal du Fort Dauphin contre les nommés Daouin et Venus," May 26, 1757, ANOM C⁹A Correspondance générale St Domingue, vol. 102, microfilm 5345, reel 91; Jean Baptiste de Laporte Lalanne, "Lettre de Mr De Laporte Lalanne au ministre sur les empoisonnements" (December 12, 1757) ANOM, F3 88, folios 224–227.

2. Joannès Tramond, *Saint-Domingue en 1756 et 1757; d'après la correspondance de l'ordonnateur Lambert* (Paris: Éditions Leroux, 1929), 24–25, cites Lambert's letter to MM. Bort et de Lalanne, in August 1757.

3. Lafarge, "Dernière lettre de Mr Lafarge [à Gérard Carbon, à Paris] qui instruit de ce qui se passe et de l'état de l'habon," March 29, 1758, ANOM 41APC-1, dossier 6.

4. Gaspard François Ardisson, "[Letter to Gérard Carbon in Paris]," October 20, 1757, ANOM 41APC-1, dossier 6, p. 4.

5. Lebrun de la Fortière, "[Letter to Gérard Carbon in Paris]," November 4, 1758, ANOM 41APC-1, dossier 6, folios 6–7; M. L. E. Moreau de Saint-Méry, *Loix et constitutions des colonies françoises de l'amérique sous le vent* (Paris: l'Auteur, 1784), 4:234.

6. Gaspard François Ardisson, "[Letter to Gérard Carbon in Paris]," October 20, 1757, ANOM 41APC-1, dossier 6.

7. [Anonymous], *Relation d'une conspiration tramée par les nègres dans l'Isle de S. Domingue* (S.l.: s.n., 1758), 4.

8. François Philippe Bart and Jean-Baptiste Laporte Lalanne, "Lettre des Adrs au ministre sur les empoisonnements," June 30, 1758, ANOM, F3 88, folios 231–234, folio 231, emphasis added.

9. Moreau de Saint-Méry, *Loix*, 2:337.

10. Moreau de Saint-Méry, *Loix*, 3:221, also 674.

11. Raymond Delaborde, "Effet dangereux de l'erreur et de la superstition dans les colonies françaises de l'Amérique" (Cayenne, January 31, 1775), ANOM C 8B, 14, n. 4, folio 2 r.

12. Laporte Lalanne, "Lettre de Mr De Laporte Lalanne."

13. [Anonymous], *Relation d'une conspiration*, 6.

14. Marie François L'Huillier de Marigny, "Mémoire sur les poisons qui règnent à Saint-Domingue," 1762, ANOM, F3 88, folios 260–264; on October 21, 1757, off the coast of Cap Français, three British ships destroyed a French fleet of seven ships and killed more than five hundred men. See Vincent Brown, *Tacky's Revolt: The Story of an Atlantic Slave War* (Cambridge, MA: Harvard University Press, 2020), 77.

15. Gaspard François Ardisson, "[Letter to Gérard Carbon in Paris]," May 15, 1757, ANOM 41APC-1, dossier 6.

16. Michel-René Hilliard d'Auberteuil, *Considérations sur l'état présent de la colonie française de Saint-Domingue*, 2 vols. (Paris: Grangé, 1776), 1:138–139.

17. [Anonymous], *Relation d'une conspiration*, 5.

18. [Anonyme], *Relation d'une conspiration*, 4. This pamphlet quotes a colonial letter dated June 24, 1758, which claims that the courts had executed twenty-four slaves and three free Black people since Makandal's execution on January 21. After Makandal's execution, there were more than two hundred

accused poisoners in Cap's prisons, according to the royal attorney of Port de Paix, a neighboring town. Regnier DuTillet, "Letter dated Port-de-Paix, 6 April 1758," April 6, 1758, ANOM C⁹A Correspondance générale St Domingue, vol. 102, microfilm 5345, reel 91.

19. Nicolas Lejeune fils, "Mémoire adressé à MM les administrateurs de St Domingue par Nas Lejeune fils habitant à Plaisance," May 27, 1788, ANOM F3 90 n. 5, folios 202–206, folio 205 v. When Lejeune wrote this, he was being tried for torturing people he thought were poisoners, so he cited this history to justify his conduct.

20. Laporte Lalanne, "Lettre de Mr De Laporte Lalanne."

21. "Arrêt de surséance en faveur de Prosper de Rastel, vicomte de Rocheblave, sous-gouverneur des pages de la Grande écurie du roi, et de Marie Aimée Lallemand, sa femme, veuve en premières noces de Pierre Alexandre Delaye, conseiller au conseil supérieur du Cap, à Saint-Domingue (n° 28) (20 avril 1779)," 1779, ANOM COL A 17 F° 106; see also Delaye, "À vendre," *Affiches américaines*, February 5, 1766, sec. Avis divers.

22. The lawyer lived in the hills but was active at court, eventually becoming a Superior Council judge. Delaye, "Déclaration du Sr Delaye au sujet d'un nègre à lui appartenant accusé d'empoisonnement" (Extrait des Registres du greffe du siège royale du Cap, June 8, 1757), ANOM C⁹A Correspondance générale St Domingue, vol. 102, microfilm 5345, reel 91; Delaye eventually sold the estate when he could not manage to grow sugar there; Delaye, "À vendre," February 5, 1766.

23. Laporte Lalanne, "Lettre de Mr De Laporte Lalanne."

24. Tramond, *Saint-Domingue en 1756 et 1757* (1929), 25–26.

25. Philibert Le Blondain, "Extrait des registres du Greffe de la Chambre criminelle du Fort Dauphin," September 25, 1757, C9A Correspondance générale St Domingue, vol. 102, microfilm 5345, reel 91. The location of Le Blondin's estate is taken from *Carte topographique de la région du Cap-Français et du Fort-Dauphin, au Nord-est de la colonie française ou St. Domingue*, 1:58000 ([s.n.][s.n.], 1760), manuscript, Bibliothèque nationale de France, département Cartes et plans, GE SH 18 PF 150 DIV 2 P 8.

26. Moreau de Saint-Méry, *Loix*, 3:856; see the discussion of hospitalières in Karol K. Weaver, *Medical Revolutionaries: The Enslaved Healers of Eighteenth-Century Saint-Domingue* (Urbana: University of Illinois Press, 2006), 1–3, 41–46.

27. Aymard et al., "Extrait des pièces déposées"; Blondain, "Extrait des registres du Greffe"; Philibert Le Blondain, "Nouvelles d'Amérique," *Affiches américaines*, June 8, 1768.

28. Laporte Lalanne, "Lettre de Mr De Laporte Lalanne." These were not the nontoxic "poisons" that Baradat tested after Daouin's leaves; that second test had already occurred by the time Le Blondain arrested Fanchon and Thomas.

29. Michel Philippe de Beaufort et al., "Interrogatoire de la négresse Marie Jeanne. Extrait des minutes déposés au Greffe du siège royal du Cap," October 26, 1757, ANOM, F3 88. The location of the Chiron estate is given in *Carte topographique de la région du Cap-Français et du Fort-Dauphin* (1760).

30. The reference to René is from Beaufort et al., "Interrogatoire de la négresse Marie Jeanne"; the reference to Yoruba men and the Delacoursière estate is from Delabrillon, Taillac, le chevalier Daux et de Blosnay, "Interrogation du nègre Hauron. Extraits des minuttes déposés au siège royal du Cap," November 1, 1757, ANOM, F3 88.

31. Delabrillon et al., "Interrogation du nègre Hauron."

32. Delabrillon et al., "Interrogation du nègre Hauron"; Michel Philippe de Beaufort et al., "Interrogatoire de la nommée Nanon. Extrait des minutes déposés au Greffe du siège royal du Cap," October 26, 1757, ANOM F3 vol. 88, folios 221–223.

33. Beaufort et al., "Interrogatoire de la nommée Nanon," and Beaufort et al., "Interrogatoire de la négresse Marie Jeanne"; Marie Jeanne is identified as a free woman in Sébastien Jacques Courtin, "Extrait [prison inspection]," November 9, 1757, ANOM C9A, vol. 102, microfilm 5345, reel 91.

34. Beaufort et al., "Interrogatoire de la nommée Nanon."

35. Beaufort et al., "Interrogatoire de la négresse Marie Jeanne."

36. Delabrillon, "Interrogation du nègre Hauron."

37. Courtin, "Extrait [prison inspection]," November 9, 1757, 8.

38. We know Valette's first name because he burned the words "Jean Valete" into the skin of a Congo man named Joseph who escaped from the Soufrière estate in 1784. See Valette, "[Marronnage report]," *Affiches américaines*, May 19, 1784, http://www.marronnage.info/fr/document.php?id=6853; for the location of the Valette estate, spelled "Valet," see René Gabriel Rabié, *Carte de la plaine du nord de l'isle St. Domingue, depuis le Limbé jusques au Fort Dauphin*, 1770, manuscript, 1:36, 300, Cartographic Items Maps K.Top.123.37.2 TAB., British Library, St Pancras.

39. See Médéric-Louis-Elie Moreau de Saint-Méry, *Description topographique, physique, civile, politique et historique de la partie française de l'isle Saint-Domingue* (Philadelphia: Chez l'auteur, 1797), 1:639.

40. Sébastien Jacques Courtin, "Interrogatoire de négresse Assam," September 27, 1757, ANOM C9A, correspondance générale St. Domingue, microfilm 5345, reel 91.

41. Charles Arthaud, ed., *Recherches, mémoires et observations sur les maladies épizootiques de Saint-Domingue* (Cap-François: Imprimerie royale, 1788), 38–44.

42. Moreau de Saint-Méry, *Description topographique*, 1:291.

43. Moreau de Saint-Méry, *Description topographique*, 1:640; see Chapter 5 for more on this epidemic.

44. Courtin, "Interrogatoire de négresse Assam"; Valette, "Extrait de minutes déposées au greffe du Siege Royal du Cap; Déclaration des Srs Valette Dezieller et Dufeu contenant ce qu'ils ont vus dire à la négresse Assam sur le compte du nommé Pompé," September 17, 1757, ANOM C⁹A, correspondance générale St. Domingue, microfilm 5345, reel 91.

45. [Raymond] de Delaborde, "Effet dangereux de l'erreur et de la superstition dans les colonies françaises de l'amerique" (Cayenne, January 31, 1775), ANOM Col E 238, folio 2.

46. Courtin, "Interrogatoire de négresse Assam," September 27, 1757.

47. For "Diola" but not "Lemanoir" or "Valette," see *Carte topographique de la région du Cap-Français et du Fort-Dauphin, au Nord-est de la colonie française ou St. Domingue*, document cartographique manuscrit, 1: 58 000 environ ([s.n.][s.n.], 1760), Bibliothèque nationale de France, département Cartes et plans, GE SH 18 PF 150 DIV 2 P 8; another map shows the "Valet" and "Le Manoye" estates; Rabié, *Carte de la plaine du nord de l'isle St. Domingue*, 1770.

48. For discussion of another enslaved Poulard woman in Saint-Domingue, see Rebecca J. Scott and Jean M. Hébrard, *Freedom Papers: An Atlantic Odyssey in the Age of Emancipation* (Cambridge, MA: Harvard University Press, 2012), 8–10. David Geggus found fewer than 1 percent of people from Assam's ethnic group listed on North Province plantation slave lists. The Mandingue group, which corresponds to the coastal region where Jola people lived, made up just over 2 percent. David P. Geggus, "Slave Society in the Sugar Plantation Zones of Saint Domingue and the Revolution of 1791–93," *Slavery & Abolition* 20 (1999): 39.

49. The location of the Laplaine estate is shown in *Carte topographique de la région du Cap-Français et du Fort-Dauphin*.

50. This was not the same Marie Jeanne interrogated on the Chiron estate, who was Creole, born in Saint-Domingue. For modern equivalents of the ethnic categories used by French colonists, see David P. Geggus, "Sugar and Coffee Production and the Shaping of Slavery in Saint Domingue," in *Cultivation and Culture: Labor and the Shaping of Slave Life in the Americas*, ed. Ira Berlin and Philip D. Morgan (Charlottesville: University of Virginia Press, 1993), 73–100, table 2.8.

51. Losange, blue vervain, and pois puant referred to *Chloroleucon mangense, verbena hastata*, and *senna occidentalis*, respectively. P. Acevedo-Rodriguez and Mark T. Strong, "Flora of the West Indies: Catalogue of Seed Plants," National Museum of Natural History, accessed February 16, 2018, http://botany.si.edu/antilles/WestIndies/catalog.htm.

52. One interrogator was Duzuttre, a local landowner who leased a farm to Pompée. The other, Dufau, left no documentary trace. Valette, "Extrait de minutes déposées au greffe."

53. [Anonymous], *Relation d'une conspiration*, 6; everything we know about Assam from this point comes from this pamphlet. A transcript of her final interrogation sent to the French Naval Ministry disappeared in transit. Nicolas Berryer, "Lettre du ministre à MM. Bart et Elias, au sujet des empoisonnements qui se sont produits à Saint-Domingue," April 6, 1759, ANOM, F3 88, folios 252–255.

54. On judicial torture, see Sophie White, *Voices of the Enslaved: Love, Labor, and Longing in French Louisiana* (Chapel Hill: University of North Carolina Press, 2019), 36.

55. [Anonymous], *Relation d'une conspiration*, 7.

56. Courtin, "Extrait [prison inspection]," 4.

57. Gabriel Debien, *Les esclaves aux Antilles françaises, XVII-XVIII siècles* (Basse-Terre: Société d'histoire de la Guadeloupe, 1974), 260.

58. When Courtin summoned Duquesnoy to the prison to respond to Assam's testimony, the Jesuit Superior came instead. When the governor tried to send Duquesnoy back to France, the Superior refused. Only after repeated requests by the administrators did he transfer Duquesnoy to a new post, away from his work with slaves. François Philippe Bart and Jean-Baptiste Laporte Lalanne, "Lettre des Adrs au ministre sur les empoisonnements," June 30, 1758, ANOM, F3 88, folios 231–234, and Nicolas Berryer, "Lettre du ministre à MM. Bart et Elias, au sujet des empoisonnements qui se sont produits à Saint-Domingue," April 6, 1759, ANOM, F3 88, folios 252–255.

59. The following year, Louis XV evicted the Jesuit order from France and all its other colonies. D. G. Thompson, "The Lavalette Affair and the Jesuit Superiors," *French History* 10, no. 2 (June 1, 1996): 206–239; for the 1763 expulsion from Saint-Domingue, see Moreau de Saint-Méry, *Loix*, 4:626. In 1776, some colonists still remembered the Jesuits as collaborating with enslaved poisoners. Michel-René Hilliard d'Auberteuil, *Considérations sur l'état présent de la colonie française de Saint-Domingue* (Paris: Grangé, 1776), 2:69–70.

60. Jean-Baptiste de Laporte Lalanne, "Lettre de Mr De Laporte Lalanne au ministre sur les empoisonnements," December 12, 1757, ANOM, F3 88, folios 224–227.

4. MAKANDAL, CONGO DIVINER

1. "Origins of Slaves Disembarked in Cap Français, 1700–1756," Trans-Atlantic Slave Trade Database, https://slavevoyages.org/voyages/fKrLhuZg.

2. "Slaves Embarked Bound for Saint-Domingue, 1680–1793," Transatlantic Slave Trade Database, http://slavevoyages.org/voyages/1F9M5UrG.

3. I use the term "Congo" because French slavers used it. On identity in West Central Africa, see Wyatt MacGaffey, "Constructing a Kongo Identity: Scholarship and Mythopoesis," *Comparative Studies in Society and History* 58, no. 1 (2016): 159–180, and Dunja Hersak, "There Are Many Kongo Worlds:

Particularities of Magico-Religious Beliefs among the Vili and Yombe of Congo-Brazzaville," *Africa* 71, no. 4 (January 2001): 614–640.

4. Kathryn M. De Luna, "Sounding the African Atlantic," *William and Mary Quarterly, 3rd Ser* 78, no. 4 (October 2021): 581–616, 593.

5. Sébastien Jacques Courtin, "Mémoire sommaire sur les prétendus pratiques magiques et empoisonnements prouvés au procès instruit et jugé au Cap," 1758, ANOM, F3 88, folio 249.

6. Courtin, "Mémoire sommaire," folio 241.

7. For "sausages," see Courtin, Mémoire sommaire," folio 141; for woolen balls, see Charles Fournier de la Chapelle, "Mémoire pour servir à l'information des procés contre les négres devins, sorciers et empoisonneurs" (1758), ANOM, F3 88 folio 236.

8. Courtin, "Mémoire sommaire," folio 248.

9. Courtin, "Mémoire sommaire," folio 242.

10. Fournier, "Mémoire," folio 236.

11. De Luna, "Sounding the African Atlantic," 600–601; the description of mistreatments characteristics comes from her explanation of the terms *ouaie/wáyi* and *mayangangue*, which Courtin attributed to Makandal.

12. Courtin, "Mémoire sommaire," folio 243.

13. Courtin, "Mémoire sommaire," folio 244.

14. Courtin, "Mémoire sommaire," folio 244.

15. Jean-Charles Laveaux, *Nouveau dictionnaire de la langue française* (Deterville, 1820), 590.

16. Courtin, "Mémoire sommaire," folio 244.

17. Robert Muchembled, *A History of the Devil: From the Middle Ages to the Present*, trans. Jean Birrell (Cambridge, UK: Polity, 2003), 15.

18. Courtin, "Mémoire sommaire," folio 246.

19. Courtin, "Mémoire sommaire," folios 242, 248, 249–250.

20. De Luna, "Sounding the African Atlantic," 596, 600.

21. De Luna, "Sounding the African Atlantic," 598.

22. No source records Le Tellier's first name. Médéric-Louis-Elie Moreau de Saint-Méry, *Description topographique, physique, civile, politique et historique de la partie française de l'isle Saint-Domingue*, vol. 1 (Philadelphia: Chez l'auteur, 1797) 641; on Makandal's master, see [Anonymous], *Relation d'une conspiration tramée par les nègres dans l'Isle de S. Domingue* (s.l.: s.n., 1758); in 1721, the governor invited Le Tellier to discuss establishing a convent in Cap Français. M. L. E. Moreau de Saint-Méry, *Loix et constitutions des colonies françoises de l'Amérique sous le Vent*, vol. 2 (Paris: l'Auteur, 1784), 716. Le Tellier's estate is marked "Le Normand" in *Carte topographique de la région du Cap-Français et du Fort-Dauphin, au Nord-est de la colonie française ou St. Domingue*, ([s.n.][s.n.], 1760), manuscript, Bibliothèque nationale de France, département Cartes et plans, GE SH 18 PF 150 DIV 2 P 8.

23. Simon P. Newman, *A New World of Labor: The Development of Plantation Slavery in the British Atlantic* (Philadelphia: University of Pennsylvania Press, 2013), 204–206.

24. Moreau de Saint-Méry, *Description topographique*, 1:651–652.

25. The April 23, 1742, sale is described in "Roche, Pierre, habitant du quartier de l'Acul à Saint-Domingue et François Auge Le Normant, intendant des armées navales du Roi 1754," December 9, 1754, ANOM Col E 355. Elisabeth Lescoffier was possibly the daughter of Louis l'Escoffier, who served as Cap Français district judge in 1697. Moreau de Saint-Méry, *Loix*, 1:570; in 1742, as a widow, Lescoffier made a large donation to the new convent in Cap Français. Moreau de Saint-Méry, *Description topographique*, 1:432; on her land grants and purchases, "Roche et Le Normant." This property is identified as "La hatte de M De Normand" on *Carte topographique de la région du Cap-Français et du Fort-Dauphin*, (1760).

26. Quotation from "Roche et Le Normant." As part of this lawsuit, in 1753, a surveyor and a Lescoffier employee searched the property fruitlessly for markers an earlier surveyor had placed in 1743.

27. These men are mentioned in "Roche et Le Normant."

28. Sébastien-François-Ange Le Normant de Mézy was second in command of civil affairs for the Cap Français region. See Moreau de Saint-Méry, *Loix*, 3: 561; on the move to Cap, see Sanson, "[Letter to naval minister]," June 1746, Colonies C9A Correspondance générale St Domingue, microfilm 5345, reel 68. On the 1748 Morne Rouge purchase, see James S. Pritchard, "Le Normant De Mézy, Sébastien-François-Ange," in *Dictionary of Canadian Biography* (Toronto, Canada: University of Toronto/Université Laval, 1979), http://www.biographi.ca/en/bio/le_normant_de_mezy_sebastien_francois_ange_4E.html. The Morne Rouge estate is marked "Le Normand" on *Carte topographique de la région du Cap-Français et du Fort-Dauphin*, (1760).

29. See the January 27, 1758, letter from Bart and Laporte-Lalanne cited by Pierre Pluchon, *Vaudou, sorciers, empoisonneurs: De Saint-Domingue à Haïti* (Paris: Karthala, 1987), 168, and Regnier DuTillet, "Letter dated Port-de-Paix, 6 April 1758," ANOM C9A Correspondance générale St Domingue, vol. 102, microfilm 5345, reel 91; [Anonymous], *Relation d'une conspiration*, 2, claims Makandal had been a fugitive for seventeen years, but this would mean he escaped before 1742, when LeTellier died.

30. David P. Geggus, "The French Slave Trade: An Overview," *William and Mary Quarterly* 58 (2001): 128; see also David P. Geggus, "Sugar and Coffee Production and the Shaping of Slavery in Saint Domingue," in *Cultivation and Culture: Labor and the Shaping of Slave Life in the Americas*, ed. Ira Berlin and Philip D. Morgan (Charlottesville: University of Virginia Press, 1993), 80.

31. De Luna, "Sounding the African Atlantic," 598.

32. Moreau de Saint-Méry, *Description*, 1:670–684.

33. Julien Guillaume Dufresne de Pont-Brillant managed sugar plantations in Limonade and Trou parishes owned by a merchant firm in his native city of Saint-Malo, France; Alain Roman, *Saint-Malo au temps des négriers* (KARTHALA Editions, 2001), 168; Roman cites a 1768 inventory of these sugar plantations. A lawsuit by Dufresne's heirs does not mention the sugar estates; Julien Guillaume Dufresne de Pontbrillant, "Dufresne de Pontbrillant, Julien Guillaume, propriétaire d'une habitation à Saint-Domingue et ses héritiers (1785)," 1785, ANOM COL E 147. The location of Dufresne coffee estate in Limbé is given on *Carte topographique de la région du Cap-Français et du Fort-Dauphin*, (1760).

34. In 1748, Jean-François Dufresne de Pontsieux captained the slave ship *Le Cerf* from Saint-Malo to the west-central African port of Loango, where he purchased 590 people; Roman, 155, 297–309; Voyage 33171 in "Slave Ship Captains Named Dufresne," Trans-Atlantic Slave Trade Database, http://slavevoyages.org/voyages/5ThCctGc. Jean-François disembarked 499 surviving Africans, more captives than Cap had received in the previous year; in 1751 and again in 1753, Jean-François sailed from Saint-Malo to Cabinda, farther down the "Congo" coast, and then to Martinique, carrying a total of 967 captives. "Slave Voyages to Saint-Domingue, 1700 to 1800," Trans-Atlantic Slave Trade Database, http://www.slavevoyages.org/voyages/nWBeKMkj.

35. Voyages 33179 and 33193, "Slave Ship Captains Named Dufresne"; Roman, *Saint-Malo au temps des négriers*, 297–309.

36. "Slave Ship Captains Named Dufresne."

37. Geggus, "French Slave Trade," 128.

38. Jean-Baptiste de Laporte Lalanne, "Lettre de Mr De Laporte Lalanne au ministre sur les empoisonnements," letter, December 12, 1757, ANOM, F3 88, folios 224–227.

39. Pierre de Vaissière, *Saint-Domingue: la société et la vie créoles sous l'ancien régime (1629–1789)* (Paris: Perrin, 1909), 247.

40. John Thornton, "Cannibals, Witches, and Slave Traders in the Atlantic World," *William and Mary Quarterly* 60 (April 2003): 273–294; Robert W. Slenes, "A Árvore de Nsanda transplantada: Cultos Kongo de aflição e identidade escrava no Sudeste brasileiro (século XIX)," in *Trabalho livre, trabalho escravo Brasil e Europa, séculos XVIII e XIX*, ed. Douglas Cole Libby and Ferreira Júnia Furtado (São Paulo, Brazil: Annablume, 2006), 287–288.

41. Jean-François Dutar, "Family Tree of Louis François Trévan," Geneanet, https://gw.geneanet.org/jfdutar?lang=en&n=trevan&oc=0&p=louis+francois.

42. This account comes from Moreau de Saint-Méry, who writes as if Makandal had two hands, even though he also wrote that Makandal's hand

was amputated after a sugar mill accident. See his *Description topographique*, 1:652, and Moreau de Saint-Méry, "[manuscript notes on Makandal]" (1788), Collection Moreau de Saint-Méry, ANOM, F3 88, folio 235.

43. Moreau de Saint-Méry, *Description*, 1:652.

44. Courtin, "Mémoire sommaire," folio 249.

45. Courtin, "Mémoire sommaire," folio 246.

46. In 1776, Hilliard d'Auberteuil advised readers that they could go to the council's archive and consult the trial records for "Macanda, Pompée, Angélique, Brigitte, Laurent, & others burned after them." Michel-René Hilliard d'Auberteuil, *Considérations sur l'état présent de la colonie française de Saint-Domingue* (Paris: Grangé, 1776), 1:137.

47. Courtin came to Saint-Domingue to make his fortune as a lawyer. He married in the colony, but his wife was not wealthy. He focused on advising colonists about contracts and inheritances. Veuve Barbaroux Courtin, "[Letter from Widow Courtin to Minister Sartine requesting judicial posts for her two sons]," 1779, ANOM E 96. In 1755, Courtin was appointed "Notary General" and charged with organizing the colony's contract archives. Moreau de Saint-Méry, *Loix*, 4:165. When the Cap Français judge died, Courtin's patrons appointed him to fill the vacancy temporarily. He hoped his poison investigation would convince the French Naval Ministry to appoint him permanently. Courtin, "Letter to naval minister de Massiac," December 26, 1758, ANOM C9A Correspondance générale St Domingue, vol. 102, microfilm 5345, reel 91; Jean Baptiste Estève, "Estève, Jean Baptiste, sénéchal et lieutenant de l'amirauté du Cap-Français, à Saint-Domingue et son neveu, écrivain des colonies 1757/1786," ANOM Col E 172.

48. Moreau de Saint-Méry, *Loix*, 4:217–218.

49. [Anonymous], *Relation d'une conspiration*, 3.

50. Moreau de Saint-Méry, *Description*, 653.

51. DuTillet, "Letter dated Port-de-Paix, 6 April 1758."

52. Hein Vanhee, "Central African Popular Christianity and the Making of Haitian Vodou Religion," in *Central Africans and Cultural Transformations in the American Diaspora*, ed. Linda M. Heywood (New York: Cambridge University Press, 2002), 264; on the deep history of this concept, see John M. Janzen, "Minkisi at the Articulations of Individual and Societal Stress Points," in *Fragments of the Invisible: The René and Odette Delenne Collection of Congo Sculpture*, ed. Constantine Petridis (Cleveland, OH: Cleveland Museum of Art, 2013), 46.

53. Wyatt MacGaffey, *Art and Healing of the Bakongo, Commented by Themselves: Minkisi from the Laman Collection* (Bloomington: Indiana University Press, 1991), 4.

54. Hein Vanhee, "Agents of Order and Disorder: Kongo Minkisi," in *Re-Visions: New Perspectives on the African Collections of the Horniman Museum*, ed. Karel Arnaut (London: Horniman Museum and Gardens, 2000), 93.

55. Wyatt MacGaffey, "The Personhood of Ritual Objects: Kongo 'Minkisi,'" *Etnofoor* 3, no. 1 (January 1990): 51.
56. Wyatt MacGaffey, "African Objects and the Idea of Fetish," *RES: Anthropology and Aesthetics* 1994, no. 25 (1994): 128.
57. Wyatt MacGaffey, *Kongo Political Culture: The Conceptual Challenge of the Particular* (Bloomington: Indiana University Press, 2000), 112.
58. MacGaffey, *Kongo Political Culture*, 109; Vanhee, "Agents of Order," 99; MacGaffey, "The Personhood of Ritual Objects," 54.
59. Vanhee, "Agents of Order,"93.
60. Jan Raymaekers, "A Changing World," in *Mayombe: Ritual Sculptures from Congo*, ed. Jo Tollebeek (Tielt, Belgium: Lanoo, 2010), 21; Wyatt MacGaffey, "Lulendo: The Recovery of a Kongo Nkisi," *Ethnos* 52, nos. 3–4 (1987): 339; Vanhee, "Agents of Order," 100.
61. John M. Janzen, *Lemba, 1650–1930: A Drum of Affliction in Africa and the New World* (New York: Garland, 1982), 5, 13, 58, 76–79.
62. Courtin, "Mémoire sommaire," folio 244.
63. Geoffroy Heimlich, "The Kongo Cross across Centuries," *African Arts* 49, no. 3 (July 2016): 26.
64. Cécile Fromont, "Under the Sign of the Cross in the Kingdom of Kongo: Religious Conversion and Visual Correlation in Early Modern Central Africa," *RES: Anthropology and Aesthetics* 5960 (2011): 109–123, 114.
65. Wyatt MacGaffey, "Complexity, Astonishment and Power: The Visual Vocabulary of Kongo Minkisi," *Journal of Southern African Studies* 14, no. 2 (1988): 191, 202; Wyatt MacGaffey and John M Janzen, "Nkisi Figures of the Bakongo," *African Arts* 7, no. 3 (1974): 88; Vanhee, "Central African Popular Christianity," 257.
66. Todd Ramón Ochoa, *Society of the Dead: Quita Manaquita and Palo Praise in Cuba* (Berkeley: University of California Press, 2010), on feeding, 185, on ritual insults, 190, and Ochoa, "Prendas-Ngangas-Equisos: Turbulence and the Influence of the Dead in Cuban-Kongo Material Culture," *Cultural Anthropology* 25, no. 3 (August 2010): 400.
67. Ochoa, *Society*, 216.
68. Ochoa, *Society*, 208, 216.
69. Ochoa, *Society*, 71.
70. Courtin, "Mémoire sommaire," folio 246.
71. Courtin, "Mémoire sommaire," folio 246.
72. DuTillet, "[Letter to the Naval Minister]."
73. Courtin, "Mémoire sommaire," folio 250.
74. Pierre-François-Xavier de Charlevoix and Jean-Baptiste Le Pers, *Histoire de l'isle espagnole ou de S. Domingue: écrite particulièrement sur des mémoires manuscrits du P. Jean-Baptiste Le Pers, jésuite*, vol. 4 (Amsterdam: François L'Honoré, 1733), 366–368; for malefice, see Caroline Oudin-Bastide, *L'effroi*

et la terreur: Esclavage, poison et sorcellerie aux Antilles (Paris: La Découverte, 2013), 23–31.

75. [Anonymous], *Relation d'une conspiration*, 8.
76. Moreau de Saint-Méry, *Description*, 652.

5. AN EPIDEMIC OF THEIR OWN MAKING

1. Charles Frostin, *Histoire de l'autonomisme colon de la partie française de St-Domingue aux XVIIe et XVIIIe siècles* (Lille, France: Service de reproduction des thèses, 1973), 602.
2. Quote from Thomas M. Truxes, *Defying Empire: Trading with the Enemy in Colonial New York* (New Haven, CT: Yale University Press, 2008), 75; Richard Pares, *War and Trade in the West Indies, 1739–1763* (London: Cass, 1936), 388.
3. Philippe-François Bart, "Lettre de Mr Bart au ministre touchant un essay de poisons fait sur des negres condamnés au feu," letter, December 25, 1759, ANOM, F3 88, folios 258–259.
4. [Raymond] de Laborde, "Effet dangereux de l'erreur et de la superstition dans les colonies françaises de l'amerique" (Cayenne, January 31, 1775), ANOM Col E 238, folio 4.
5. Antoine Gisler, *L'esclavage aux Antilles françaises (17e-19e siècle): Contribution au problème de l'esclavage* (Fribourg, Switzerland: Éditions Universitaires, 1965), 113, cites a memorandum by the lower-court judge Jean-Baptiste Estève, ANOM F3_90, folios 149–158.
6. Estève's memorandum, cited in Gisler, *L'esclavage*, 114.
7. Malick W. Ghachem, *The Old Regime and the Haitian Revolution* (New York: Cambridge University Press, 2012), 133–138, cites the same Estève memorandum referenced by Gisler.
8. Ghachem, *The Old Regime*, 132; Pierre Pluchon, *Vaudou, sorciers, empoisonneurs: de Saint-Domingue à Haïti* (Paris: KARTHALA, 1987), 198.
9. Ghachem, *The Old Regime*, 138.
10. Antoine Fritz Pierre, *Le commerce de la viande dans la colonie française de Saint-Domingue aux XVIIe et XVIIIe sièclest* (Paris: CIDHICA France, 2018), 214–217; this was probably not the man who supplied deadly meat in 1756 because the city auctioned off the butcher's monopoly every few years; Médéric-Louis-Elie Moreau de Saint-Méry, *Description topographique, physique, civile, politique et historique de la partie française de l'isle Saint-Domingue*, vol. 1 (Philadelphia: Chez l'auteur, 1797), 237.
11. [Jean Louis Polony], "[Letter to the colonial minister]," January 7, 1779, ANOM Col E388.
12. McClellan, *Colonialism and Science: Saint-Domingue in the Old Regime* (Baltimore: Johns Hopkins Press, 1992), 144.

13. Regnaudot, "Description d'une maladie épizootique," qui régnoit à Saint-Domingue, dans la dépendance du Cap-François dans les années 1772 & 1773 & 1774," in *Recherches, mémoires et observations sur les maladies épizootiques de Saint-Domingue*, ed. Charles Arthaud (Cap-François: Imprimerie royale, 1788), 198.

14. Regnaudot, "Description d'une maladie épizootique, 196–205; Karen Bourdier, *Vie quotidienne et conditions sanitaires sur les grandes habitations sucrières du nord de Saint-Domingue à la veille de l'insurrection d'août 1791* (Paris: Indes Savantes, 2019), 261. The locations of Carré, Dupaty, Sacanville, Laplaigne and Macarty plantations are shown in *Carte topographique de la région du Cap-Français et du Fort-Dauphin, au Nord-est de la colonie française ou St. Domingue,* ([s.n.][s.n.], 1760), Bibliothèque nationale de France, département Cartes et plans, GE SH 18 PF 150 DIV 2 P 8.

15. Moreau de Saint-Méry, *Description*, 219.

16. Moreau de Saint-Méry, *Description*, 543; McClellan, *Colonialism and Science*, 144; Karen Bourdier, "Les conditions sanitaires sur les habitations sucrières de Saint-Domingue à la fin du siècle," *Dix-huitième siècle* n° 43, no. 1 (2011): 364.

17. [Jean Louis Polony], "[Letter to the colonial minister]," January 7, 1779.

18. Yvan Debbasch, "Le crime d'empoisonnement," *Revue d'histoire d'outre-mer* 52 (1963), 171 cites letter from Delribal to Bréda, October 12, 1773, Arch. Nat., 18 AP 3.

19. On the three arrested men, see Philippe R. Girard, *Toussaint Louverture: A Revolutionary Life* (New York: Basic Books, 2016), 39, who cites a November 13, 1773, letter from Delribal to Bréda in Archives National 18AP/3; on the two attempted suicides and the quote, see Jean-Louis Donnadieu, *Un grand seigneur et ses esclaves: le comte de Noé entre Antilles et Gascogne, 1728–1816* (Toulouse, 2009), 84, who cites an August 18, 1773, letter in 18AP/3.

20. Philippe R. Girard and Jean-Louis Donnadieu, "Toussaint before Louverture: New Archival Findings on the Early Life of Toussaint Louverture," *William and Mary Quarterly* 70, no. 1 (2013): 68; there were 154 people enslaved at Haut-du-Cap in the 1780s, but this followed a period of expansion. David P. Geggus, "Toussaint Louverture and the Slaves of the Bréda Plantations," *The Journal of Caribbean History* 20 (1985–86): 35, 42.

21. Girard and Donnadieu, "Toussaint before Louverture": 69.

22. The Bréda livestock deaths stopped in 1775. Girard, *Toussaint Louverture*, 39–40; Bayon's quote from Bourdier, *Vie quotidienne*, 253, who cites an October 12, 1773, letter in 189/AP/3 dossier 12.

23. Pierre Étienne Bourgeois de Boynes, "Lettre du ministre de la Marine à Bertin, ministre," March 10 1774, ANOM Col., F3, vol. 89, folio 140.

24. François Vallat, "An Outbreak in France in the XVIIIth Century: Rinderpest," *Comptes Rendus Biologies* 335, no. 5 (2012): 343–349, 347–348; Jean Lompagieu Lapole, *Observations relatives à la santé des animaux ou Essai sur leurs maladies* (Paris, 1788), 286.

25. Lapole, *Observations*, 283–284.

26. D. C. Dragon and R. P. Rennie, "The Ecology of Anthrax Spores: Tough but Not Invincible," *Canadian Veterinary Journal = La Revue Veterinaire Canadienne* 36, no. 5 (May 1995): 299–300; Sarah Friebe, F. Gisou van der Goot, and Jérôme Bürgi, "The Ins and Outs of Anthrax Toxin," *Toxins* 8, no. 3 (2016): 5.

27. N. Metcalfe, "The History of Woolsorters' Disease: A Yorkshire Beginning with an International Future?" *Occupational Medicine* 54, no. 7 (2004): 489–492; Robert E. Levin, *Anthrax: History, Biology, Global Distribution, Clinical Aspects, Immunology, and Molecular Biology* (Sharjah, UAE, 2014), 27–28.

28. The first documented use of the term was in 1772, according to Trésor de la Langue Français, "ÉPIZOOTIE: Définition de ÉPIZOOTIE," ORTOLANG: Outils et Ressources pour un Traitement Optimisé de la Langue, 1994, https://www.cnrtl.fr/definition/%C3%A9pizootie; Caroline C. Hannaway, "Veterinary Medicine and Rural Health Care in Pre-Revolutionary France," *Bulletin of the History of Medicine* 51, no. 3 (1977): 431–447, 431.

29. [Jean] Fournier, *Observations sur les fièvres putrides et malignes* (Dijon, France: Frantin, 1775), 145.

30. Bourdier, *Vie quotidienne*, 152, cites ANOM 107AP/128, January 8, 1775, letter from Nicolas Odeluq to the Marquis de Galliffet.

31. Antoine Baradat, "[Test of chocolate, from Laurin and Marie Louise and Dau of the Galliffet plantation]," November 22, 1774, Bibliothèque de l'Académie national de médecine, SRM 180B, dr 21, pièce 14.

32. Baradat, "[Test of chocolate]."

33. Lapole, *Observations* (1788), 290–291.

34. Bourdier, *Vie quotidienne*, 242, cites Odelucq's May 1774 letter in CARAN 107/AP/128.

35. On slaves poisoning other slaves to hurt their masters, Jean-Baptiste Mathieu Thibault de Chanvalon, *Voyage à la Martinique contenant diverses observations . . . faites en 1751 et dans les années suivantes* (Paris: C.J.-B. Bauche, 1763), 64, copied by S.-J. Ducoeurjoly, *Manuel des habitans de Saint-Domingue*, vol. 1, 2 vols. (Paris: Arthus-Bertrand, 1802), 29.

36. Félix Vicq d'Azyr, *Exposé des moyens curatifs & préservatifs qui peuvent être employés contre les maladies pestilentielles des bêtes à cornes* (Paris: Merigot l'aîné, 1776), 181; Baradat's report is printed on pp. 174–175.

37. Moreau de Saint-Méry, *Description*, 525.

38. Quote is from Matthew Mulcahy, "'Miserably Scorched': Drought in the Plantation Colonies of the British Greater Caribbean," in *Atlantic Environments and the American South*, ed. Thomas Blake Earle and D. Andrew Johnson (Athens: University of Georgia Press, 2020), 76; Richard Sheridan, "The Crisis of Slave Subsistence in the British West Indies during and after the American Revolution," *William and Mary Quarterly*, 3d ser., 33, no. 4 (1976): 615–641.

39. The one exception to this was Irish beef. Bertie Mandelblatt, "How Feeding Slaves Shaped the French Atlantic," in *The Political Economy of Empire in the Early Modern World*, ed. Sophus Reinert and Pernille Røge (Basingstoke, UK: Palgrave Macmillan, 2013), 205, 209–210.

40. Moreau de Saint-Méry, *Loix*, 5:729; Bertie Mandelblatt, "'A Land Where Hunger Is in Gold and Famine Is in Opulence': Plantation Slavery, Island Ecology, and the Fear of Famine in the French Caribbean," in *Fear and the Shaping of Early American Societies*, ed. Lauric Henneton and L. H. Roper (Leiden, Netherlands, 2016), 243–264, and Joseph Horan, "The Colonial Famine Plot: Slavery, Free Trade, and Empire in the French Atlantic, 1763–1791," *International Review of Social History* 55, s18 (2010): 103–121.

41. Quoted in Charles Frostin, "Saint-Domingue et la révolution américaine," *Bulletin de la société d'histoire de la Guadeloupe* 22 (1974): 74, 79–80.

42. Arthaud, *Recherches*, 35, 44, 46, 47, 72, 78–79, 173, 180.

43. Arthaud, *Recherches*, 48.

44. Arthaud, ed, *Recherches*, 36.

45. Moreau de Saint-Méry, *Loix*, 5:701; Worlock, "Mémoire," in Arthaud, *Recherches*," 173–174.

46. Moreau de Saint-Méry, *Loix*, 6:3–4; Pierre Ulric Dubuisson and Laurent-François Lenoir (Marquis de Rouvray), *Lettres critiques et politiques sur les colonies & le commerce des villes maritimes de France* (Genève, 1785), 122.

47. Arthaud, *Recherches*, 180.

48. Bourdier, *Vie quotidienne*, 262, cites a letter of 1776.

49. Garrigus, "'Like an Epidemic One Could Only Stop with the Most Violent Remedies': African Poisons versus Livestock Disease in Saint Domingue, 1750–88," *William and Mary Quarterly* 78, no. 4 (2021): 617–652.

50. Richard M. Swiderski, *Anthrax: A History* (Jefferson, NC: McFarland, 2004), 88, and Anthony Karabanow MD, "Anthrax in Haiti," CRUDEM Foundation, Inc., January 31, 2012, http://crudem.org/anthrax-in-haiti/.

51. De Paroy was one of Saint-Domingue's richest planters, holding nearly seven hundred people in slavery by the 1770s. See Rafael De Bivar Marquese, "A Tale of Two Coffee Colonies: Environment and Slavery in Suriname and Saint-Domingue, ca. 1750–1790," *Comparative Studies in Society and History* (March 2022): 21–22. The De Paroy estate is labeled "LeGentille" on *Carte topographique de la région du Cap-Français et du Fort-Dauphin*, (1760).

52. Marc-Antoine Avalle, "Memoire instructifs des faits d'opposition et trouble apporté au maintien de l'execution de l'arret du conseil d'Etat du Roi du 27 nov 1779" (Limonade, 1780), ANOM 164APOM_LeGentilDeParoy.

53. See John Garrigus, *Before Haiti: Race and Citizenship in Saint-Domingue* (New York: Palgrave Macmillan, 2006), 40, 64–66, 83–86.

54. [Marc-Antoine] Avalle, "[Letter to Governor and Intendant]," November 20, 1776, ANOM 164APOM_LeGentilDeParoy.

55. Lizette, "Extrait des minutes du Siege royal du Cap Suplie humblement Lisette negresse demeurante à la Savanne de Limonade" (Cap Français, November 28, 1777), ANOM 164APOM_LeGentilDeParoy.

56. On the encounter with Kangal, see Avalle, "Relevé des noms des negres et negresses qui sont morts dans le courant de l'an 1776 sur les deux sucreries de M le Marquis de Paroy [with attached] 'Observation,'" ANOM 164APOM_LeGentilDeParoy; on Kangal's "prejudicial business," Avalle, "[Letter to Governor and Intendant]," November 20, 1776.

57. Avalle, "Relevé des noms des negres et negresses."

58. Avalle, "Relevé des noms des negres et negresses."

59. Caznau, "Dépositions qui ont été fait par les Negres ci-apres dénommées" (Limonade, October 20, 1776), ANOM 164APOM_LeGentilDeParoy.

60. My transcription from Caznau, "Depositions": "À fouturasse à blanc yo. Bouté dans savanne pou tormenté monde autant moi té ici yo tomenté moi yo chicanné, nous avons jourd'huy quai sa yo va faire moi."

61. Caznau, "Dépositions."

62. Avalle, "[Letter to Governor and Intendant]," November 20, 1776.

63. Avalle, "[Letter to Governor and Intendant]," November 20, 1776.

64. Lizette, "Extrait des minutes du Siege royal du Cap" (November 28, 1777).

65. For wealthy free planters of color in Limonade, see Stewart R. King, *Blue Coat or Powdered Wig: Free People of Color in Pre-Revolutionary Saint Domingue* (Athens: University of Georgia, 2001), 46–48, 144–145, 163, 174, 188, 222.

66. From 1770 to 1778, de Paroy and Avalle were involved in a violent feud with the agent of the neighboring estate over surveying errors that dated from the 1730s. Bitterness over this affair undoubtedly provided Lizette with many local allies for her case. See Avalle, "Extrait des minutes du Conseil d'Etat," October 31, 1778, ANOM 164APOM_LeGentilDeParoy.

67. Lizette, "Extrait des minutes du Siege royal" (November 28, 1777).

68. Avalle, "Relevé des noms des negres et negresses."

69. Conseil Supérieur de Cap Français, "Extrait des registres du Conseil superieur du Cap," February 5, 1779, ANOM 164APOM_LeGentilDeParoy.

70. Avalle, "Extrait des registres du Conseil d'Etat," October 31, 1778, ANOM 164APOM_LeGentilDeParoy; on authorship of the letter, see de

Paroy, "Copie d'une lettre à mon fils le Vte," December 19, 1777, ANOM 164APOM_LeGentilDeParoy.

71. Conseil des depêches, "Dispositif de l'arret du Conseil des depêches rendu en faveur de M le Mis de Paroi le 27 9bre 1779 dans l'affaire du Negre Antoine," November 27, 1779, ANOM 164APOM_LeGentilDeParoy.

72. Lizette, "Extrait des minutes du Greffe du Siege royale de Cap," June 6, 1780, ANOM 164APOM_LeGentilDeParoy.

73. Avalle, "Memoire instructifs des faits d'opposition et trouble apporté au maintien de l'execution de l'arret du conseil d'Etat du Roi du 27 nov 1779," ANOM 164APOM_LeGentilDeParoy.

74. François Bordier, "Extrait des minutes du Greffe du Siege royale de Cap [Procès verbale de visite]," June 9, 1780, ANOM 164APOM_LeGentilDeParoy.

75. "Arrêt qui casse et annule celui du conseil supérieur du Cap du 5 février 1779, obtenu par la négresse Lizette, contre Guy Le Gentil, marquis de Paroy," 1779; ANOM COL A 17 F° 214; Avalle, "Memoire instructifs des faits d'opposition et trouble."

76. Avalle also arrested Bayonne, one of Kangal's fellow house slaves who was freed around the same time. A visitor to the de Paroy estate heard Bayonne trying to escape from a cell where he was being held and wrote down what Bayonne had told him. See Blanleuil, "[Report on interrogation of Bayonne]" (Limonade, July 3, 1777), ANOM 164APOM_LeGentilDeParoy.

77. "Arrêt qui casse et annule celui ... du 5 février 1779," cited in Frédéric Charlin, "La nature juridique de l'affranchissement de l'esclave dans les colonies françaises," in *Journées internationales de la Société d'histoire du droit: Droit naturel et droits de l'homme* (Grenoble, France: CERDHAP, 2009), 253.

78. "[Letter from Versailles to the Superior Conseil of Cap Français]," December 9, 1780, ANOM 164APOM_LeGentilDeParoy.

6. MAKANDAL'S GHOST

1. David P. Geggus, "Sugar and Coffee Production and the Shaping of Slavery in Saint Domingue," in *Cultivation and Culture: Labor and the Shaping of Slave Life in the Americas*, ed. Ira Berlin and Philip D. Morgan (Charlottesville: University of Virginia Press, 1993), 75; Keith Anthony Manuel, "Slavery, Coffee, and Family in a Frontier Society: Jérémie and Its Hinterland, 1780–1789" (MA thesis, University of Florida, 2005), 33; Pierre Joseph Laborie, *The Coffee Planter of Saint Domingo* (London: T. Cadell and W. Davies, 1798), 92.

2. Laborie, *Coffee Planter*, 164.

3. Charles Arthaud, ed., *Recherches, mémoires et observations sur les maladies épizootiques de Saint-Domingue* (Cap-François: Imprimerie royale, 1788), 44, 64–65.

4. On the estate deaths, see Philippe Haudrère, "Les tribulations de Paul Jean-François Le Mercier de la Rivière, ancien ordonnateur de la Marine, devenu habitant de Saint-Domingue, 1787–1791," in *L'esclave et les plantations: De l'établissement de la servitude à son abolition*, ed. Philippe Hrodĕj (Rennes, France: Presses universitaires de Rennes, 2019), 194; for de la Rivière's negotiations with Santo Domingo authorities about livestock trade, see Jean-Baptiste de Tastes de Lilancourt, Joseph-Alexandre Le Brasseur, and Chevalier De La Rivière, "Pièces concernant les négociations entreprises . . . par le chevalier de La Rivière en vue d'obtenir à nouveau la liberté d'importation des bestiaux espagnols," August 1781, ANOM $F3\_79$ folios 162–174.

5. Julien-François Duchemin de L'Étang, *Gazette de médecine pour les colonies* (Cap Français, Saint-Domingue: Imprimerie royale du Cap, 1778), 5–6.

6. Duchemin de L'Étang, *Gazette de médecine*, 10–11.

7. Alexandre de Vincent de Mazade and François Barbé de Marbois, "Lettre de MM. de Vincent et de Marbois au sujet de l'affaire du sieur Lejeune et du régime de l'esclavage," August 29, 1788, ANOM F3 90, folios 258–268, folio 258.

8. Cappé retired from the army in 1767 and moved to Marmelade to develop the land owned by his wife, an island-born woman named Laurignac. See Charles François Pichot de Kerdisien-Trémais, "No1 Cappé. Précis de la conduite tenue et des excés commis par M. Cappé envers l'habitation Trémais," [undated], ANOM E 62, folio 1 r; the land was marked "Corail" in the 1779 manuscript map by Laurent François Le Noir Rouvray, *Chemins de St Domingue (Soufrière; Marmelade)*, ANOM 15DFC0107B; the Laurignac farm is also visible on the 1760 manuscript map *Carte topographique de la région du Cap-Français et du Fort-Dauphin*, Bibliothèque nationale de France, département Cartes et plans, GE SH 18 PF 150 DIV 2 P 8.

9. See the second of Trémais's documents about Cappé, Charles François Pichot de Kerdisien-Trémais, "Mémoire sur la conduite du S. Cappé," June 25, 1780, ANOM E 62, folio 2 r; for the path; 10b r for the sugar syrup.

10. On the town of Gonaïves, see Moreau de Saint-Méry, *Description topographique*, 2:110; the journey from Marmelade to Cap Français was 12 French leagues or 30 miles; from Marmelade to Gonaïves, 14 French leagues or 35 miles. Moreau de Saint-Méry, *Description*, 1:274.

11. Trémais, "No1 Cappé. Précis de la conduite," folios 2 and 3.

12. Trémais assumed control of his wife's plantation in 1769, so these deaths occurred in the early 1770s. See Trémais, "No1 Cappé. Précis de la conduite," folios 4–6; on Trémais's career, see Michel Roberge, "Biography— PICHOT DE QUERDISIEN TRÉMAIS, CHARLES-FRANÇOIS," in vol. 4 *Dictionary of Canadian Biography* (Toronto: University of Toronto/ Université Laval, 1979), http://www.biographi.ca/en/bio/pichot_de_querdisien_tremais_charles_francois_4E.html.

13. Trémais, "Mémoire sur la conduite," folios 10 and 11.
14. Trémais, "No1 Cappé. Précis de la conduite," folios 6–8.
15. Trémais, "Mémoire sur la conduite," folio 4.
16. Trémais, "Mémoire sur la conduite," folios 7–8.
17. Trémais also never mentioned his first wife's name, referring to her only as the widow Romieu. She died soon after their marriage in 1769, and Trémais married Marie-Elizabeth Lamarenx. See Pierre Force, *Wealth and Disaster: Atlantic Migrations from a Pyrenean Town in the Eighteenth and Nineteenth Centuries* (Baltimore: Johns Hopkins University Press, 2016), 38.
18. Trémais, "Mémoire sur la conduite," folio 7.
19. John Thornton, "Cannibals, Witches, and Slave Traders in the Atlantic World," *William and Mary Quarterly* 60 (April 2003), 278; Wyatt MacGaffey, *Art and Healing of the Bakongo, Commented by Themselves: Minkisi from the Laman Collection* (Bloomington: Indiana University Press, 1991), 9.
20. Some colonists described these ceremonies as a form of "magnetism," referring to the techniques of Anton Mesmer, recently imported from France. See Moreau de Saint-Méry, *Description*, 274–275.
21. Gabriel Debien, "Assemblées nocturnes d'esclaves. La Marmelade, 1786," *Annales historiques de la Révolution française* 44, no. 208 (April-June 1972), 269, 278–279.
22. Debien, "Assemblées nocturnes," 279–280. This was probably owned by the brother of Judge Jean-Baptiste Estève; see this marronage report Saint-Domingue, *Affiches américaines*, July 15, 1767, http://www.marronnage.info/fr/document.php?id=1991. Locations for these events on Map 6.1 are approximate.
23. Gressier de la Jalousière, "Extrait d'une déclaration faite par le Sr Gressier de la Jalousière, habitant à la Marmelade, et remise à Mr Baratte, habitant du même quartier, du 26 mai 1786," *Revue de l'histoire des colonies françaises*, 1929, 72–74.
24. Debien, "Assemblées nocturnes," 280.
25. Trémais, "No1 Cappé. Précis de la conduite," folio 4 r, claims that a Sieur de la Jalousière was Cappé's bookkeeper (*économe*) in 1780.
26. M. Thomas J. Desch-Obi, *Fighting for Honor: The History of African Martial Art Traditions in the Atlantic World* (Columbia: University of South Carolina Press, 2008), 143–150; Moreau de Saint-Méry, *Description*, 53, describes the sticks and how enslaved men used them. Gressier, "Extrait d'une déclaration," 74.
27. Philippe Haudrère, "Les tribulations de Paul Jean-François Le Mercier de la Rivière, ancien ordonnateur de la Marine, devenu habitant de Saint-Domingue, 1787–1791," in *L'esclave et les plantations: De l'établissement de la servitude à son abolition*, ed. Philippe Hrodĕj (Rennes, France: Presses

universitaires de Rennes, 2019), 187–208. The location shown in Map 6.1 is approximate.

28. Nicolas-Louis François de Neufchâteau, "Magnétisme proscrit à S. Domingue parmi les nègres," in *Causes célèbres, curieuses et intéressantes, de toutes les cours souveraines du royaume, avec les jugemens qui les ont décidées,* ed. Nicolas Toussaint LeMoyne Des Essarts, vol. 144 (Paris: Nyon, 1786), 61–65.

29. Moreau de Saint-Méry, *Description,* 272, says Marmelade parish had seven thousand slaves.

30. Nicolas-Louis François de Neufchâteau, "[Instructions to arrest Kingué]," September 16, 1785, AN AP27/ Neufchâteau 12, dossier 2.

31. Lemay, "[Letter about Marie Kingué]," September 17, 1785, AN AP27/ Neufchâteau 12, dossier 2.

32. Lemay, "[Letter about Marie Kingué]." Kingué's locations on Map 6.1 are approximate.

33. John K. Thornton, "'I Am the Subject of the King of Kongo': African Political Ideology and the Haitian Revolution," *Journal of World History* 4 (1993): 181–214, 193.

34. James Sweet, "Research Note: New Perspectives on Kongo in Revolutionary Haiti," *The Americas: A Quarterly Review of Latin American History* 74, no. 1 (January 2017): 94; Louis-Narcisse Baudry Des Lozières, *Second voyage à la Louisiane: Faisant suite au premier de l'auteur de 1794 à 1798,* 2 vols. (Paris: Charles, 1803), 2:130.

35. Nicolas-Louis François de Neufchâteau, "Lettres au sujet de plaintes contre une sorcière noire, Marie-Catherine ou Kingué, 1785," AP27/ Neufchâteau 12, dossier 2, AN Pierrefitte-sur-Seine.

36. Nicolas Louis François de Neufchâteau, "[Instructions to arrest Kingué]," September 16, 1785, AN AP27/ Neufchâteau 12, dossier 2.

37. Anon, "[Letter about Marie Kingué]," September 3, 1785, AN AP27/ Neufchâteau 12, dossier 2; Neufchâteau, "[Instructions to arrest Kingué]."

38. Chevalier de Dugrès, "Mémoire de M Chailleau, et du certificat du lieutenant de Roy du Cap," 1783, ANOM Col. E 68.

39. Neufchâteau, "Lettres . . . contre une sorcière noire."

40. Anon, "[Letter about Marie Kingué]."

41. Chevalier de Dugrès, "Mémoire de M Chailleau" and Guillaume-Léonard de Bellecombe, "Lettre de M. de Bellecombe," both in ANOM Col. E 68. The location of Chailleau's estate in Map 6.1 is approximate.

42. Anon, "[Letter about Marie Kingué]."

43. Anon, "[Letter about Marie Kingué]."

44. Lemay, "[Letter about Marie Kingué]."

45. M. L. E. Moreau de Saint-Méry, *Loix et constitutions des colonies françoises de l'amérique sous le vent* (Paris: Chez l'auteur, 1784), 6:655–67.

46. Anon, "[Letter about Marie Kingué]."
47. Lemay, "[Letter about Marie Kingué]."
48. Both quotes from Neufchâteau, "Lettres au sujet de plaintes contre une sorcière noire."
49. Lemay, "[Letter about Marie Kingué]."
50. Lejeune's location on Map 6.1 is approximate, but details are shown in Dumoutier, arpenteur du roi, [Plan des terres du quartier de Plaisance, île de St. Domingue, entre le quartier des Gonaïves et la Grande Rivière de Plaisance], 1788, manuscript map, Bibliothèque nationale de France, département Cartes et plans, GE C-9250.
51. Lejeune, "[Maroon notice]," *Affiches américaines*, May 8, 1781, http://www.marronnage.info/fr/document.php?id=5958.
52. "[Maroon notice]," *Affiches américaines*, November 20, 1782, http://www.marronnage.info/fr/document.php?id=6607.
53. Jean-Baptiste Julien Busson, "Addition continuation dinformation [Allard Belin]," March 27, 1788, FR ANOM COL E 274 bis, ark:/61561/up424qklnlq; Nicolas Lejeune fils, "Mémoire adressé à MM les administrateurs de St Domingue par Nas Lejeune fils habitant à Plaisance. Au Cap le 27 mars 1788," May 27, 1788, ANOM F3 90, folios 202–206, folio 202 *r*; on poisonings of white employees, see Nicolas Lejeune père, "Requête dintervention," May 21, 1788, ANOM COL E 274 bis, folios 107–142; folio 110.
54. "[Maroon notice]," *Affiches américaines*, April 9, 1783.
55. "[Maroon notice]," *Affiches américaines*, April 9 and 30, 1783.
56. "[Maroon notice]," *Affiches américaines*, April 9, 1783.
57. Nicolas Lejeune fils, "Mémoire adressé à MM les administrateurs de St Domingue par Nas Lejeune fils habitant à Plaisance," May 27, 1788, ANOM F3 90, folio 202 *v*.
58. Moreau de Saint-Méry, *Loix*, 6:370.
59. Quote from Lejeune fils, "Mémoire adressé à MM les administrateurs," folio 203 *v*; on the drought, see Lejeune père, "Requête d'intervention," May 21, 1788, ANOM COL E 274 bis, folios 107–143, folio 110; on Lejeune's food expenses, see Jean-Baptiste Julien Busson, "Addition continuation d'information [Allard Belin]," March 27, 1788, ANOM COL E 274 bis, 4.
60. "[Maroon notice]," *Affiches américaines*, June 23, 1784.
61. "Negres marrons entrés à la geole," *Supplément aux Affiches américaines*, October 4, 1786.
62. "Nègres marrons entrés à la geole," *Supplément Affiches américaines*, March 24, 1787.
63. The white informants, including the former overseer, claimed that these two died of poison, like so many others. Busson, "Information," March 20, 1788, FR ANOM COL E 274 bis, folios 46–48.

64. Jean-Baptiste Julien Busson, "Information," March 20, 1788, ANOM COL E 274 bis, folios 50–51.

65. Testimony of Jean Chaussepied, the overseer, in Busson, "Information," folio 47; Jean Baptiste Louis Augustin Couet de Montarand, "Procès verbale de transporte de M. Couet de Monteran sur l'habitation du S Lejeune," March 10, 1788, ANOM COL E 274 bis, folios 9–11.

66. Vincent and Marbois, "Lettre de MM. de Vincent et de Marbois au sujet de l'affaire du sieur Lejeune et du régime de l'esclavage," August 29, 1788, ANOM F3 90, folios 258–268, folio 258 v.

67. Lejeune fils, "Mémoire adressé à MM les administrateurs," folio 203 v.

68. Testimony of Darius, in Busson, "Information," folio 51 r.

69. Busson, "Information," unlabeled recto between 48 and 49; veterinarian Jean Lompagieu Lapole found it did not harm animals; see his *Observations relatives à la santé des animaux ou Essai sur leurs maladies* (Cap Français, Saint-Domingue: Serviere, 1788), 289. Physician Charles Arthaud did his own tests and concurred; see his *Recherches*, 212–214.

70. Lejeune fils, "Mémoire pour MM. les administrateurs," folio 203 v.

71. Jean-Baptiste Julien Busson, "Proces Verbal de transport et contenant la declaration de quelques des negres de l'habitation le Jeune," March 9, 1788, ANOM COL E 274 bis; Lejeune fils, "Mémoire adressé à MM les administrateurs," folio 203 v.

72. Testimony of Darius, in Busson, "Information," March 20, 1788, f. 51 v.

73. Busson, "Répétition par forme d'information des 14 esclaves du Sr Lejeune," March 19, 1788, f. 38 v.

74. Busson, "Répétition par forme d'information," f. 39v.

75. Moreau de Saint-Méry, *Loix*, 6:655–667.

76. Maurice Begouën Demeaux, *Mémorial dune famille du Havre. Stanislas Foäche, 1737–1806: négociant de Saint-Domingue* (Paris: Société française dhistoire doutre-mer, 1982), 109.

77. Gabriel Debien, *Les esclaves aux Antilles françaises, XVII–XVIII siècles* (Basse-Terre: Société d'histoire de la Guadeloupe, 1974), 485.

78. Moreau de Saint-Méry, *Loix*, 6:918–928.

79. Moreau de Saint-Méry, *Loix*, 6:655 and 6:928.

80. Jean Baptiste Louis Augustin Couet de Montarand, "PV de transport de M Coues de Montarand chez le Sr Dudemaine," March 13, 1788, ANOM COL E 274 bis.

81. Cossié, "Mémoire par les habitants de Plaisance," March 23, 1788, ANOM F3 90, folios 197–187.

82. Malick W. Ghachem, *The Old Regime and the Haitian Revolution* (New York: Cambridge University Press, 2012), 200–201.

7. THE HAITIAN REVOLUTION BEGINS

1. Jean-Louis Donnadieu calls this the Manquets plantation, but I use the name Noé, which appears on many contemporary maps. This chapter is deeply indebted to Donnadieu's publications, listed below.

2. Karen Bourdier, "Vie quotidienne et conditions sanitaires sur les grandes habitations sucrières du nord de Saint-Domingue à la veille de l'insurrection d'août 1791" (Université de Pau, 2005), 299.

3. Médéric-Louis-Elie Moreau de Saint-Méry, *Description topographique, physique, civile, politique et historique de la partie française de l'isle Saint-Domingue*, vol. 1 (Philadelphia: Chez l'auteur, 1797), 640.

4. Jean-Louis Donnadieu, "Entre Gascogne et Saint-Domingue: Le Comte Louis-Pantaléon de Noé, grand propriétaire créole et aristocrate gascon (1728–1816)" (doctorate thesis, Université de Pau, 2006), 370, cites an August 2, 1782, letter from Bayon de Libertat; in 1791, the Noé estate had 345 slaves, and probably around 400 in the 1770s, according to Donnadieu, "Jean-Jacques et Hippolyte, deux commandeurs meneurs de grève, ou comment sonner l'alarme à la sucrerie des Manquets (Saint-Domingue, 1782)," *Transatlantica. Revue d'études américaines*, no. 2 (2012): 3, 10.

5. Jean-Louis Donnadieu, *Un grand seigneur et ses esclaves, le comte de Noé entre Antilles et Gascogne, 1728–1816* (Toulouse, France: Presses universitaires du Mirail, 2009), 297; Jean-Louis Donnadieu, "Entre Gascogne et Saint-Domingue," 366, letter of May 19, 1782, and 356, letter of December 2, 1779.

6. Philippe Girard, *Toussaint Louverture: A Revolutionary Life* (New York: Basic, 2016), 54.

7. Donnadieu, "Entre Gascogne," 356, letter of December 2, 1779.

8. Donnadieu, "Entre Gascogne," 361–362, letter of March 10, 1781.

9. Donnadieu, "Entre Gascogne," 366, letter of May 19, 1782; for depletion of the Santo Domingo herd, see Antonio Sanchez Valverde, *Idea del valor de la Isla Española, y utilidades, que de ella puede sacar su monarquia* (Madrid: P. Marin, 1785), 62; for the aborted invasion of Jamaica, see Trevor Burnard and John D. Garrigus, *The Plantation Machine: Atlantic Capitalism in French Saint-Domingue and British Jamaica* (Philadelphia: University of Pennsylvania Press, 2016), 215–218.

10. Donnadieu, "Entre Gascogne," 367, letter of May 9, 1782.

11. Donnadieu, "Entre Gascogne," 367, 369, letter of May 27, 1782.

12. Donnadieu, "Entre Gascogne," 366, 368, letter of May 19, 1782.

13. Donnadieu, "Entre Gascogne," 370, letter of August 2, 1782.

14. Donnadieu, "Entre Gascogne," 366–367, letter of May 19, 1782; the number 140 comes from research showing that roughly 40 percent of the people enslaved on a sugar plantation worked in the fields.

15. Donnadieu, "Entre Gascogne," 366–367, letter of May 19, 1782.
16. Donnadieu, "Entre Gascogne," 367, letter of May 27, 1782.
17. Donnadieu, "Entre Gascogne," 368; letter of August 2, 1782.
18. David P. Geggus, *The Haitian Revolution: A Documentary History* (Indianapolis: Hackett, 2014), 25–28, cites Archives Nationales, Paris, 505 Mi 86 and 107 AP 128, Galliffet notebook. The locations of the striking plantations shown on Map 7.1 are taken from René Phelipeau, Plan de la plaine du Cap François en l'Isle St. Domingue, rédigé d'après les dernieres opérations géométriques des ingénieurs du roy, (Paris, 1786).
19. Geggus, *Haitian Revolution*, 26.
20. Geggus, *Haitian Revolution*, 28; on continuing deaths, see Geggus, "Les esclaves de la Plaine du Nord à la veille de la révolution française Partie III," *Revue de la société d'histoire de géographie d'Haïti*, no. 144 (September 1984): 15–44, 34, and Karen Bourdier, *Vie quotidienne et conditions sanitaires sur les grandes habitations sucrières du nord de Saint-Domingue* (Indes Savantes, 2019), 246–250.
21. Donnadieu, "Entre Gascogne," 370, August 2, 1782.
22. Donnadieu, "Entre Gascogne," 367, letter of May 27, 1782.
23. Donnadieu, "Entre Gascogne," 370, letter of August 2, 1782.
24. Donnadieu, "Entre Gascogne," 374, letter of October 8, 1783.
25. Today, a small Haitian town named Dutty sits on the old Dutilh site. US Army Map Service, *Marmelade (Haiti) Sheet 5574, Series E732*, 1:50,000 (Washington DC: US Army Map Service, 1963).
26. See, for example, Crystal Nicole Eddins, *Rituals, Runaways, and the Haitian Revolution: Collective Action in the African Diaspora*, Cambridge Studies on the African Diaspora (Cambridge: Cambridge University Press, 2021), 277.
27. Sources claimed that Boukman was enslaved on the Clément estate. The Dutilh/Clément family connection is documented in "CLÉMENT frères », du Dauphiné à la Martinique et à Marseille, négociants puis habitants à Saint Domingue, descendants réfugiés à Philadelphie," *Généalogie et histoire de la Caraibe*, 2018, http://www.ghcaraibe.org/articles/2018-art42.pdf.
28. Donnadieu, "Entre Gascogne," 375–376, undated letter from late 1783 or early 1784.
29. Donnadieu, "Entre Gascogne," 378, April 15, 1786.
30. Donnadieu, "Entre Gascogne," 379, April 15, 1786; in the letter in which Bayon told Noé he forced the slaves to accept his orders, he noted that none of the mills on the local river had enough water to run.
31. Donnadieu, "Entre Gascogne," 381, June 1787.
32. Gabriel Debien, "Les débuts de la révolution à Saint-Domingue, vus des plantations Bréda," in *Études Antillaises* (Paris: Armand Colin, 1956), 163.

33. Debien, "Les débuts," 167.
34. Donnadieu, "Jean-Jacques et Hippolyte," 10.
35. John D. Garrigus, "Vincent Ogé Jeune (1757–91): Social Class and Free Colored Mobilization on the Eve of the Haitian Revolution," *Americas* 68 (July 2011): 33–62, 54; "Procuration à MM. Grenouillaud et Chavanne," October 30, 1789, Archives Départementales de la Gironde, Collection Chatillon 61J 15, piece 21; Chavanne and Castaing, "Lettre aux messieurs du comité colonial séant au Cap," October 30, 1789, Collection Chatillon 61J 15, piece 24, Archives départementales de la Gironde; on Chavanne's family, see Stewart R. King, *Blue Coat or Powdered Wig: Free People of Color in Pre-Revolutionary Saint Domingue* (Athens: University of Georgia, 2001), 221; on Chavanne's work in the cattle trade, see Antoine Dalmas, *Histoire de la révolution de Saint-Domingue depuis le commencement des troubles*, vol. 1, (Paris: Mame frères, 1814), 71.
36. John D. Garrigus, "Vincent Ogé Jeune (1757–91)": 33–62.
37. Martin-Ollivier Bocquet de Frévent, "Extrait des minutes du Conseil Supérieur du Cap" (CARAN Dxxv58/ 574, January 1791).
38. See Conseil Supérieur de Cap Français, *Arrêt de Conseil Supérieur du Cap contre le nommé Ogé jeune & ses Complices* (Cap Français, Saint-Domingue: Imprimerie Royale, 1791).
39. See ANOM on-line research site IREL; http://anom.archivesnationales.culture.gouv.fr/caomec2/; Grande-Rivière, Dondon, Marmelade, and Limonade.
40. Their racial category and home parish were identified by Ogé's brother Jacques. Antoine-Etienne Ruotte and Marie-François Pourcheresse de Vertières, "Ogé, Jacques, dit Jacot, quarteron libre, habitant de Saint-Domingue 1791," ANOM COL E 325, folio 2. It isn't clear if Quiquo Lapeyre was married, but he and Marguerite Déclain had a free Black son, Léon, who was twelve years old in 1790; see Conseil Supérieur de Cap Français, *Arrêt de Conseil Supérieur du Cap contre le nommé Ogé jeune & ses Complices* (Cap Français, Saint-Domingue: Imprimerie Royale, 1791), 21.
41. On October 18, 1784, "Ambois Declin" served as godfather for a free Black girl in Grande-Rivière; his brother François, also indicted in the revolt, presented his son Augustin Remy for baptism in the parish on February 25, 1784; ANOM, DPPC, État civil, Grande-Rivière, 1784.
42. Debien, "Les débuts de la révolution," 157, 158.
43. Ruotte and Pourcheresse de Vertières, "Ogé, Jacques, dit Jacot," 1791, ANOM COL E 325; Jacques Ogé's testimony is critiqued in Jean-Philippe Garran de Coulon, *Rapport sur les troubles de Saint-Domingue, fait au nom de la Commission des colonies, des Comités de salut public, de législation et de marine, réunis* (Paris: Imp. nationale, 1797), 2:59–62.

44. For Marc Chavanne's marriage, see ANOM DPPC, État civil, L'Acul, December 18, 1780. Marie-Marthe Chavanne married Romaine Poisson. See ANOM DPPC, État civil, L'Acul, July 3, 1782.

45. Jean-Baptiste Millet et al., *Discours fait a l'Assemblée nationale, le 3 novembre 1791* (Paris: Imprimerie nationale, 1791), 2.

46. David P. Geggus, *Haitian Revolutionary Studies* (Bloomington: Indiana University Press, 2002), 84–86.

47. Millet, *Discours*, 2; the Chabaud plantation was located where the Soufrière River joined the main Limbé valley; see René Phelipeau, *Plan de la plaine du Cap François en l'Isle St. Domingue* (Paris, 1786).

48. See the Grieu estate marked on CARAN, "Fonds Rochambeau; IV- Fonds de documentation cartographique. 135AP/4." https://www.siv.archives-nationales.culture.gouv.fr/siv/media/FRAN_IR_004312/d_57/FRAN_0257_0774_L.

49. Garran de Coulon, *Rapport sur les troubles*, 2:1, and Millet, *Discours*, 2–3, say they came from the Flaville plantation, which is labeled on the Phelipeau 1786 map of the Cap Français plain as the Héron de la Filière estate; the confusion over these names stems from a marriage between Elisabeth Nogérée de la Filière, the stepdaughter of Elisabeth-Antoinette Héron, and Marc-Antoine Guillaumeau de Flaville; see the lawsuit settled in 1779, "Arrêt de surséance en faveur de Flaville, ancien lieutenant de vaisseaux, et des héritiers Nogérée, copropriétaires d'une moitié d'habitation située à Saint-Domingue, dans le quartier de l'Accul," 1779, ANOM COL A 16 F° 284, ark:/61561/ka455wsqwwl.

50. Olivier Gliech, "The de Grieu Family in Saint-Domingue," September 13, 2021, personal material, cites ANOM F3 267 (folio 311 et s.).

51. Garran de Coulon, *Rapport sur les troubles*, 2:212.

52. Dalmas, *Histoire de la révolution de Saint-Domingue*, 1:116–20.

53. David Geggus generously shared with me a digital photograph of Baron, *Tableau général des habitations en sucrerie qui forment les paroisses de la Petite Anse, Limonade, et Quartier Morin*, n.d., manuscript, n.d., AN, Fonds de la Marine, 6 JJ 60/61; Geggus, *Haitian Revolutionary Studies*, 85, clarifies the confusion between Morne Rouge and the Bois Caïman ceremony. The Haitian government has a site commemorating Bois Caïman on the former LeNormant plantation in Morne Rouge; see the map in Paul Clammer's excellent guidebook *Haiti*, 2nd ed. (Bradt Travel Guides, 2016), 185.

54. Dalmas, *Histoire*, 1:117.

55. Robin Law, "La cérémonie du Bois Caïman et le 'pacte de sang' dahoméen," in *L'insurrection des esclaves de Saint-Domingue (22–23 août 1791)*, ed. Laënnec Hurbon (Paris: Karthala, 2000), 131–147; Geggus, *Haitian Revolutionary Studies*, 86, describes the literature on Boukman's presence.

56. Garran de Coulon, *Rapport sur les troubles*, 2:212–213; Garran and subsequent historians refer to the Clément estate, but the 1786 Phelipeau map and others label it as Dutilh.

57. Garran de Coulon, *Rapport*, 2:212; the other leader was a man named Auguste, from the estate labeled Héron de la Filière on Phelipeau's 1786 map.

58. Pierre Force specifies that the rebels first went to the Trémais warehouse on the river and shot a carpenter there but didn't kill him. See his *Wealth and Disaster: Atlantic Migrations from a Pyrenean Town in the Eighteenth and Nineteenth Centuries* (Baltimore: Johns Hopkins University Press, 2016), 89.

59. Millet, *Discours*, 3–4; Jeremy D. Popkin, *Facing Racial Revolution: Eyewitness Accounts of the Haitian Insurrection* (Chicago: University of Chicago Press, 2007), 55, points out that colonists later executed Jean-Jacques for being involved in Dumenil's death; Garran-Coulon, *Rapport sur les troubles*, 2:213.

60. Popkin, *Facing Racial Revolution*, 54.

61. Translation from Popkin, *Facing Racial Revolution*, 52–53.

62. Jacques de Cauna, "Autour de la thèse du complot: Franc-maçonnerie, révolution et contre-révolution à Saint-Domingue, 1789–1791," in *La Franc-maçonnerie au siècle des lumières: Europe-Amériques*, ed. Charles Porset and Cécile Révauger (Bordeaux 3, 2006), 289–310, and Girard, *Toussaint Louverture*, 109–113.

63. Popkin, *Facing Racial Revolution*, 52–53.

64. Fick, "Saint-Domingue Slave Insurrection," 688, spells it Pillât. For poisoning charges against people enslaved by Pillat in 1758, see Sébastien Jacques Courtin, "Mémoire sommaire sur les prétendus pratiques magiques et empoisonnements," ANOM, F3 88, folio 250r.

65. Fick, *Making of Haiti*, 105; Fick, "Saint-Domingue Slave Insurrection," 687. The location of Belin plantation shown in Map 7.2 is taken from René Phelipeau, *Plan de la plaine du Cap François* (Paris, 1786).

66. Dalmas, *Histoire*, 1:122–123; Fick lays out the chronology in "Saint-Domingue Slave Insurrection," 691.

67. Millet et al., *Discours*, 5. The Philibert story may be apocryphal. Dalmas, who worked with Odelucq, says he was killed by a rebel named Mathurin. Dalmas, *Histoire*, 1:123; Fick, "Saint-Domingue Slave Insurrection," 691, sides with Millet.

68. Laurent Dubois, *Avengers of the New World: The Story of the Haitian Revolution* (Belknap, 2004), 112; Fick, *Making of Haiti*, 108.

69. Girard, *Toussaint Louverture*, 114–115.

70. Lejeune attended a parish political meeting less than a year before the uprising; Citoyens de Plaisance, "Extrait des Archives de l'Assemblée provinciale du Nord" (Imprimerie de l'Assemblée provinciale du Nord, November 13, 1790), ANOM 87 Miom 83.

71. Fick, "Saint-Domingue Slave Insurrection," 689.
72. Fick, "Saint-Domingue Slave Insurrection," 699.
73. For Jean-Jacques, see Popkin, *Facing Racial Revolution*, 55; for Boukman, see Fick, "Saint-Domingue Slave Insurrection," 704.
74. Laurent Dubois and John D. Garrigus, *Slave Revolution in the Caribbean, 1789–1804: A Brief History with Documents*, 2nd ed. (New York: Bedford St. Martin's, 2017), 87–89; see the summary of these positions in Jeremy D. Popkin, "A Haitian Revolutionary Manifesto? New Perspectives on the 'Letter of Jean-François, Biassou, and Belair,'" *Slavery & Abolition* 43, no. 1 (January 2022): 12–15.
75. Dubois and Garrigus, *Slave Revolution*, 103–104.
76. Popkin, "Haitian Revolutionary Manifesto?" 10–11.
77. Popkin, *Concise History*, 52–53.
78. Popkin, *Concise History*, 54.
79. See the detailed account in Jeremy D. Popkin, *You Are All Free: The Haitian Revolution and the Abolition of Slavery* (New York: Cambridge University Press, 2010), 189–245.

CONCLUSION

1. Laurent Dubois, *Avengers of the New World: The Story of the Haitian Revolution* (Cambridge, MA: Belknap Press of Harvard University Press, 2004), 97, cites Mossut to Galliffet, September 19, 1791, AN 107 AP 128, folder 3.
2. Randy M. Browne, *Surviving Slavery in the British Caribbean* (Philadelphia: University of Pennsylvania Press, 2017), 3; Carolyn E. Fick, *The Making of Haiti: The Saint Domingue Revolution from Below* (Knoxville: University of Tennessee Press, 1990), 75; David P. Geggus, *The Haitian Revolution: A Documentary History* (Indianapolis: Hackett, 2014), 15–35.
3. Browne, *Surviving Slavery*, 190.
4. Burnard, *Mastery, Tyranny, and Desire*, 155.
5. Médéric-Louis-Elie Moreau de Saint-Méry, *Description topographique, physique, civile, politique et historique de la partie française de l'isle Saint-Domingue*, vol. 1 (Philadelphia: Chez l'auteur, 1797), 48; on West African blood oaths in Saint-Domingue, see Robin Law, "La cérémonie du Bois Caïman et le 'pacte de sang' dahoméen," in *L'insurrection des esclaves de Saint-Domingue (22–23 août 1791)*, ed. Laënnec Hurbon (Paris: Karthala, 2000), 131–147. David P. Geggus, "Haitian Voodoo in the Eighteenth Century: Language, Culture, Resistance," *Jahrbuch für Geschichte von Staat, Wirtschaft und Gesellschaft Lateinamerikas* 28 (1991): 21–51; p41 analyzes a chant at this ceremony and reveals that it is in Congo language. Nevertheless, Geggus notes that the ceremony was still likely guided by West African ideas.

6. "Saint-Domingue on the Eve of the Haitian Revolution," in *The World of the Haitian Revolution*, ed. David P. Geggus and Norman Fiering (Bloomington: Indiana University Press, 2009), 3–20, 15.

7. Burnard, *Mastery, Tyranny, and Desire*, 252.

8. The document reads: "Et qu'il y a un secret parmi eux qui ne tend qu'à faire perir la colonie et que les blancs l'ignorent, et dont les negres libres sont la cause principalle, faisant jouer tous les ressorts pour augmenter leur nombre à fin d'être en état de faire face aux blancs en cas de besoin." See Louis Auguste Aymard et al., "Extrait des déclarations de Médor," May 26, 1757, ANOM, Col., F3 88, folio 212. The same phrase is found in a similar though not identical copy of this document in ANOM C9A Correspondance générale St Domingue, vol. 102, microfilm 5345, reel 91.

9. John D. Garrigus, *Before Haiti: Race and Citizenship in Saint-Domingue* (New York: Palgrave Macmillan, 2006), 141–170, especially 167–168.

10. Habitant de St Domingue, *Testament de mort d'Ogé et adresse de Pinchinat aux hommes de couleur* (Philadelphia: Parent, 1793), 3.

11. Marlene L. Daut, *Tropics of Haiti: Race and the Literary History of the Haitian Revolution in the Atlantic World, 1789–1865* (Liverpool: Liverpool UP, 2015), 4–5.

12. John K. Thornton, "'I Am the Subject of the King of Kongo': African Political Ideology and the Haitian Revolution," *Journal of World History* 4 (1993): 181–214.

13. Johnhenry Gonzalez, *Maroon Nation: A History of Revolutionary Haiti*, Yale Agrarian Studies (New Haven: Yale University Press, 2019); Laurent Dubois, *Haiti: The Aftershocks of History* (New York: Henry Holt, 2012); Jean Casimir, *The Haitians: A Decolonial History*, trans. Laurent Dubois (Chapel Hill: University of North Carolina Press, 2020).

14. Gonzalez, *Maroon Nation*, 16–18, 27–30.

Acknowledgments

I've been fortunate enough to publish three books with wonderful coauthors and coeditors. As enjoyable as those projects were, I was looking forward to writing this book as a solo project. Very happily, it has been anything but. More than any other book, I've written this one with the support of dozens of people. The most important of them is Susan Fletcher. Anyone who has read my other publications will notice her influence on my writing and ideas. We worked on these chapters daily, for months.

This book also owes its existence to David Geggus, Jeremy Popkin, Lynn Hunt, and Laurent Dubois, who inspired me with their scholarship and encouraged me to push my own research further. Trevor Burnard's patience allowed me to make Makandal part of our book *Plantation Machine*. The interpretation here replaces that earlier version. Conversations with Jim Sidbury and Philippe Girard over the years motivated me to write this account, which has benefited from their careful reading. French friends and colleagues have had a huge influence on my work, especially Anne Pérotin-Dumon, Dominique Rogers, and Gérard Lafleur. Thank you, Jane Landers, for asking me where the Clément plantation was located and forcing me to realize I had no idea where Boukman was enslaved! It was Jeremy Popkin who pointed me toward the 1786 Phelipeau map, while David Geggus generously shared his copy of the manuscript map that shows the location of Bois Caïman on the Choiseul plantation.

I wrote Chapters 2 and 3 at the National Humanities Center, and their librarians, especially Brooke Andrade, procured some of the maps and other digital sources that shaped my subsequent research. Laurent Dubois, Daphne Lamothe, Barry Gaspar, Todd Ochoa, and others participated in a very helpful seminar at the center, discussing an early version of Chapter 2. Thanks to Todd for introducing me to the literature on Congo religion.

Chapter 5 builds on ideas I first presented in "'Like an Epidemic One Could Only Stop with the Most Violent Remedies': African Poisons versus Livestock Disease in Saint Dominque, 1750-88," the *William & Mary Quarterly*, 78:4 (2021), 617–652.

This book was made possible in part by a grant from the Carnegie Corporation of New York. The statements made and views expressed are solely the responsibility of the author. As a Carnegie Fellow, I tried to write this book to advance scholarship while engaging a broad spectrum of readers. Elisabeth Cawthon, Dean of the University of Texas at Arlington (UTA) College of Liberal Arts, nominated me to represent UTA in the Carnegie competition. She, Antoinette Sol, and Scott Palmer helped me extend the generous Carnegie award over two years. Thanks to Andy Milson for including me on a research grant from UTA's College of Liberal Arts that helped consolidate my cartographic work on Saint-Domingue.

The UTA History Department has long heard about this project at our research brown-bag meetings. At one of those meetings, Christopher Malmberg, then a doctoral student, urged me to consider anthrax as a possible cause of sudden deaths in Saint-Domingue. Joshua Piker at the *William & Mary Quarterly* also challenged me to rethink my earlier theory about the cause of these deaths.

I presented the material that went into Chapters 4 and 5 at the Dallas Area Social History group, with very useful advice from attendees there, including Ed Countryman and Kathleen Wellman as well as my colleagues Andy Milson, Chris Morris,

Stephanie Cole, and David Lafevor. Alberto Ortiz-Diaz read a late draft of Chapter 4 and contributed discerning comments. A version of Chapter 5 benefited enormously from readers at the Early Americanists of Texas meeting in Austin. Thanks to Bob Olwell, Julie Hardwick, Jim Sidbury, Ron Johnson, Ed Countryman, and Cynthia Bouton, among others.

I've been very fortunate to have friends like Chris Conway and Desiree Henderson who shared and sustained my enthusiasm for this work. Chris and Antoinette Sol started this project many years ago by asking me to make a presentation at a UTA graduate conference about cultural constructions of resistance. Chris Hodson pushed my work forward by sending me his archival images of Makandal's interrogation and related documents. Julia Gaffield generously gave me her archival material on Vincent Ogé. Fredrik Thomasson shared innumerable materials and many ideas from his work on the Swedish West Indies. Because of COVID restrictions, I relied on fellow researchers in France to send me digital photos. Emmanuelle Lizé, Kamil Perrussel, Jakob Burnham, and Dhouha Djerbi were lifesavers in this regard. Oliver Gliech provided me with his data on a key Limbé family involved in the August 1791 revolt.

My editor, Kathleen McDermott of Harvard University Press, urged me to reframe my evidence about Médor and Makandal as a history of slave resistance. Her suggestion made this book possible. Thanks to Ben Meader and Vincent Falardeau of Rhumb Line Maps for their excellent cartography.

Finally, this book is dedicated to my sweetheart, Susan, who made it come alive.

Index

Page numbers in italics refer to illustrations.

absinthe bâtarde, 51
Acul parish, 66, 67, 104, 140, 145, *146*, 150, 153, 150, 154, 157, 158, *159*, *162*, 177
Agnès (enslaved woman in Delavaud household), 15, 44–47
American Revolutionary War, 148, 152
Angelique (enslaved woman in Cap Français), 40
Angélique (enslaved woman on Delaviviaud estate), 43–44
anthrax: animal management practices and, 108; Baradat on dissections of infected animals, 109; Bréda estate and, 103–104; coffee plantations and, 120; consumption of, 18, 110–111, 172; food management practices and, 109–111; humans and, 105–106, 109–110; knowledge of, 100–101; map of outbreaks of, *102*; Marmelade parish and, 123; mechanism of, 105; misconstrued as poisoning, 99–101, *102*, 103–104, 106–109, 124; modern-day Haiti and, 112; response of enslaved people in Marmelade to, 129–130; as source of intentional poison, 108, 143; strain of, 111–112; *tassau*, 110
Archival records, 3, 4, 10, 58, 120, 190n10, 201n46, 202n47
Assam (enslaved woman on Valette estate): livestock disease on Valette estate and, 66–67; role of on estate, 64, *65*, 67, 70; search for medicine of, *65*, 68–70, 75; story in testimony about being urged to kill enslaver, 70–71; suspicion of, 2, 70; swelling disease on Valette plantation and, 67–68; testimony of, 2, 70–74, 173; torture of, 72–73
Assassin's Creed video game, 8
Avalle, Marc-Antoine, 113–119
Aymar, Louis August, 36

Baradat, Antoine, 51, 61, 107–109
Baudin, Philippe, 84
Bayon de Libertat (estate agent), 104, 147–150, 152–154, 166
Belhumeur (free associate of Kingué), 132–135
Belin sugar plantation, 159, 165
Biassou, Georges, 167–168

Black Jacobins, The (James), 8
blue vervain, 69
Bois Caïman ceremony, 161–162, 174, 218n54
Bonaparte, Napoleon, 169–170
Bongars plantation, 165
Bonnemain (enslaver from Les Perches), 49
Borel de Neuilly, Francois, 36
Boucard, François, 19
Boukman (Dutty): actions in Haitian Revolution and, 3, 164–166; Bois Caïman ceremony and, 162; community and revolt of, 12, 153; death of, 167; Dutty name origin, 153, 216n28; Jean-Jacques and, 153; Morne Rouge meeting and, 158–161
Boutin, Father, 23
branding, 21
Bréda Haut du Cap sugar plantation, 103–104, 142, 154
Brigitte (wife of Makandal), 78–79, 88, 92
Brinvilliers, Marquise de, 40–41
Brown, Vincent, 9, 11
Browne, Randy, 10–11, 172–173
Burnard, Trevor, 174–175

Cabeuil sugar estate, 151
Cadiz (free Black man in Soufrière), 84
calendas (dances), 24, 42, 54, 87, 127–128
Cap Français: community and, 18; disease in, 17; economic opportunities at market for slaves and people of color, 18; free population of color in, 16; Haitian Revolution and, 167; legal system and, 16, 21; livestock disease and, 31; map of, *16*; meat sales and, 18–19, 31; Petite Guinée (Little Africa) neighborhood, 21; Place d'Armes, 18–19; plantation economy and, 15–16; population of, 15; as slave trade center, 14, 17, 121
Cap Français Superior Council: appeals to Code Noir laws and, 4, 9, 16, 21, 98–100, 112–120, 135–137, 139–142, 175; Code Noir laws of 1785 and, 141; death sentences and, 60, 88; Jesuits and, 22, 74; Kangal's case and, 117–118; Lejeune case and, 140, 142; Lejeune overseer's murder and, 137; Trémais and, 126
Cappé, Pierre, 124, *125*, 126–128, 210n8
Carbon, André, 44–47, 53–54
Carbon, Gérard, 25–27, 44, 54, 187n50, 191n13
Carpentier, Alejo, 8
Carré plantation, 100–101
Casimir, Jean, 179
Cassarouy (plantation owner), 99
Catholic Church, 92. *See also* Fathers of Charity; Jesuits
Cautant, Jacques, 158, *159*, 160, 165
Le Cerf, 86
Chailleau, Antoine, 134, 136
charms (*gry*), 76
Chastenoy sugar plantation, 151
Chaussepied, Jean, 141
Chavanne, Jean-Baptiste, 116, 155–156, 176
Chavanne, Marc, 157–158
Chavanne, Marie-Marthe, 157–158
Chiron, Monsieur, 62–64
Choiseul plantation, 165

INDEX

Clément plantation, 216n28
Cléricy plantation, 165
Code Noir. *See* French slave laws
coffee plantations: anthrax and, 120; drivers on, 122–123; enslaved children and, 86; Haitian Revolution and, 165, 167; Kingué and, 133–134; life for slaves on, 14, 28; in Marmelade parish, 121–123; pictured, 29
Colas Jambes Coupées (Colas Cut Legs), 27–28
colonial courts, 4, 9, 16, 21, 98–100
Congo ritual practice: Christian symbols in, 91; communities sharing, 9, 75–76, 79, 85–86, 92–93, 174; Cuban Palo and, 91–92; Kingué and, 132–136; Minkisi and, 89–91; prenda judía minkisi, 92; punishment for ritual meetings and, 131–132; response to anthrax and, 129–130
Courtin, Sebastian, 60, 71–72, 74, 88–95, 201–202n47
Crillon family, 187n50
Cruon, Jean, 51
Cuban Palo, 91–92

Dainé (free Black man in Cap Français), 41
Daouin (slave in Les Perches), 42, 46, 51, 53, 108, 173, 175
Darius, Pierre, 141
Dau (slave on Galliffet plantation), 106–107, 175
Daut, Marlene, 177
Déclain, Amboise (Yamé), 157, 217n41
Declaration of the Rights of Man and Citizen, 155, 178
Delaborde, Raymond, 55–56, 67, 98

Delavaud, Augustine, 34–35, 42, 45–46, 48, 190n8
Delavaud, Philippe, 14, 28, 30, 33–36, 38, 42, 44–46
Delaviviaud, François, 43–44
Delaye, Pierre-Alexandre, 59–60
Delribal, 103–104
de Luna, Kathryn, 79–80
de Paroy, Marquis le Gentil, 112–113, 115–116
Dessalines, Jean-Jacques, 170, 179
Dessources (plantation owner), 99–100
d'Héricourt, Chevalier, 147
Diola (free Black man), 68, 75
diseases: in Cap Français, 17; innoculation against, 100, 103; livestock disease, 31–32, 95–96, 100–101; nkisi as part of ritual against, 90; scarlet fever, 41; smallpox, 17, 41, 100, 103; swelling disease and, 67–68, 86; tassau and, 18; yellow fever, 17. *See also* anthrax
driver role: autonomy of, 14–15; Cappé's accusations and, 126–128; coffee plantations and, 122–123; interaction with slaves and, 14; lifespan of, 26; Noé sugar plantation and, 147; resistance and, 27; risks of, 15; sugar plantations and, 26
drought, 97, 105, 109–110, 148, 152, 154
Duchemin de l'Etang, Julien-François, 123–124
Dudemaine, François, 134–135, 141
Dufresne, Jean-François (slave ship captain), 86, 200n34
Dufresne, Julien, 86, 200n33
Dufresne plantation, *81*, 86–87, 147

Dumenil (estate agent on Noé sugar plantation), 162
Dupaty plantation, 101
Duplessis (surveyor on Dufresne plantation), 87
Duquesnoy, Father (Jesuit), 23, 73–74
Dutilh, Jean, 153
Dutilh sugar plantation, 160, 162, 216n28

Eddins, Crystal, 6
enslaved people: ability to mobilize of, 143; accusations of magical weapons and, 130–131; children, 86; coffee plantations and, 14, 28; communities of resistance and, 11, 119–120, 143, 145, 161, 171, 174–175, 178; competition among, 173–174; Congo ritual practice community of, 75–76, 79, 92–93, 174; culture of torture of, 55–56; effect of Seven Years' War on, 30, 54; historical record and, 3–4; lifespans of, 26–27; livestock guardians, 27; origins of, 75–76; Paris and, 27; promise of manumission and, 38–39; punishment for ritual communities and, 131; remedies of, 129–130; skilled laborers/artisans, 27; sugar plantations and, 14, 25; West African, 58–60. *See also* poisoning investigations
Estève, Henry, 131
Estève, Jean-Baptiste, 98–100, 107, 129

faire diable ritual, 78–79, 91
Fanchon (hospitalière on LeBlondain estate), 60–61

Fathers of Charity, 107, 165
Ferou (slave in Les Perches), 42, 46
Fick, Carolyn, 173
Flaville plantation, 217n50
Food, 14, 18, 49, 138; chocolate, 106–107; insecurity of, 110, 111, 172; market gardening, 18, 59, 66, 124; meat, 18, 32, 54, 70, 110–111, 172; slave provisions, 31, 33, 54, 124, 149; smuggling of, 30–31, 97, 110; war and, 31, 54, 97, 110, 149, 172. *See also* drought
Fort Dauphin courts, 36–38, 51, 53
Fournier, Jean, 106
Fournier de la Chapelle, Charles, 54, 72, 88, 103
French National Assembly, 155, 167–169
French Revolution, 154–155, 168
French Revolutionary Army, 169
French slave laws: of 1785, 140; appeals to, 4, 9, 16, 21, 98–100, 112–120, 135–137, 139–142, 175; Code Noir of 1685, 20; destruction of slave trial records and, 4; plantation strikes and, 151

Galbaud, Etienne, 168–169
Galliffet sugar complex, 151, 165–166
Gaou (slave in Les Perches), 34–35, 42, 46, 48, 50, 108, 175
gardes de corps, 133
Gastine, Civique de, 7
Gazette de Médecine, 123–124
Geggus, David, 5–6, 173–174
Geneviève (follower of Makandal), 79, 88

INDEX

Goma (enslaved man on Lejeune estate), 138
Gonzalez, Johnhenry, 179
Gordon-Reed, Annette, 8
Grande-Rivière, *36*, 47, 123, 155–157, *159*, 161, 167, 170, 177
gry (charms), 76
Guyana records of complaints of enslaved and, 10

Haiti, 170, 179–180
Haitian Revolution: Bois Caïman ceremony and, 161–162, 174; Choiseul plantation and, 165; colonialist narratives about, 171; community of resistance and, 9, 11, 119–120, 143, 145, 161, 171, 174–175, 178; declaration of independence for Haiti and, 170; Dutilh plantation and, 164–165; emancipation decree and, 169; Galliffet sugar complex, 151, 165–166; historical record loss and, 4; Makandal mythos and, 7–8, 95–96; maps of, *159*, *163*; Morne Rouge meeting and, 158–161; Napoleon and, 169–170; Noé sugar plantation and, 162, 164; "Ogé" revolt and, 155–157, 176–177; Port Margot and, 166; protection of individual enslavers and, 166; rebel camps of, 167; role of maroonage in, 5–6; start of, 3, 165–166; war with Spain and, 168
Hamelin, Jacques, 36
Hauron (slave on Delacoursière estate), 62–64
Héron de la Filière plantation, 160, 165, 217n50

Hippolyte (field driver on Noé estate), 3, 147–150, 152–153

Ignace (enslaved man on La Gossette estate), 161
indigo plantations, 14, 80, *82*, 86
irrigation, 25–26, 30, 59. *See also* drought

Jacob (enslaved man on Lejeune estate), 137
Jacques (enslaved man on Lejeune estate), 137
Jamaica, 5, 9, 149
James, C. L. R., 8
Jean à Tessereau (follower of Makandal), 70, 89
Jean-Baptiste (enslaved man on Bréda plantation), 103–104
Jean-Baptiste (enslaved man on Lejeune estate), 136
Jean (enslaved man on Laplaine plantation), 68–70, 75
Jean-François (rebel leader), 167, 168
Jean-Jacques (driver on Noé estate), 3, 145, 147–150, 152–154, 158, 162, 164, 166–167
Jeannot (enslaved man on Lejeune estate), 138
Jean-Pierre (enslaved by Fathers of Charity), 107
Jean-Pierre (enslaved man on Delaye estate), 59–60
Jean-Pierre (enslaved man on Lejeune estate), 137
Jean the diviner, 129–132, 147
Jean Yoquo (enslaved man on Carbon plantation), 44
Jérôme (enslaved man on Béliers estate), 130–132, 147, 174

Jesuits, 21–23, 23, 74, 198n57
Jolicoeur (slave in Cap Français), 79, 88, 94
Julie (enslaved woman on Lejeune estate), 138–139
Julien (enslaved man on Trémais estate), 131
Jupiter (enslaved man on De la Selle plantation), 44
Jupiter (enslaved man on de Paroy plantation), 114–115

Kangal (Antoine, free Black man from de Paroy estate), 2, 112–119, 175, 177–178
Kingdom of this World, The (Carpentier), 8
King Louis XV, 26
Kingué (diviner), 132–136, 147, 173–174

Ladot, Jean, 129
La Gossette sugar plantation, 151, 161. *See also* Galliffet sugar complex
language: African languages spoken among slaves, 14; description of medicine as "poison" and, 34–35; Jean (slave on the Laplaine plantation), 68; Médor's testimony to Delavaud's neighbors and, 37; names and, 14–15, 80, 85
Lapeyre, Quiquo, 157, 217n40
Lapole, Jean, 104–105
Larival, 7
La Rouderie (free Black man in Soufrière), 84
Larue, Dame, 40
Laurin (living near Galliffet plantation), 106–107, 175

LeBlondain, Philibert, 60–61
legal system: African medicines and, 60–61; appeals to French, 4, 9, 16, 21, 98–100, 112–120, 135–137, 139–142, 175; magic and, 35; manusmission and, 20, 39–40
Lejeune, Nicolas, 136–137, 141, 166
Lejeune, Nicolas (son), 137–138
Le Mercier de la Rivière, Paul Jean-François, 123, 209n4
Le Normant de Mézy, 84, 158, 200n28, 218n54
Lescoffier, Elisabeth, 83–84, 200n25
Les Perches, 28–30
LeTellier (indigo plantation owner), 80, 84, 199n22, 200n29
Leveillé (follower of Makandal), 79, 88, 93–94
Lhér, Etienne, 51
Limbé parish, 65, 66, 68, 79, 80, *81*, 83, *124*, 140, 145, 150, 153, 154, 157, 158, 159, 160, *162*, 165, 166, 167, 177
livestock: disease, 31–32, 95–96, 100–101, *102*, 105–106; drought and, 30; food management and, 109–111; Seven Years' War and, 30. *See also* anthrax
livestock guardians, 27
Lizette (enslaved woman on de Paroy estate), 2, 112–113, 116–119, 142, 177–178
Lombard sugar plantation, 151
losange, 69
Louis XIV, 35, 41
Louis XV, 105–106
Louis XVI, 154–155, 160, 168

Louverture, Toussaint, 104, 147, 166, 167–169
Lucas, Jacques, 177

Macaya (enslaved man on Lejeune estate), 138
Magdelaine (slave in Cap Français), 40
magic: accusations of using spells, 27–28, 133; criminal statutes and, 35; magical weapon accusations, 130–131; testimony of accused poisoners and, 64
Magre, Jean, 138–139, 141
Makandal: background of, 79–80; capture of on Dufresne plantation, 87–88; charge of sacrilege and, 91; colonist-killer myth of, 6; Congo ritual practice community and, 9, 75–76, 79, 85–86, 174; divination and, 2, 8; execution of, 88–89; *faire diable* ritual and, 78–79, 91; heroic revolutionary myth of, 7–8; Kingué described in terms of, 132; as livestock guard, 84; madman myth, 6–7; makandals (bundles) of, 76–79; map of life in Saint-Domingue, *81*; as maroon, 84–86; minkisi and, 89–91; myth of, 95–96; name and, 80, 85; Noé estate and, 147; plantation work and, 82–84; possible loss of hand and, 83; torture of, 88
"Makandal: True Story" (Larival), 7
makandals (bundles), 76–79, 130
manumission, 19–20, 38–40
Margot (enslaved woman in Cap Français), 40
Marianne (enslaved woman in Cap Français), 79

Marie Jeanne (enslaved child in Delavaud household), 46–48, 53–54, 173
Marie Jeanne (enslaved woman in Chiron household), 62–64, 73
Marie-Louise (living near Galliffet plantation), 106, 175
Marie Rose (enslaved woman on Lejeune estate), 139, 141
Marmelade parish, 121–123, 126–128
maroons, 5–6, 27–28, 28, 173
Medical cultures: African medicines, 33, 42, 60–61; African practitioners, 33, 42, 45, 68, 71, 72, 73, 74, 75, 76, 85, 133–134, 135; French medicines, 35, 51, 103; French practitioners, 14, 17, 32, 33, 51, 52, 55, 67, 96, 98, 100, 101, 103, 106, 110, 123, 139, 154, 172; hospitalière role, 59, 60, 67, 70, 75, 127; plantation "hospital," 67, 113–114, 153; plantation surgeons, 60, 61, 67, 110, 123, 139, 164, 192n31; veterinarians, 104–105, 106, 123, 139. *See also* anthrax, smallpox, yellow fever
Médor: calendas and, 24; confession about poison and, 2, 33, 42, 173; conspiracy to help Marie Jeanne escape Delavaud household and, 46–48; conspiracy to increase number of free Blacks and, 41, 57, 155, 170, 175–176; death of, 50; events from testimony of, *36*; on free Blacks in Petite Guinée, 21; household role of, 14; hysteria of poisoning investigations caused by, 52, 55–57; implication

of Augustine Delavaud and, 45;
implication of other slaves and,
40, 42–45, 173; market opportunity and, 19; medicine for
diseased slaves and, 33; motives
for poisoning, 46; move to coffee
plantation and, 1, 28–29; origin
of, 15; second day of interrogation and, 48–50; testimony given
to Delavaud's neighbors and,
36–38; written confession signed
by, 49–50
ménagère role, 26–27
Mentor sugar plantation, 151
Mercure (follower of Makandal),
88, 92
Michel (enslaved man in Cap
Français), 79
Miles, Tiya, 3
minkisi, 89–92
Morne Rouge meeting, 158–161,
159
Mossut, Pierre, 171

Nanon (enslaved woman in Chiron
household), 62–64, 73
Neufchâteau, Nicolas Louis
François de, 132
Nicolas (driver on Lejeune estate),
2, 139–141
nkisi, 89–91
Noé, Louis-Pantaléon de, 145, 147
Noé sugar plantation: anthrax
outbreak and, 145; conditions
before strikes, 145, 147–149;
drought and, 148, 152, 154;
Haitian Revolution and, 162,
164; Jean-Jacques and, 3, 145,
147–150, 152–154; labor strike
and, 144, 149–150; livestock
deaths and, 154; ritual communities and, 145, 147

Ochoa, Todd, 91–92
Odelucq, Nicolas, 107, 111, 151,
161, 166
Ogé, Jacques, 157
Ogé, Vincent, 155–156, 176
Olivier, Jérôme, 23

pakets congos, 76
Pantin, 98
Paris, enslaved labor and, 26
Pascault (overseer on Noé estate),
149
Paul (from Belin/Blin estate), 159,
165–166
Pelagie (enslaved woman on Delaye
estate), 59–60
Pelissot (Galliffet estate surgeon),
110–111
Petite Anse parish, 62, 64, 66–67,
100, *102*, 107, 111, *146*, 150,
155, 161, 165
Petite Guinée (Little Africa) neighborhood, 21
petiveria alliacea (guinea weed), 45
Philibert (enslaved coachman of
Odelucq), 166, 219n68
Pierre (enslaved man on Lejeune
estate), 136
Place d'Armes, 18–19
Plaisance parish, *124*, 132–138, 142,
145, 157, *159*, *163*, 166
plantation surgeons, 60, 61, 67, 110,
123, 139, 164, 192n31
Plants, used for healing, 45, 51, 69,
76–77. *See also* quebec
poisoning: African medicine and,
60–61; anthrax misconstrued

as, 2, 100–101, *102*, 103–104, 106–109, 124; Baradat's examination of substances found on implicated slaves, 51; Cappé and, 126–127; extrajudicial torture upon suspicions of, 55–56; French familiarity with, 40–41; to gain manumission, 40, 45, 61–64, 175; with goal of influencing enslavers, 45, 143; intentional use of anthrax as, 108, 143; language and, 34–35; legal statutes regarding witchcraft and, 35; possibility of contamination by livestock disease and, 51–52; Trémais's view of, 126

poisoning investigations: accusations after Médor's death and, 52, 55–58, *58*; after Makandal, 194n18; autopsies and, 60–61; Cappé and, 126–128; chocolate and, 106–107; commonalities of testimonies in, 58–59; communities of enslaved and, 173; destruction of records of slave criminal trial records and, 4, 58; focus on household slaves and, 57–59; torture and, 55–56, 126–127; as ways of targeting individuals/communities, 98–99, 114, 116–117, 126–128, 136. *See also* Assam; Makandal; Médor

pois puant, 69

Poissy, Marianne, 47

police force/constables, 18, 20–21, 50, 86, 88, 99, 108, 110, 117–118, 127–128, 141, 151

Polidor (associate of Kingué), 135–136

Polony, Jean Louis, 100, 103

Polverel, Etienne, 168

Polydor, 28

Pompee (free Black man), 68–72

Port-au-Prince, 4, 158

Port Margot parish, 76, 79, *81*, 85, *126*, 132, 140, 145, 158, *159*, *163*, 166

Pouppé-Desportes, Jean-Baptiste, 31

quebec, 139, 213n68

Quessy (slave on De la Selle plantation), 44, 46

Raimond, Julien, 155, 176

Régent, Frédéric, 10

Regnaudot, Jean-Marie, 101

resistance: ability of enslaved to mobilize and, 143; Bois Caïman ceremony and, 161–162, 174; colonial court challenges, 4, 9, 16, 21, 98–100, 112–120, 135–137, 139–142, 175; community and, 11, 119–120, 143, 145, 161, 171, 174–175, 178; debate about what constitutes, 9–10; enslavement due to economic conditions and, 10–11; food instability and, 109–111, 171–172; forms of, 9–10, 172; free Black people and slave, 177–178; goals of, 11, 176; in Haiti, 179; locations of, 9, *146*; Morne Rouge meeting and, 158–161; "Ogé" revolt and, 155–157, 176–177; precursors to Haitian Revolution and, *159*; strikes and, 103–104, 120, 142, 144, *146*, 149–152, 175; survival efforts as, 10; uprising on La Gossette sugar plantation, 161; vodou and, 174. *See also* Haitian Revolution

Richer, Augustin, 36
Rosette (enslaved woman on Lejeune estate), 137

Saint-Barthélemy, 45
Saint-Domingue: Black militia and, 20; culture of torture and, 55–56; destruction of records of slave criminal trials, 4, 58; effect of Seven Years' War on, 29–30; emancipation decree for, 169; food management and, 109–111, 171–172; French Revolution and, 155; Jesuits and, 21–23, 23, 74, 198n57; makeup up of in 1730s, 13–14; "Ogé" revolt and, 155–157; Revolutionary Commission and, 168–169; rights of citizenship for free Black Frenchmen and, 167–168; sanction of Catholicism and, 22–23; smuggling during Seven Years' War and, 97. *See also* Haiti; Haitian Revolution
Saint-Méry, Moreau de, 24, 95, 174
scarlet fever, 41
self-purchase, 19–20
Seven Years' War, 1, 29, 97, 109–110
smallpox, 17, 41, 100, 103
Sonthonax, Léger, 168–169, 176
Soufrière, 66, 68, 70, 72, 75, 76, 79, 80, 84–86, 109, 121, 129, 140, 144–145, 150, 154, 158
Spain, 168
strikes, 3, 9, 103–104, 120, 142, 144, *146*, 149–152, 175
sugar plantations: accessibility of Cap Français to, 24; life for slaves on, 14, 25–26, 83, *83*; planting and, 82; strikes on, 149–152; sugar processing and, 25, 82–83, *83*. *See also individual plantations*
Superior Council of Léogane, 4
Sweet, James, 38

tassau, 18, 54, 110
Télémaque (driver on Béliers estate), 130–132, 147
Thomas (enslaved man on LeBlondain estate), 61
Toussaint (enslaved man on Lejeune estate), 137
Toussaint Louverture. See Louverture, Toussaint
Tranquille (overseer on Lejeune estate), 138
Trémais, Charles-François Pichot de Kerdisien de, 126–129, 162, 210n17, 218n59
Trévan, Louis-François, 87

Valette, Jean, 66–74, 85, 111, 196n38
Venus (enslaved woman in Delavaud household), 47–50, 53, 173
Vicq d'Azyr, Félix, 108–109
Vinba (enslaved man on Lejeune estate), 136
Vincent (participant in Haitian Revolution), 164
vodou, 174

Walsh sugar plantation, 151
Worlock, Simeon, 103

Zabeth (enslaved woman on Lejeune estate), 138–139, 141
Zinga (enslaved man on Lejeune estate), 136